W9-AQN-944

Simple Ways to Protect Yourself from Lawsuits

A Complete Guide to Asset Protection

WITH FORMS

Mark Warda
Attorney at Law

SPHINX PUBLISHING
Sphinx International, Inc.
1725 Clearwater-Largo Rd., S.
Post Office Box 25
Clearwater, FL 34617
Tel. (813) 587-0999
Fax (813) 586-5088

WITHDRAWN

Tennessee Tech Library
Cookeville, TN

Note: The law changes constantly and is subject to different interpretations. It is up to you
to check it thoroughly before relying on it.
Neither the author nor the publisher guarantees the outcome of the uses to which this
material is put.

Copyright © 1996 by Mark Warda

All rights reserved. No part of this book, except for brief passages in articles that refer to author
and publisher may be reproduced without written permission of the author. Purchasers of the
book are granted a license to use the forms contained herein.

First Edition, 1996

ISBN 1-57248-020-3
LCCN: 95-74590

Manufactured in the United States of America.

This publication is designed to provide accurate and authoritative information in regard to the
subject matter covered. It is sold with the understanding that the publisher is not engaged in
rendering legal, accounting or other professional services. If legal advice or other expert
assistance is required, the service of a competent professional person should be sought.

-From a Declaration of Principles jointly
adopted by a Committee of the American Bar
Association and a Committee of Publishers.

Published by Sphinx Publishing, a division of Sphinx International, Inc., Post Office Box 25,
Clearwater, Florida 34617-0025. This publication is available by mail for $24.95 plus Florida sales
tax if applicable plus $3.75 shipping. Credit card orders call 1-800-226-5291.

Table of Contents

Part One Overview of Asset Protection Planning

Chapter 1
Our Current Crisis

To say that there is a crisis in America regarding liability is not an exaggeration. People who have worked hard for a lifetime are being wiped out for a single incident. Whole industries are going out of business because they cannot afford the high cost of liability insurance.

This is not a partisan issue. People ranging from Dan Quayle to George McGovern have noted that the current system is in crisis, that it is crippling American businesses. Manufacturers of such items as football helmets and small aircraft have gone out of business because they could not afford the insurance to cover the outrageous judgments which juries in our nation are awarding.

America is different today. The American ethic used to be that if you worked hard you would eventually be well off. Today Americans believe that if you are lucky you will suddenly become rich. You can be lucky with a lottery ticket or you can be lucky enough to trip on someone else's property. As we have seen in both civil and criminal cases, our jury system doesn't always work

These people have observed the lifestyles of the rich and famous and think they deserve to live the same way. They have forgotten that it takes work and perseverance to make it big. They have taken in an instant what it took another a lifetime to achieve.

Years ago people were only held liable if they were at fault for an injury. But a couple of decades ago some law professors and judges decided that injured people deserved compensation no matter who was at fault. They decided to make compensation of injured people a burden, not on society as a whole, but on successful members of society. In a matter of decades they completely revolutionized the legal system without a single vote in any legislature. Such a rapid change was previously unheard of in the whole history of law.

In this new system billions of dollars are transferred each year from people who run businesses or own property to those who suffer injuries in society. But not all of the money goes to the victims. Lawyers siphon off up to 40% of most awards. No wonder they are fighting tooth and nail against reform of the system.

The unsophisticated jury is their tool and they work their jury with precision, using juror profile psychologists, gory photographs and computer simulations. They work not with the law or the facts but with the emotions of the jurors. Of course the "victim" wins and whoever has the most money loses.

The system is like a lottery. Even if a person has a meritless claim there is a chance a sympathetic jury will award him a windfall. And if he lose it costs him nothing.

The system is much more favorable to people filing suit than to people defending themselves. Attorneys will work for a contingent fee (no fee unless they win) for someone with a claim. But to defend a suit one must pay an attorney by the hour as the work is done. And even if you win you have to pay your own attorney fees, which can amount to hundreds of thousands or even over a million dollars. Something is wrong when an innocent person can be financially wiped out by a frivolous claim, while the losing claimant suffers no loss.

In England the loser must pay the winner's attorney fees, so only serious claims are filed. But here there is no risk to bringing a weak or even false claim. It is so expensive to defend a suit that often innocent people pay a large settlement rather than pay twice as much in attorney fees to win.

England (and most other countries) also forbid contingent fees for attorneys. In our system the lawyer agrees not to charge for his work unless he wins, but then he takes a big piece, often one-third to one-half of the entire amount awarded. Think of it, if a person is made a quadriplegic in an accident and a jury says he is entitled to millions of dollars compensation to last the rest of his life, should his lawyer get half if it for doing one year's work on the case?

The amounts of the verdicts are also getting out of hand. It is almost like play money the juries are giving away. Don't they realize that there are not unlimited piles of money to be given away? That each big award raises the price we all pay for insurance and products and services in society?

These are the kinds of awards juries are giving today:

• Defamation of a former employee resulted in a $1.9 million judgment

• Failing to diagnose skin cancer resulted in a $4.17 million judgment

• Sponsoring a Christmas party where a guest later had a traffic accident resulted in a $5.87 million judgment

Even if you have insurance it may not be enough to cover the kinds of awards juries are handing out today. For example:

• $41 million for a misdiagnosis of abdominal pain

• $49 million for a stillborn baby

• $77 million for giving an anti-asthma drug which caused the patient to become mute, blind and paralyzed.

• $84.5 million for children drowned and brain damaged in a swimming pool accident

• $569 million judgment against a lawyer for sexually abusing his son

Even people who have done nothing wrong are being held liable. It used to be that only people who were at fault were liable. Today whoever has money, the "deep pocket," is liable, no matter who was at fault. The courts are inventing new theories of liability to transfer money from those who have it to those who are "victims" of unfortunate accidents. Some examples are:

• $986,000 awarded to a woman who "lost her psychic powers" after a CAT scan

• $2.3 million awarded to a woman after radiation treatment for uterine cancer, including $1.2 million for "loss of life's pleasures"

• $300,000 for slapping a daughter twice on face

- $500,000 for causing emotional stress to wife in divorce

- $456,000 for letting a 27-year-old son drive a car, causing an accident

- $75,000 for spraying perfume on a person without permission

- $60,000 for cursing which caused "emotional distress"

A new type of law which has been passed in recent years in some states is a "product disparagement" law. This means that if you say something disparaging about, for example, Florida oranges, you could be sued. Suppose you discover that a new pesticide which has been sprayed on Florida oranges causes cancer. If you publicize this and it hurts the orange industry, you may be liable for millions in damages. What about freedom of speech? You might win the suit, if you can afford all of the legal fees to win both the case and the appeal.

What is wrong with this country? Has our success as a nation caused us to become lazy, greedy and selfish? Is it natural for our system to break down and decay like the Roman Empire?

Whatever the reason we do not all have to be swept along with it. For nearly every law there is a legal loophole. That is how it has been for thousands of years. The Romans had lawyers and loopholes and the people in the middle ages had lawyers and loopholes. Lawyers write laws and other lawyers find ways to get around those laws. Lawyers change the laws and then other lawyers find ways around *those* laws. And one thing you can be sure of is that lawyers who are working for private citizens or for themselves are much more enterprising than those who would work for the government.

In using legal loopholes to protect yourself from an unfair system you are following a fine tradition of people who have stood up for their individual rights. This book will teach you about the loopholes that can be used to protect your wealth.

Chapter 2
The Risks We Face

The following is a summary of some of the most likely sources of liability which you face. Some of them, such as loans you sign for, are under your control. Others, such as accidents or acts of your employees, are out of your control. Still others, such as slandering or injuring someone, may only happen if you lose control.

Debts:

- Business loans
- Personal loans
- Real estate loans
- Personal guarantees
- Alimony
- Child support
- Medical bills
- Legal bills
- Taxes

In most cases debts are under your control and can be kept reasonable. However, when combined with unexpected liabilities they may overwhelm your ability to meet all of your obligations.

Alimony and child support are supposed to be reasonable, but there have been cases where these amounts have totaled 85% of a person's earnings. Medical and legal bills can strike without warning and can reach astronomical levels. Taxes should be simple to calculate but bad advice or a miscalculation can result in a surprise assessment along with interest and penalties.

In some states spouses are liable for each other's necessaries such as food and medical care. This means you can be liable for your spouse's medical bills even if you do not sign a guaranty. In a least one state (Florida) the husband is liable for his wife's necessaries but a wife is not liable for her husband's necessaries. The Florida Supreme Court said that this was not fair but that it was up to the legislature to change it!

Accidents:

- Professional malpractice
- Auto accidents
- Homeowner accidents
- Rental property accidents
- Recreational vehicle accidents
- Sporting accidents

Accidents can happen without warning and wipe you out when you least expect it. On a Sunday outing a chiropractor accidently drove his boat over a smaller boat which crossed in front of him, killing three teenagers. It cost him over a million dollars in legal fees defending against manslaughter charges, even before he faced the civil liability.

Legal violations and wrongful acts:

- Environmental violations
- Civil rights violations
- Labor law violations
- Criminal violations
- Sexual harassment violations
- Committing slander against someone
- Inflicting violence on someone

Today there are so many laws it would be impossible for you know all the ones which you must obey. But "ignorance of the law is no excuse" so you can be liable, even for criminal penalties, for an act you thought harmless.

Liability for acts of others:

- Partners
- Employees
- Family members
- Those who use your vehicles

While the law considers you to have some control over the acts of others, in reality you have little control over much of what your employees or family members do. If your employee infects someone with AIDS, your partner commits malpractice or your child runs your car into a school bus, you may be held responsible.

And then there are potential liabilities which you probably couldn't even imagine. Did you know that if toxic chemicals flow underground from another property to under your back yard you may have to pay an unlimited amount to have it cleaned up? It may cost $100,000, $500,000 or even $1,000,000. And you cannot escape the liability by going bankrupt or giving the property away. The law in America today says that property owners are responsible for the cleanup of environmental hazards on their property.

People have told me that this is clearly not fair and that someone who is stuck with such liability should appeal the case. But people have appealed and they have lost. The courts have upheld such a system. Why? Congress has declared that pollution is a national crisis, it has realized that our government does not have the money to pay for it and has decided that sticking it to a few property owners is politically easier than raising taxes on the rest of the country.

One aspect of our legal system which is unusual is the doctrine of "joint and severable liability." Under this rule, *anyone* with *any* negligence in an incident can be liable for 100% of the damages if the other parties cannot pay. For example, a woman was killed at Disney World. She was 79% at fault for the accident, her husband was 20% at fault and Disney World 1% at fault. Disney World had to pay her husband damages for her death because it was the only one with money.

The fact is, in America today you can lose everything you have worked for in your life if you make one little mistake, or even if someone else makes a mistake and they do it on your property or can find some other reason to blame you.

But this same system which can take away your wealth can also protect it if you know the laws and the loopholes. This book will explain in simple language each protection available to you and how to use it.

Divorce

While seeking to keep assets safe from creditors, you must not overlook the risk of divorce. Roughly half of first marriages and 75% of second marriages end in divorce. Some clearly do not work from the beginning, but the saddest ones are those where one party thinks that the relationship is fine, but the other party finds that "something" is missing.

In setting up your asset protection plan, you should not disregard the risk of divorce. Putting everything in your spouse's name may protect it from creditors, but you would probably rather have them get it if your spouse runs off with someone else.

Loss of Purchasing Power

With the risk of sounding like an alarmist, it must be pointed out that one risk that every American faces today is that of currency devaluation. While our economy appears to be running smoothly, there is a very real danger that it could unravel at any time. Did you realize that the *interest* on our national debt now takes up about 60% of all income tax taken in by the federal government. When interest rates rise from their currently depressed levels, the interest alone may be more than our government takes in.

Two ways this crisis could be alleviated would be to either stop paying the interest or to print more money to pay it with. The first way would be the biggest embarrassment in the history of this country and the second way could be blamed on uncontrollable forces, greedy investors, and currency speculators. Which one do you think our American politicians would choose?

A good analogy to our nation's situation is a person who has been living beyond his means by borrowing on his credit cards. He never pays down the debt but keeps borrowing to pay the interest on the current debt. Eventually the interest alone becomes more than he can afford. For this individual the only option is bankruptcy. Bankruptcy is also an option for our nation. It would mean defaulting on treasury bonds, notes and bills. Those who think most of these are held by foreigners or the wealthy think it would not be a bad idea. But a great portion of treasury securities are held by banks, savings and loans and pension funds. Default would cause a national crisis.

Inflation, on the other hand, could happen relatively slowly. And each politician could point his finger at someone else. The easiest targets would be politicians who are dead.

If you are concerned about asset protection, you should also seek to protect yourself from this type of loss. One way to do this is to invest some of your assets in things other than the U. S. dollar. This means things like real estate, gold and foreign currencies. All of these investments can be made through asset protection devices described in this book.

Chapter 3
Why I Wrote This Book

As a lawyer I read reports of new court cases every week. And the more cases I read the more frightened I became for my own financial well being. A landlord took three days to fix a water heater and was liable for $775,000 in damages because a tenant was careless enough to boil a pot of water and spill it on her grandchild. A man earning $74,000 a year was ordered to pay $64,000 a year in alimony, child support and marital bills. A purchaser of a small piece of property was liable for hundreds of thousands of dollars in environmental cleanup costs.

Our legal system obviously is out of control and I was scared of becoming a victim of it. But as a lawyer I knew that the same system which could take everything from me could protect everything I own. That is the nature of law and always has been.

So I undertook the most detailed research I ever did in my career. My entire life savings was at stake as was my future ability to retire and enjoy my final years. I read cases of people who were successful their whole lives and then lost their life savings at the age of 60 or 70. What is a person to do then, live on social security in a small tenement, hoping not to be mugged by underclass thugs of the future?

I have read every book and article I could find on protecting assets. I wrote to every expert I could find and asked questions. I called them. I wrote to hundreds of banks and trust companies in foreign countries to see what they had to offer. I analyzed all of this material and figured out which systems were the simplest, easiest and safest. Then I used the methods which fit my circumstances to protect what I own.

But I still read every week of others whose lives are being ruined by outrageous lawsuits. And I have thought of how useful this information could be to them. So I decided to condense everything I have learned into this book in the hope that others can use it to protect themselves.

I know it is lawyers who are partly to blame for this crisis in this country. Too many are pursuing ridiculous claims and pressing unfair arguments. So perhaps I can help with this book to make up for what they are doing.

This is not a book of theory. It is not a product thrown together because there might be a market for it. It is the material I researched for my own use, to protect everything I own from possible claims which might arise in the future in our crazy legal system. You can find no better legal device than one a lawyer uses for himself.

Chapter 4
What You Can Do
to Protect Yourself

The ultimate goal of asset protection planning is to set up your affairs so that no one can get your property. There are many simple ways to do this. In some states your home cannot be taken from you no matter what it is worth. In others, annuities, life insurance, or property owned jointly with a spouse may be untouchable. For more substantial interests a limited partnership or trust may be set up which is untouchable by even the most determined creditor. By knowing the rules and setting up your affairs accordingly you can own a substantial estate and have it totally free from claims of creditors.

This chapter summarizes what you can do to protect yourself, and later chapters explain in detail exactly how to do it.

Three Ways to Protect Your Assets

There are three main approaches to protecting your assets from those who wish to take them. The first is to keep the claims from reaching you. The second is to be sure that property you own in your name is immune from claims which do reach you. The third is to take property out of your name (but retain control). All of these methods can be used legally, and to be totally safe you must utilize all three approaches in your planning.

Keeping Claims from Reaching You

You can keep claims from reaching you by avoiding risky activities as often as possible, by conducting the risky activities you do have in separate entities such as corporations, by having enough insurance to pay for any claims that may arise against you personally, and by limiting your liability by contract.

Additionally, you can avoid being a target of lawsuits by keeping a low profile and not showing off your wealth. A huge home, expensive cars and furs may be fun to show off, but such a lifestyle may make you the target of someone who covets your wealth. Sure, it is fun to show off your success, but is it worth losing it over?

Being conservative rather than boastful on your financial statements will also make you a less desirable target for lawsuits.

All of these methods of protecting yourself from suits are discussed in Part Two of this book.

Keeping Your Property Insulated from Claims Which Reach You

Not all claims can be deflected so you must be sure that the assets you own cannot be reached by claims that do get through your first line of defense. Every state allows its citizens to own certain property which is exempt from the claims of creditors. In some states, such as Texas and Florida, you may have millions of dollars in property which cannot be touched by your creditors. In other states you may keep amounts ranging from a few thousand dollars to hundreds of thousands of dollars. The laws protect such things as your home, pensions and annuities, insurance, tools, a car, and household goods.

All of the types of property which are exempt from creditors' claims are explained in Part Three of this book. A list showing how the states compare is contained in Appendix 2, and a summary for each state in Appendix 3.

Taking Property Out of Your Name

Because most states only exempt limited amounts of property, most people need other ways to protect their wealth. And because creditors can only seize property owned by their debtor, taking property out of your name can make it untouchable by your creditors. However, there are strict rules covering how this can be done legally and what can get you into trouble. In fact, certain actions are criminal.

Some of the ways you can take property out of your name are to make gifts of it to your spouse, children or other relatives, or to convey it to a limited partnership or to a trust.

How to do this legally is explained in Part Four of this book.

After You Have a Creditor

Once you know that a creditor has a claim against you your legal rights change. There are certain things which you can no longer do. At this point people often do desperate things, and these things get them into more trouble.

Your options after a creditor appears are discussed in Part Five of this book.

Your Action Plan

It is easy to read a book like this, to agree with it, and then to put it down and not take any action. Deciding which action to take and actually going through the steps takes a lot of effort. But asset protection is important and you should not procrastinate. Everything you have worked for your entire life can be lost if you are the defendant of a single lawsuit, even a frivolous one.

To make it easy for you, I have put together an action plan. This is a checklist you can follow step-by-step to protect your assets. If you follow it through, you can protect everything you own. If you take even a few of the steps you can be sure you have a few things left for yourself which cannot be touched should you be successfully sued. You can use these to start your life over if the worst happens.

The action plan is contained in Part Six of this book.

Diagram on how asset protections work

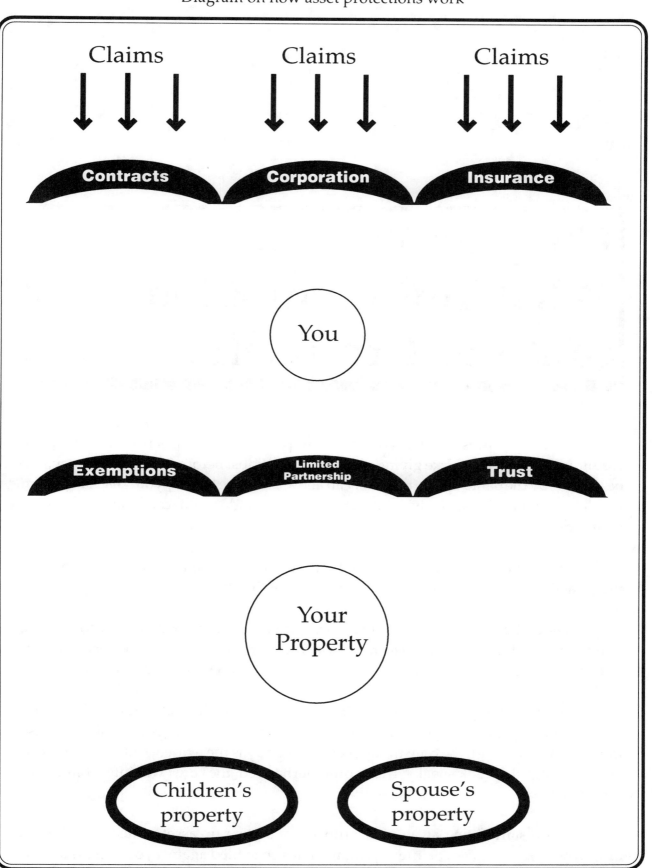

Chapter 5
What You Cannot Do
to Protect Yourself

There are limits to what you can do to protect your assets from the claims of creditors. Some actions, like giving away your assets just before filing bankruptcy, can be undone by the bankruptcy trustee or can allow the judge to deny your discharge from the debt. Other things, like lying about your assets under oath, can result in criminal penalties.

You can usually protect most of your assets legally so there is no need to take illegal actions or to do things which won't hold up in court.

One of the most important things considered in determining whether something is legal or illegal is *when it was done*. It is always better to do something sooner than later. In fact, in some instances there are exact dates as to when you can do things legally.

The other important thing considered is your *intent* when taking an action. If you had an intent to defraud your creditors, your action will be judged illegal. Because intent is in your mind, the only thing a court can go by is the evidence of your intent. If you do things that look sneaky, tricky or underhanded, the court will infer fraudulent intent.

If you start giving away your property or setting up asset protection schemes after you have been sued or after a judgment has been filed against you there is a good chance that a court will undo your actions. But if you arrange your affairs to protect your assets before anyone makes any claim against you, then your assets will more likely be safe.

The following is a summary of the laws which limit the actions you may take in protecting your assets.

Fraudulent Transfer Laws

The most important laws determining how you may protect your assets are the Uniform Fraudulent Transfer Act (UFTA) and the Uniform Fraudulent Conveyances Act (UFCA). Versions of either or both of these laws were enacted by all of the states.

The purpose of these laws is to protect creditors from people who might give away their assets to avoid losing them to creditors. The first thing some people think of doing when a creditor tries to claim their property is to give it to their spouse, children, parents, siblings or friends. But under fraudulent transfer laws the property can be recovered by the creditor.

Fraudulent transfer laws define what types of transfers of property are illegal. They contain a list of "badges of fraud" which a court will look at in determining if a transfer constitutes a fraud on creditors. A summary of the badges which courts look for is as follows:

- A family or close relationship between the parties
- Little or nothing paid for the property
- Continued use or benefit by the debtor
- Secrecy of the transaction
- Debtor disappearing or leaving the area
- Financial condition of the debtor before and after the transfer
- A pattern of transactions after financial difficulties begins
- The general chronology of the transfers
- Transfer of all of one's property

Under the law, if even one of these badges is present the court might find that the transfer was illegal. If several are present it is even more likely the transfer will be found to be fraudulent.

Even if there is not found to be actual fraud, a court may find **constructive fraud** if certain factors exist. Constructive fraud is activity which legally amounts to fraud, even if there is not enough evidence to prove actual fraud. The factors which indicate constructive fraud are:

- The person is insolvent either before or after the transfer of property
- The person is left with an unreasonably low amount of capital after the transfer of property
- The person begins to incur debts beyond his or her ability to pay them as they come due.

The most important of these is whether or not the debtor is insolvent. In simple English, insolvency means that a person's debts exceed his assets. However, in court many factors are weighed in this determination.

For one thing, property which cannot be reached by creditors is not included in determining whether debts exceed assets. This would be exempt property such as a homestead and property in a trust outside of the country. Also, there is an important difference between the UFTA and the UFCA in this area. The UFCA finds fraud if the "probable liabilities" exceed the "present salable value" of the assets. But the UFTA finds fraud if the sum of "current debts" exceeds the "fair value" of the assets not including exempt property.

The difference here is that probable liabilities are usually much greater than current debts, and the present salable value of the assets is usually much less than their fair market value.

Example: If a person has assets of $1 million and debts of $500,000 he would appear to be solvent. But under the UFCA, if some of the assets include a partnership interest (which is not salable) and a vacant subdivision (which would be worth one-third as much when sold in bulk, rather than separately) then the person may actually be considered insolvent under the law.

By inflating the liabilities and discounting the assets the UFCA makes it more likely that a person will be guilty of fraud. However, the UFCA has been replaced by the UFTA in the following 26 states: Alabama, Arizona, Arkansas, California, Florida, Hawaii, Idaho, Illinois, Maine, Minnesota, Nebraska, Nevada, New Hampshire, New Jersey, New Mexico, North Dakota, Ohio, Oklahoma, Oregon, Rhode Island, South Dakota, Texas, Utah, Washington, West Virginia and Wisconsin.

However, the courts in some of the UFCA states (and the bankruptcy laws) allow persons to avoid some of the harsh results of this law. If an accountant using generally accepted accounting practices can testify that you are solvent, it is less likely that you would be found to be insolvent.

It is not necessary that a person obtain a judgment against you before you can be stopped from transferring your assets. Fraudulent transfer laws protect anyone who "has a claim" against you. These may include claims which are "unliquidated, contingent, unmatured disputed, undisputed, legal, equitable, secured or unsecured." This is quite broad and again shows the importance of taking action early.

Bankruptcy Law

Another law which determines whether your transfers of property are legal is the Bankruptcy Act. If you file for bankruptcy, the bankruptcy trustee is given title to your property, and if you made any transfers which were not legal, they can be set aside. This means that the trustee can get a court order requiring people who hold property which had been yours to return it.

Section 548 of the bankruptcy law states that any transfer of property within one year of filing for bankruptcy can be set aside. This law protects creditors of people who think that they can give all their property to their spouse and children and then file bankruptcy saying that they have no assets to pay their bills.

Under the law the bankruptcy trustee can order recipients of property to surrender it to him and can have the property seized if the recipient refuses to return it. If the recipient of the property has lost, damaged or destroyed it he or she can be held liable for the value of that property.

Section 544(b) of the bankruptcy law says that the bankruptcy trustee can use state law to determine if a transfer was fraudulent. This means that the UFTA and the UFCA adopted by the state in which the bankruptcy court is located can be used by the trustee to determine if a transfer was fraudulent.

Defense

A defense to a charge of fraudulent conveyance is that there was fair consideration paid for the property. This means that if you sold your expensive car to your son for a fair price, the transfer should not be considered fraudulent, even if you spent the money on a trip to Europe.

Statutes of Limitations

A **statute of limitations** is a law which limits the time in which a suit can be brought. Fortunately, fraudulent transfer laws also have limitations. The UFTA requires that claims be brought within four years of the conveyance or two years after it was discovered or should have been discovered, whichever comes later. The statute of limitations under the UFCA varies by state. Under the bankruptcy law, transfers within one year prior to filing can be set aside. Countries which offer asset protection, such as the Bahamas and the Cook Islands, have very short statutes of limitations.

Nondischargeable Debts

Certain debts are not dischargeable in bankruptcy. This means that these debts will remain as claims against you until you pay them, and upon your death they will be claims against your estate. Nondischargeable debts can include the following:

- liabilities based upon fraud
- income taxes and excise taxes for the last three years
- alimony and child support
- liabilities for willful and malicious injuries
- liabilities from drunk driving
- government fines, penalties or forfeitures
- environmental fines
- student loans which matured less than seven years ago
- debts incurred with false statements
- debts which were nondischargeable in a previous bankruptcy
- credit card cash advances taken just before bankruptcy
- debts which were taken over by you in a divorce (if your ex-spouse objects)

Of course, if you have no property in your name, and there is no property in your estate at death, these debts do not have to be repaid. By properly arranging your affairs you can assure that no property is in your name, but still have control of it.

Some people are unaware that one's children do not have to pay one's debts. If a person dies with large debts and no property in their estate, in most cases the creditors are out of luck.

More specific rules about what can and cannot be done in exchanging nonexempt property for exempt property and out of your hands are contained in Chapters 15 and 29.

Chapter 6
Understanding the
Asset Seizure System

Before discussing the system for protecting assets it would help to understand a few of the legal terms involved when someone tries to collect money from you.

Someone claiming that you owe him money is a **claimant** who has a mere **claim** against you. If he files a lawsuit against you he becomes the **plaintiff** and you will be the **defendant**.

If he wins the suit the judge will sign a **judgment** against you, which is a statement of what you legally owe the plaintiff. The plaintiff will then be your **creditor** and you will be his **debtor**.

There is no law forcing you to pay a judgment against you. Debtors' prison has been abolished and you cannot be jailed for failing to pay your debts. However, in some matters, such as failure to pay child support, you can be held in jail in **contempt of court** if a judge thinks you are intentionally disobeying a court order.

If there is a judgment against you, you can pay it voluntarily or your creditor can try to locate and seize any assets which are titled in your name. There are various procedures for seizing the assets of a debtor. **Garnishment** can be used to seize money held by a third party, such as a bank account held by a bank or wages held by an employer. In some states a judgment can be **docketed** with the sheriff. Then the sheriff can be instructed to **levy** on the property and sell it. The sheriff may levy by either seizing it and putting it in storage or by posting a notice on or near the property that it is under the sheriff's control.

To find out what property you own, the court can order you to attend a **deposition,** where you must answer questions about your financial affairs under oath. The creditor can **subpoena** your personal records such as tax returns, deeds, bank statements, cancelled checks, and so forth. If you fail to come to a deposition or to supply your records after being subpoenaed, you can be held in contempt of court and jailed. If you lie under oath you can be found guilty of **perjury**.

Some of the property you own is **exempt** and may not be seized by a creditor. In most states your **homestead** or a portion of it is exempt. In some states you may own your property as **tenants by the entireties** with your spouse, and in some of those states such property may only be seized by creditors who have a judgment against both spouses.

You may take your property out of your name and transfer it to another entity, such as a **trust**, a **corporation** or a **limited partnership**. If the property is not in your name it usually cannot be seized unless the transfer was fraudulent.

A trust is an arrangement whereby one person, the **trustee**, holds property for another, the **beneficiary**. The person giving the property to the trustee is called the **grantor** or the **settlor**. The creditors of the trustee usually cannot reach the trust property because it is not the trustee's own property, he is merely holding it for others. The creditors of the beneficiaries, however, can often reach the beneficiaries' interest in the trust because they can seize the beneficiaries' interests, unless the trust is set us as a **spendthrift** trust. In a spendthrift trust a beneficiary cannot assign his interest and a creditor cannot seize it. But a person cannot set up a spendthrift trust for himself. More on trusts is explained in Chapters 33 through 37.

A corporation is a legal entity which is owned by its **shareholders** and run by its **officers** who are chosen by its **directors** (who are chosen by the shareholders). Personal creditors of the officers and directors usually cannot reach the property of the corporation because they are not owners of it, only employees. Creditors of a shareholder can seize the stock of the shareholder, and may or may not be able to reach the assets of the corporation. More on corporations is explained in Chapter 11.

A limited partnership is an arrangement between one or more **general partners** and one or more **limited partners** whereby the general partner controls the enterprise and incurs the liability and the limited partner puts up property hoping for future profits, but without further liability. Creditors of the partners can usually only have a **charging order** against the interests in the partnership and may not seize the partnership assets. This is explained in more detail in Chapter 32.

If you have a claim or a judgment against you and you give away your property or sell it for less than it is worth, that is considered a **fraudulent conveyance**. If it is considered fraudulent, your transfer of property may be set aside by a court and the property may be seized by your creditors.

If you have claims or judgments against you that you do not expect to be able to pay off, you can declare **bankruptcy**. **Chapter 7** bankruptcy allows you to wipe out your debts and start over. You can wipe out all of your debts except certain kinds, such as student loans, alimony, child support, income taxes less than three years old, debts incurred through fraud or false statements, debts from drunk driving, government fines and penalties such as environmental cleanup, and willful and malicious injuries. In Chapter 7 bankruptcy you can keep all of your exempt property but you must surrender your nonexempt property. Filing Chapter 7 bankruptcy takes about 90 days and wipes out all of your debts except those listed above.

Chapter 13 bankruptcy is used by persons with less than $1,000,000 in debts to restructure their payments to allow them to pay them off over a longer period of time. **Chapter 11** bankruptcy is similar but used by persons who have over $1,000,000 in debts. Often people try to restructure their debts under Chapter 13 then discover it is hopeless and switch to Chapter 7. This is euphemistically called **Chapter 20** bankruptcy. More on bankruptcy is explained in Chapter 41 of this book.

Chapter 7
The Four Most Important Rules of Asset Protection

If you are to successfully protect your assets from creditors you must follow four important rules.

1. Set up your asset protection plan as soon as possible

Once a suit has been filed against you it is too late to do most things which would best protect your assets. Even before a suit has been filed, but after you have committed an act which could give rise to a claim, it is too late to protect much of your property. To be completely safe you must set up your asset protection system before any possible claimant is known.

It is so easy to delay. You have never been sued. You might never be sued. Those millions of lawsuits filed each year are always against others. But each year, each day, the odds become greater that it is your turn to be handed those dreaded papers by the sheriff or process server.

I was very uncomfortable until I protected my own assets. The thought of some undeserved person and his lawyer taking what I had worked my life to attain was unacceptable. I worked late into the night on so many occasions, shopped carefully and never wasted anything, for what? To give it to someone else?

2. Get professional advice on your state's current exemptions

The easiest protections you have are the state exemption laws. These are laws which protect certain of your property from creditors. In some states these can shield hundreds of thousands of dollars worth of property. In other states there are limits on each exemption.

The laws are complicated and are subject to change both by the legislature and by court decisions. In some cases a minor detail on how the property is titled can make all the difference as to whether it is protected.

To be sure your property is set up correctly you should have a short consultation with an attorney who specializes in this area of law. He or she will have read all the most recent laws and cases in your state and will be able to tell you what investments are safe.

Chapter 46 explains how to find and work with an attorney.

3. Review your plan often

The makeup of your property changes, the laws covering what is exempt change, and the risks in your life change. Therefore you must occasionally review your asset protection to be sure that all of your property is covered from all of the risks.

For example, as a young surgeon your greatest risk may be of malpractice, but a few years later you may face a greater risk of divorce. Putting your assets in your spouse's name may protect you in the beginning but not from divorce.

4. Don't look like the "bad guy"

I have read numerous court cases of people in lawsuits with creditors. In some the judge let them keep their property; in others they lost their property, even though the facts looked the same. Why? Judges have discretion in these cases and they can make a decision on who appears to be the most honest and deserving.

If your actions make you look like a scoundrel who did everything to get out of paying a judgment, your asset protection plans will probably not work. But if you look honest and appear only to have acted prudently, to protect your family, you will probably win.

Chapter 8
The Cost of Asset Protection

While some of the strategies in this book for protecting your assets will be as simple as signing a bill of sale, other methods will involve some cost. There might be legal fees, service fees, lost interest or extra taxes. While some people cannot bear to get a quarter-percent less interest or to pay a dollar more in taxes, you must realize that these costs are insurance payments you are making to be sure you do not risk losing everything.

If you have never been sued or gotten into financial trouble it is easy to think that it will never happen to you and that asset protection costs are a waste of money. But your house has probably not burned down and yet you pay hundreds of dollars every year for fire insurance. Today you are probably much more likely to get sued than to have a fire in your home. The price you pay for asset protection may be all that it costs you to be sure you do not enter your golden years impoverished.

This extra cost can be compared to the risk/reward ratio of any investment. Junk bonds pay much higher interest than treasury bonds, but there is a greater chance you will lose your money with junk bonds. With asset protection techniques you may have a lower overall return on your investments, but you will be much safer and not worry about losing your life savings.

The amount you will pay to protect your assets will depend upon how great they are, how flexible you are in the type of assets you wish to hold, and the state in which you live. Some states offer simple protections for many types of assets, while others offer few protections. In the latter you will need to be more creative in structuring your assets to obtain the most protection.

If you have substantial assets your best protection may be to move a portion of them overseas. Many Americans are worrying about the litigation crisis in this country and an asset protection industry has sprung up around the globe to help Americans protect our assets. Some may be scams, but many are safe, legitimate investments.

As with any type of investment you need to investigate asset protection products carefully. This book will give you an unbiased analysis of those techniques known to the author. Others you learn of should be investigated thoroughly. It won't do any good to take your assets out of the reach of your creditors if your trustee absconds with.

Part Two
Shielding Yourself Against Claims

Chapter 9
Avoiding Risk

As mentioned earlier in this book, America has changed. Things which were harmless activities a few years ago are now fraught with risk. In this dangerous new world you must change your actions if you do not want to be the victim of the new liabilities.

It may seem sad, but it now may be risky to serve in some volunteer capacities. Driving the Cub Scouts on an outing, having a fund-raising meeting at your home or sponsoring a charitable event could result in millions of dollars in liability if someone is injured. Example: A Boy Scout touch football game "quickly degenerated into a tackle game" and a 16-year-old broke his neck. Two volunteers at the outing were found to be negligent and a jury awarded $7.1 million to the boy. Fortunately, the national Boy Scouts organization was able to pay that judgment, but what about smaller organizations? And what about the volunteers' legal fees?

As explained in Chapter 2, even if you are only 1% responsible for an injury, you may be ordered to pay for 100% of a lifetime of damages. The more wealth you have the more likely you will be found guilty.

In one case several children were injured when they were playing with dynamite blasting caps. Of course, when the caps exploded there was no evidence left of who the manufacturer was, so the children's families didn't know who to sue. The court ruled that since they could not know which company to sue, all companies who made blasting caps must pay a proportionate share of the damages. Even the most careful companies, which had done nothing wrong, were found liable. The court did not require any proof of guilt or wrongdoing.

Even if you had nothing to do with the injury you could bear all the financial burden if you are the deep pocket. This was a complete reversal of hundreds of years of legal theory which said that only guilty parties must pay for injuries.

Serving on a board of directors of a corporation used to be an honor. Now it is just too risky. Numerous million-dollar judgments have been entered against people who have served as directors.

Joining in with a friend or neighbor to buy a boat or piece of property may sound like a good deal, but again the risk may be greater than the reward. If you still want to do it, you should consider using a corporation as described in Chapter 11.

Before you agree to participate in any venture, be sure to consider all of the potential risks involved. If you can be listed as a named insured on an adequate insurance, and if you can get a written indemnification agreement from the organization you would have more reason to agree, but the riskiest activities should be avoided completely.

Chapter 10
Insurance

One simple way to protect yourself from liability is to buy insurance against liability. However, in the current crisis insurance may be unreasonably priced or even impossible to get. For some products the insurance can be three times the cost of manufacturing the item. For medical specialists the premiums can be more than their take-home pay.

One problem with insurance is that you never know how much to get. A small unforeseen accident may result in a multimillion-dollar award. Several years ago a judgment over a million dollars was a rarity. Today there are hundreds of such awards each year. With so many judgments now over a million dollars it is foolish for anyone with assets to have policies with the usual limits of $100,000 or $300,000. For the cost of only a couple hundred dollars a year it is usually possible to get an umbrella policy which covers your home, vehicles and rental properties for a million dollars or more. Those with large amounts of assets should get an umbrella policy with $5 million in coverage.

While insurance can protect against liability it can also attract lawsuits. Lately some professionals have decided to go without insurance to deter patients and clients from filing lawsuits. For those with few assets or well-protected assets this may be an option.

However, in some states lack of adequate insurance is considered in an insolvency analysis so that asset protection actions may be deemed fraudulent. In these states a law may allow creditors to take your exempt assets if you do not have enough insurance or other assets to cover the usual risks of the business you are in. In other states insurance may be required by law for some professions.

Another drawback of relying on insurance is that it does not cover all possible liabilities. Legal violations such as environmental liabilities or civil rights violations, intentional acts such as slander, and other liabilities such as alimony cannot be insured against. Also, there are the risks that your insurance will be dropped after a minor claims, that coverage will be denied for some reason, or that an insurance company will not be solvent enough to cover all claims. The natural disasters in recent years caused several companies to close and others to cancel policies. A future crisis could be even worse.

For the insurance you do have, you must be sure that the correct names and risks are listed. Depending on your business structure (corporate, partnership, etc.) you must arrange your insurance accordingly. If you are an employee you must be sure you are listed on your employer's policy. If you are an employer you must be sure the acts of all employees are covered. If you have partners you must be sure all are covered. If you are an officer or director of a corporation or charitable organization, be sure you name is specifically listed on their policy and that all possible risks are covered.

Be sure that all insurance arrangements are in writing. Don't rely on your agent's verbal assurance. If you ask if something is covered, ask him to mail or fax his answer. If he fails to do so, send him a certified letter restating your understanding. The friendliest agent may forget what he told you once you have a claim.

Chapter 11
Legal Entities

One way you can protect yourself from personal liability is by setting up your affairs in a way which will shield you from claims. For example, as an individual business owner you would be liable for accidents caused by your employees. But if your business was a corporation you would not usually be personally liable for acts of employees.

From a personal liability standpoint sole proprietorships and general partnerships are the riskiest types of ventures. In either of these entities you could be personally liable if your employee had a traffic accident on the way to the post office for you, or if someone slipped on your floor. In a partnership you could be personally liable for the acts of your partners. For example, in an accounting firm, medical practice or legal practice, if one partner makes an error, all partners are liable. In a recent case, sexual harassment by one partner in a law firm resulted in a $7 million judgment against the firm for which all partners were fully liable.

You can protect against this type of liability by structuring your affairs to insulate yourself. Some entities used to insulate from liability include corporations, limited partnerships, trusts, and in most states, limited liability companies.

This chapter discusses ways in which these entities can be used to shield you from liability. With this method, the business entity incurs all the liability and there are no claims against you personally. For this to be successful, the entity should have only a limited amount of assets, because these assets will be subject to the claims.

The entities described in this chapter can also be used in a different way. They can hold your valuable assets and protect them from claims against you personally. This method is discussed in more detail in Part Four of this book.

Corporations

A corporation is one of the oldest and best shelters from liability. The purpose of a corporation is to let people put a limited amount of money into a risky venture and not worry about losing anything else they own.

For example, if a doctor sets up a practice in his or her own name then the doctor would be personally liable for all of the debts and liabilities of the business including accidents caused by employees. However, if the doctor were to incorporate, the corporation would be considered a separate legal "person" liable for its own debts and employees. If a lawsuit resulted in a million-dollar judgment against the corporation, the doctor would lose whatever capital went into the corporation, but the doctor's other property and investments could not be touched. (This does not, however, protect the doctor from liability for acts he or she performs personally.)

One of the most famous law school cases involving corporate protection from liability occurred in New York. A man who owned hundreds of taxis put each one into a separate corporation and carried only the minimum insurance on each. When one taxi caused an accident the victim could collect the insurance on that taxi, and if that was not enough, could take the taxi itself, but could not touch any of the other taxis he owned which were in separate corporations. Today it is possible that a court would hold such an arrangement to be a sham, or against "public policy," but so far courts have not abandoned the protections afforded by corporations.

Of course, some businesses need large amounts of equipment in order to conduct their operations. To avoid putting the equipment at risk you could put it in a second corporation and lease it to the first corporation. If you wish to be even more creative you could put it in a "children's trust" and avoid taxes as well as liability. See Chapter 34.

As an officer, director, or major shareholder you will also have some day to day control for which you could be held liable, if you contributed to a damaging act.

In order to enjoy the protection of a corporation you must carefully follow the rules for corporations. Some of the most important ones are:

- Be sure that stock issued to you has been paid for
- Always hold annual meetings
- Never commingle corporate funds with your personal funds
- Keep accurate records and minutes
- Always use the correct corporate name with "Inc.," "Corp.," "P.A." or whatever is registered
- Always use your corporate title after your name
- Do not use corporate property for personal matters
- Have written agreements with yourself, employees and independent contractors

For asset protection purposes, you must also be sure that your corporation is not undercapitalized. This means that it must have a reasonable amount of capital for the type of business it is in. If your business needs few assets you do not have to have a lot of capital in the business, but if it uses a lot of capital equipment, you must have enough capital or your creditors may reach you personally.

To be sure of what is adequate capital, you should check with an accountant. Then record in the minutes the reasons for the amount of capital. Note that you made an assessment of the risks of the business and discussed the insurance needs of the business with an insurance agent. Be sure the debt ratio of the business is comparable with others in the industry.

Another important thing to consider is liability for federal withholding taxes. If a corporation fails to pay the required tax for its employees, the principal officers are personally liable for all amounts unpaid and there is an additional penalty of 100% of the tax which was not withheld. Withholding taxes should be one of the first items paid by the corporation.

Limited Partnerships

Some types of ventures, such as real estate projects, are often structured as limited partnerships. A limited partnership is a partnership between one or more general partners and one or more limited partners. The general partner is personally liable for all the debts and liabilities of the venture but the limited partners are only liable for the amount of money they contributed to the venture. It is also possible to use a corporation as the general partner thereby insulating everyone. However, unless the corporation were financially strong it would be difficult to get financing for such a venture, and there could be tax problems.

Limited partnerships can be useful in two ways. By setting up a risky venture as a limited partnership you can limit your risk to the amount of capital you contribute. As a limited partner you would not be liable if the venture failed.

The other way a limited partnership can be useful is if you set one or more up to hold your other assets. Limited partnership assets cannot be taken to pay the debts of one partner, so if your assets are in a limited partnership your creditors cannot reach them. This is discussed in more detail in Chapter 32.

Trusts

While trusts are primarily known for their ability to avoid probate and the legal fees that go with probate, they can protect from some liability.

If real estate is owned by a **land trust** then liability on the financing can be limited to the assets in the trust. This is one way to obtain financing from a seller for which no one is personally liable. The way to do this is to set up a trust to buy the property you are interested in and have your trustee sign the mortgage which will be held by the seller. A third party lender and a sophisticated seller would require a personal guarantee, but if a contract is presented correctly this might not be requested.

However, land trusts do not protect against liability for accidents on the property or for environmental problems. Also, land trusts can only be used in a limited number of states.

A **business trust**, like a limited partnership, can be used either to contain liability or to protect from liability. However, because business trusts are so seldom used and the law is not clear, it is better to use them to protect from liability than to contain liability, since corporations contain liability much more effectively. Using business trusts is discussed in Chapter 37.

Living trusts and **irrevocable trusts** are not usually useful in shielding you from claims and should not be used for this purpose. They are better used for shielding your assets from claims which reach you as explained in Chapters 33 through 36.

Limited Liability Companies

The limited liability company is a new type of business entity which was just invented in the 1980s. It has the limited liability of a corporation with the tax advantages of a partnership. It has been compared to a limited partnership with no general partners.

As of 1996 nearly all states have passed laws allowing LLCs and the last seven are expected to follow suit soon. A uniform limited liability company law was prepared by delegates from each state, and this law is expected to pass in some form in most states. This would make the laws of the different states more in line with each other.

Unlike a corporation which is subject to double taxation, an LLC files a partnership tax return. All income and deductions are passed through to the individual returns of the owners. This is similar to how an s-corporation works, but the advantages are:

- it can have an unlimited number of owners
- it can have corporations as owners
- it can have different classes of owners
- it may have nonresident aliens as owners

In five states–Arkansas, Georgia, Idaho, Montana and Texas– a sole proprietor can set up an LLC. However, the IRS has not yet ruled on whether these will be taxed at individual or corporate rates. In other states at least two persons are necessary to form an LLC.

In some states the LLC may be less advantageous than the s-corporation. In Florida, for example, an LLC must pay the same 5.5% corporate income tax as a c-corporation. The s-corporation is still exempt from this tax.

Limited Liability Partnerships

the newest legal entity is the limited liability partnership. In some states professionals such as lawyers and doctors cannot practice under a corporate or LLC form, so this entity was structured to allow professionals to form a partnerships and avoid liability for the acts of their partners.

Tax Considerations

Most of the entities in this chapter which protect you from liability must file their own tax return and each has several options for taxation. You can choose the cash or accrual basis, you can adopt a fiscal year different from the calendar year, and in some cases you can choose between different methods of taxation. For example, a corporation may be taxed as a separate entity (c-corporation) or may pass its taxable income through to its shareholders (s-corporation).

To be sure to get the best advantages you should review the tax options with an accountant or tax attorney. Don't just ask them to decide what you should do. Let them explain the advantages of each choice and then you decide. Some tax advisors do things one way because they haven't learned the other ways.

If you are pressed for time you may wish to put your trust in an advisor. However, there are several books available on corporations and the tax options available and you would be much better off if you understood how your business is structured.

Resources

A Guide to Limited Liability Companies, Commerce Clearing House, $22.50 Tel: (800) 835-5224

Bagley, William and Whynott, Philip P., *The Better Alternative: The Limited Liability Company*, Limited Liability Company Law & Practice, P. O. Box 1436, Cheyenne, WY 82003-1436, Tel: (307) 634-0446. $135

Family Limited Partnerships, General American Life Insurance Co., P. O. Box 396, St. Louis, MO 63166, Tel: (800) 835-2711, Includes book, video and forms on diskette. $75 plus $4.50 shipping

Jacobs, Vern, *Tax Factors in Choosing a Form of Business*, Research Press, Inc. $29.00

Warda, Mark, *Land Trusts in Florida*, Sphinx Publishing, $19.95, 4th edition due out late 1995

Wilber, W. Kelsea and Sartorius, Arthur G., III, *How to Form Your Own Corporation*, Sphinx Publishing, $19.95, ISBN 0-913825-61-1

Chapter 12
Contracts

Some types of liability can be guarded against with contracts. If you put into a contract exactly what you are offering to do, you should not be held liable if you do not accomplish more. For example, if you put in writing that an operation has 50% chance of success and it is not successful, there is less likelihood of a suit than if nothing was in writing and the patient says you promised perfect results.

Arbitration Clauses

An arbitration clause should be included in every contract you sign. This is a clause which says that a dispute between the parties will be decided by an arbitrator, not a court. Why is this good? Because arbitration is faster and more straightforward than our court system. Court cases can be dragged out for years with all kinds of motions and investigations. And sympathetic juries can be swayed by emotional lawyers and bogus "experts." Arbitrators can settle the case quickly and cut through the smoke put up by lawyers.

Whenever you sign any contract or lease of any kind, insist that the following clause be added and initialed by all parties:

Any conflicts between the parties to this agreement shall be settled by binding arbitration under the rules of the American Arbitration Association.

Be careful how the clause is worded. If it had just said "any conflict under this agreement," a person could argue that their dispute with you was not "under the agreement" so that arbitration did not apply.

In Appendix 5 of this book is an Addendum to Contract which you can use to add an arbitration clause to any contract you sign. Just be sure the other party signs it.

Business Contracts

In some lines of work business is always handled on a handshake or a verbal agreement. But in some cases there is not the same understanding by both sides as to what the agreement is. This may work fine most of the time, especially if large sums of money are not involved. However, every so often such an agreement can get out of hand.

To protect yourself in any type of business you should have a standard contract that you give to all customers spelling out exactly what you are promising to provide and what your obligations are. This applies to all businesses whether you are a roofer, doctor, or an attorney.

This contract should be well thought out and should take into consideration everything possible that could go wrong. It should be in simple English rather than legalese. If there are any clauses which might be construed by a court as unfair or questionable, then there should be a place for the parties to initial next to them, signalling their clear agreement with each clause.

Employee Contracts

If you have employees you should have them sign employment contracts. These contracts can protect you from litigation and potential damages. Your employment contract should spell out what the employee's rights and obligations are, and it should make clear that the policy of your company is to forbid discrimination, sexual harassment, and other illegal activities. It should require them to report any offenses to you immediately so that you can take action.

As with other types of contracts, the most important clause to have in an employment contract is an arbitration clause. Arbitration clauses have been successful in protecting businesses from lawsuits under federal civil rights laws. The U. S. Supreme Court ruled in 1991* that claims under the Age Discrimination in Employment Act could be made subject to binding arbitration. This would probably also apply to

*Gilmer v. Interstate/Johnson Corp., 500 U.S. 20, 111 S.Ct. 1647 (1991)

similar types of claims and could protect you from civil rights and sexual harassment suits. If not subject to binding arbitration, such suits could drag out for ten or more years and cost you a fortune in legal fees and lost productivity.

A sample employment contract is included in Appendix 5.

Independent Contractors

There are many advantages to using independent contractors rather than employees in your business. The most important have to do with liability and taxes. You are usually not liable for the acts of independent contractors with whom you contract. They are liable for their own acts and those of their employees.

As for taxation, you can avoid social security, medicare, unemployment and other taxes by hiring independent contractors rather than employees. However, the IRS is making a special effort to investigate companies which use independent contractors. There are penalties for incorrectly calling an employee an independent contractor.

Basically, if a person is in business for himself and has other customers he will most likely be considered an independent contractor. This will be true if he decides how and when the work will be done and supplies his own tools. If you have too much control over how the work is done, he may be considered an employee.

Premarital Contracts

In a marriage, a premarital agreement is a contract which spells out what will happen in the event of divorce or death. By signing such an agreement you can protect against a catastrophic divorce judgment.

Especially in second marriages, premarital agreements are useful in protecting the rights of children born of a previous marriage.

Most people do not realize it, but everyone who gets married has a premarital agreement. It is the one contained in the divorce and probate laws of your state. Those who do not make their own have one made up by the judges and the legislature. Naturally, one size does not fit all, and the distribution of your assets in the event of divorce may not be what either of you would prefer.

Not all premarital agreements hold up in court, but if both parties have attorneys, and there is a full disclosure between them, then the agreement should be binding. If the more wealthy party springs it by surprise an hour before the wedding with a threat to cancel the whole thing if it is not signed, then it probably would be thrown out by a judge.

If you are already married it is possible to cover the same items a premarital agreement would, in a marital agreement.

Real Estate Contracts and Leases

Real estate deals are common sources of litigation. Since large sums of money are involved it is worth the time and money to hire an attorney and go to court if you have a good case. Today the courts are expanding the liabilities of persons involved in real estate deals. In some states you are required by law to disclose "all known" defects in the property. In others you need only disclose "hidden" defects. If you do not or if you cannot prove that you made the disclosure then you may be sued for thousands of dollars in damages after the sale.

In addition, there are laws requiring the disclosure of such things as lead paint on the walls, radon gas in the ground, and even former military bases in the neighborhood.

If your contract or lease is drafted properly you can protect yourself from most kinds of suits. You should not expect a real estate agent to protect you completely in such a transaction. While some are very skillful and look out for their customer, many do not know all of the risks and some look out only for their commission.

Usually an attorney's fee is well worth the protection in putting together a real estate deal. While many deals may go through smoothly, if yours has a problem and you are not protected it could cost you thousands of dollars. Another alternative is a book which explains real estate contracts or leases. However, since laws change constantly, a book would not be able to keep up with the most recent changes.

Daily contracts

Some people may consider it to be going too far but to be even more sure of avoiding litigation, some suggest that simple contract forms be used in everyday transactions.

For example, if you sell your used refrigerator in a garage sale, writing on the receipt that the item is sold "as is" with no warranties can protect you from a nuisance suit if it breaks down a week later.

Resources

Elias, Stephen and Stewart, Marcia, *Simple Contracts for Personal Use*, $16.95 Nolo Press

Haman, Edward A., *How to Write Your Own Premarital Agreement*, Sphinx Publishing, $19.95, ISBN 0-913825-69-7

Warda, Mark, *How to Negotiate Real Estate Contracts*, Sphinx Publishing, $14.95, ISBN 0-913825-59-X

Warda, Mark, *How to Negotiate Real Estate Leases*, Sphinx Publishing, $14.95, ISBN 0-913825-58-1

Chapter 13
Your Financial Statement

One of the first steps in protecting your assets is to eliminate as many assets as possible from your financial statement. Over the years you have probably added to your assets and proudly watched your wealth grow. When applying for a loan it is only natural to list everything possible and even to exaggerate its value. But for asset protection purposes this is the worst thing you can do.

Your financial statement is one of the first things your creditor will look at when trying to seize your assets. Your creditor's lawyer can force you to provide copies of all financial statements you have prepared in recent years. What if you didn't save copies, or have "lost" them? Creditors can subpoena copies from all banks you have done business with. And how will they find that out? They will subpoena copies of all checks you have written in past years and see who you have been making payments to.

If your financial statement now has things on it such as a boat, a vacation home and a coin collection, you cannot simply stop listing them and pretend they do not exist. You will be asked under oath what happened to them and will be expected to produce receipts or other proof of what you did with them.

There is little you can do today if a lawsuit has already been filed against you. Your best bet is to sell your nonexempt assets and buy exempt assets. But if you do not have any claims against you now, you can begin today to clean up your financial statement before you are hit with a future claim. If your available assets diminish slowly over the years, you will not look like a "bad guy" who tried to cheat creditors. You merely prudently shifted to other investments.

You don't have to actually rid yourself of your wealth, and you don't have to lie. Your goal is to convert what you have to forms of wealth that either do not appear on your financial statement or are untouchable by your creditors. Parts 3 and 4 of this book explain the safe ways to hold your property. For example, in some states you can take your cash and mutual funds and buy an annuity which cannot be touched by your creditors. In every state you can put your coin collection in a family limited partnership.

There are many ways to convert your assets to safe forms of ownership. The longer the time period before your potential trouble, the more flexibility you have. Immediately before wiping out your debts through bankruptcy you can convert some nonexempt assets to exempt assets (see Chapter 15). But all transfers made within a year of bankruptcy must be disclosed to the court and can be set aside. If you have no financial problems for the next year most transfers you make now will be safe, and if no problems arise for 5 or 10 years, your sales or transfers might not even be questioned.

Chapter 14
Privacy

One important way to protect your assets is to keep your affairs private. People who are obviously wealthy are at a greater risk of being sued. The most famous and wealthy in our society are constantly being sued by people trying to get some of their wealth. For them, defending such suits comes as the cost of being famous.

One of the first things an attorney does when he takes a case is to see what assets the defendant has available. If it looks like a lot of assets are available, the case is well worth taking. Even a frivolous suit might get a settlement to avoid the nuisance and legal fees. But if the defendant appears to have few assets the attorney might try for a quick settlement for a small amount, or accept the limit of the insurance policy, or not take the case at all.

Most personal injury cases in this country are taken on a contingent fee basis by attorneys. This means that the attorneys don't get paid unless the client collects. They may work for nothing for years on a case if it looks like there will be a big payoff in the end. Some of them may even put out thousands of dollars of their own money to pay the costs of trying the case. But attorneys are not likely to take cases that involve a lot of work and little money.

To protect your wealth you should keep as low a profile as possible. If you flaunt your wealth, wear expensive jewelry, drive expensive cars and live in a mansion you are

more likely to be the target of a lawsuit (and you will have more available assets to seize). Sam Walton, founder of Wal-Mart, was one of the wealthiest men in the world and yet he drove a pickup truck. Does your ego demand more?

You may be thinking, "But what good is it to be wealthy if I cannot enjoy it? I like and want a Porsche, furs, a mansion and my own jet." Okay, if you must have those things you can, but you will face a greater expense in protecting them and a greater risk of suits.

Another alternative is to live two lifestyles. Where you live and work you can live modestly, but on the weekend go to your luxury home in Manhattan, Monte Carlo, or Vail. Tell your neighbors you spend weekends with your mother, or at a cottage in the country (buy one if you have to).

Another advantage of protecting your privacy is that if you are sued your wealth can less easily be found if you have not left extensive records of it.

In our country today there are hundreds of government and private databases that contain countless facts about your life. Credit bureaus, the social security administration, banks, loan companies, department stores and numerous other entities have files on you. Did you notice how some grocery stores print out coupons based upon what you buy? Soon, if you pay by credit or debit card they will be able to keep a record of your annual food purchases. Do you buy wine? Steaks? Where did the money come from?

Look at your check book and your credit card statements. What do these say about you? Do they list investments? Jewelry purchases? Gifts? Flights overseas? The purchase of this book? All of these records will be available to parties who sue you. In most cases they cannot see them until they win. But in some situations they can subpoena your records early in the case.

If you claim to have "lost" your records they can get copies from your bank. Banks microfilm every check you write, so all of your purchases can all be traced.

The first thing you need to do is to make sure there is no permanent record of your purchases. Don't worry about the basics like your mortgage payment, electricity, water, etc. Everyone has those expenses and it would be silly to drive around town paying cash for those things. But your discretionary purchases should not be made by check or credit card. Or at least not by *your* check or credit card. How do you pay for things? By cash or by check or credit cards which are not in your name.

Legal Issues

Just like a knife, which can either be used to peel an apple or to kill someone, the information in this chapter can be used for honest or dishonest purposes. The purpose of this book is to show you how you can legally protect what you have earned from unfair claimants. It is not a book on how to avoid taxes or launder money.

One problem with using privacy techniques for asset protection is that it arouses suspicion of the IRS. If an IRS audit reveals any evidence of cash transactions which were not run through bank account, you will be suspected of tax fraud. To counter this possible claim you should keep detailed records of your cash transactions which you can produce in the event of an audit.

There are many loopholes and deductions in our tax system. It is not necessary to become a criminal to lower your taxes. Doing so puts an emotional strain on you as well as opens the possibility that you may lose your freedom completely if you are jailed for tax evasion. Don't become a criminal for a few extra dollars. Just use the legal loopholes in the tax system to pay as little as possible.

As discussed later in this chapter, there are severe penalties for money laundering. In its zest to slow the use of drugs our government has passed several laws which make innocent acts criminal. Be careful not to run afoul of these laws.

Cash

The simplest way to avoid having a record of your financial affairs is to use cash. Years ago it was expected that we would soon have a cashless society, but we are now using more cash than ever.

Other than your standard household expenses you should use cash whenever possible. Every week when you deposit your paycheck take part of it in cash. Or cash every other check. Here are some other suggestions and things to keep in mind.

- When you receive dividends, bonuses, mortgage payments, or other receivables in the form of checks, you can take them to the bank teller and get cash for them without depositing them into your account. That way they are not microfilmed along with your bank records.

- If you would like to keep your cash transactions even more discrete, you can open another account at a different bank, and then use that bank exclusively for cashing checks.

- For local checks you can go to the banks on which they are drawn to get cash, but this would not be much of an advantage over cashing them at a bank where you have an account (as long as they are not deposited into the account).

- Keep in mind that cashing a check without depositing it does not relieve you of the tax liability. In many cases you and the IRS will get 1099 statements which report this income.

- There is a law which requires all transactions of over $10,000 in cash to be reported to the federal government. If you try to break down a large transaction into several smaller ones over a few days, these are supposed to be combined and reported.

- For transactions which must be conducted by mail, money orders or cashier's checks can be used. Some banks even allow a certain number of free cashier's checks a month. However, other banks require that if you buy a money order with cash (even a $5 money order) you must fill out a form with your name, address, social security number, etc. Find a new bank.

- If you leave the country with more than $5,000 in cash or negotiable instruments with you, you are required to file a federal report. There is no limit to the amount you can take out of the country, you just have to report it.

Credit Cards

Since your credit card accounts are reported to the credit bureau, a card in your name and social security number will show up on a copy of your credit report. A creditor's attorney can get a list of your credit cards, and from these a statement of all of your purchases. Therefore, to ensure privacy you need a card which is not listed in your name. These are some possibilities:

- If you can get a credit card in a foreign country, it will not be reported to the U.S. credit bureaus. Visa, Master Card and American Express issue cards all over the world which are good in nearly every country. This means that if you get a foreign card you can use it here in the U.S. as a normal card for meals, travel, investments, gifts or anything else.

The problem with this is that it is very hard to get a card elsewhere as a nonresident. Possibly if you open a bank account at the same bank (and authorize payments to be debited from the account) it may help. But in some places you may have to establish a local address. (Any plans for an extended vacation or intensive language study abroad?)

In using a foreign credit card you must consider the possibility of currency fluctuation. While the long term prospects of the dollar seem risky in light of the national debt, short term the dollar could gain against some currencies. If you are concerned about this you might wish to get an account denominated in U. S. dollars.

- If you have a trusted friend, or rather a friend who trusts you, you can get a credit card in his or her name. For example, ask your parent or child to apply for a credit card and put you on the account as an additional user. Once the card is issued, destroy their card and have the address of the account changed to a post office box to which you have access. Then use the card as your own and pay the bill each month with a money order purchased for cash.

- A spouse would not be a good choice because in a divorce all of your records could be disclosed. Also, in a suit against both of you, the records would be available to creditors.

- If you have an interest in a corporation you might be able to get a card in the corporation's name. While the corporation's records might be subpoenaed, if you held only a minor interest it might be ignored. However, be careful when using a corporate account for personal expenses. If not reimbursed scrupulously, it might result in tax problems or a "piercing of the corporate veil."

Checking Account

The ideal checking account is one that is not in your name or social security number and does not pay interest (which would result in a 1099 which must go on your tax return). These are some possibilities:

- As with credit cards above, if you have a trusting friend you can open an account in their name and then make all the deposits and checks yourself. (Be sure to be listed as a signatory on the account.)

- A corporate checking account could be used for some purposes, but you would need to repay amounts used for personal expenses.

- If you set up a trust you may be able to obtain a separate Federal Employer Identification Number for it. Then you could open a bank account for the trust and use its FEIN instead of your social security number.

- You can open an account under a "fictitious name." In most states the name must be registered with either the county or the state, but it puts up one more wall of privacy which must be climbed.

- While a local bank may be useful for local bills, the bulk of your transactions could be done through a money market account with check writing privileges in another state. This would make it harder for a local creditor to subpoena records or garnish funds.

Whether any or all of these methods work will depend on how clever the attorney is who is after you. It will depend on whether his deposition questions ask for "your personal checking account records," "all checking accounts in your name," or "all checking accounts on which you can sign."

Real Estate

In county courthouses around the country, copies of deeds and the taxes paid on them are public records which allows anyone to look up what was paid for a piece of property. Property appraisers' offices sometimes have data which includes the layout of the house and the value of the fixtures. There are no public records of the stocks, bonds or bank accounts people own, so why are real estate records open to public view? They don't have to be. There are ways to keep some of this information private.

Land Trusts

One of the best ways is the "Illinois-type" land trust. This device allows you to put property in the name of another person or bank, keeping your name off the public records. When the property is transferred, the "deed stamps" can be put on the assignment of the trust certificate, which is not recorded in the public records. No one need know who owns the property, how much it sold for, or even how many times it sold. Unfortunately, land trusts are only available in a few states, for example, Arizona, California, Florida, Hawaii, Illinois, Indiana, North Dakota, and Virginia.

Living Trusts

If land trusts are not available in your state you can use a living trust with someone other than yourself, such as a bank, as the trustee.

Corporations

If a corporation owns a piece of property, stock in the corporation could be sold with no record of the price paid or the purchaser. In most states corporations must disclose their officers and directors, but not the names of their stockholders. If you are buying a piece of property you could arrange for the seller to convey it to a corporation and then transfer the stock to you. However, there are numerous tax considerations involved and such a transaction should be set up by your accountant.

Keep in mind that while the stockholders of a corporation are not registered anywhere, the officers are directors are public record. In many states someone could search the corporate records for all corporations in which you are an officer or director. Therefore it may be advisable to use a relative or friend for these positions.

Limited Partnerships

Because of the strong asset protection benefits of a limited partnership, it is one of the best ways to hold real property. Limited partnerships are discussed in more detail in Chapter 32.

Aircraft and Boats

If you own an aircraft or boat in your own name it is easy for a creditor to find. It often takes just one phone call. Owning these items through a corporation or limited partnership can offer both privacy and protection from liability.

Gold and Collectibles

One of the best ways to keep your wealth private is to invest in something of which there is no record. Gold coins, rare stamps, gemstones, and all types of collectibles can be bought for cash at both shops and collectibles shows. Most of these can be easily hidden from thieves. Some collectibles, such as rare toys, porcelain or other antiques can be worth tens of thousands of dollars, yet be ignored by burglars who are unaware of their value.

If you plan to invest in collectibles of this type, be sure it is something you are interested in and willing to learn about. You cannot safely invest in collectibles and expect to rely on the goodwill of dealers. Dealers in collectibles make the most profit from customers who do not know the value of the items. To do well you must enjoy the items enough to become knowledgeable about them.

If you own valuable items you will need to protect them from loss. If you insure them there will be a record of the insurance. If you keep them in a safe deposit box there will be a record of the box. Although only you will know what is in the box, if you have a large size box it will be hard to claim you only kept your deed and insurance papers in it.

Some items such as gold and gems can be safely hidden in your home. A secret compartment in a door frame or fake receptacle box will be safe from most burglars. Burying them in the basement under the concrete will probably survive most natural disasters. Just be sure there is a map for your heirs in case you die. You wouldn't want your prize possessions to go to some demolition worker 50 years from now!

Other Ways to Protect Your Privacy

The above are the best things you can do to protect your financial privacy. Some other suggestions are:

- Use a post office box. If you can conveniently use one in a different town than that of your home that is even better.

- Do not list your phone number. Or, list your number under a fake name. Then you can tell friends "If you need to look up my number, I'm under 'Bill Ding.'" Today it is possible to buy a CDROM containing nearly every phone listing in the country for less than $30.

- Use a signature which is unreadable, especially on your checks.

- You can use different versions of your real name to confuse persons trying to search your records. For example, Harold Robert Jones could be Harold R. Jones, Harry Jones, H. Robert Jones, H. R. "Bob" Jones or even Bob Jones. This would not be foolproof, since searchers are supposed to check all variations, but it could be missed.

- When you call an individual or business they may be able to get a display of your phone number and name. Eventually they will automatically be able to download other information about you. To thwart this you can dial a special code which will prevent your information from being given out. In most areas it is "*67" for touch tone service or "1167" for pulse service. Check your phone directory or with your phone company on how this may be done in your area. You cannot block 800 or 900 numbers from getting your number.

How People Find You

To know how to avoid being found you must know the techniques used to track people down. I have read different books explaining how to find a person and from these learned the following:

- The most important piece of information needed to track someone down is their social security number and their date of birth. Therefore, you should never give these out to anyone unless absolutely necessary. Sometimes, people who say that you must give them this information are mistaken. If you are a sole proprietor you have the choice of using your social security number or getting a Federal Employer Identification Number. By using the latter you can keep your business separate from your personal affairs.

- It is sometimes possible to get a birth date and social security number from a state department of motor vehicles with only a name. Therefore, if you do not want to be found you may have to go without a driver's license. (See "Changing Your Name" which follows).

- If you file a change of address form with the post office, anyone can obtain this by paying $1 or by writing "Address correction requested" on a letter sent to you. There are also plans to enter this into a national database. To avoid disclosing your new address this way, you should notify correspondents individually or have your mail forwarded to a post office box. If the box is in a state other than the one you are moving to, you can really throw them off!

- Today there are inexpensive databases available to private investigators which contain every phone listing in the country. To avoid being included you should have an unlisted phone number or list your phone under a name other than your own.

- If you are in any type of regulated profession or hold any type of license, the state records on you are probably open to the public.

- With the rapidly advancing computer technology, more and more databases are being computerized. Soon it will be possible to access records of all types with a computer over the phone lines. These will include court cases, recreational permits, tenant records and many others.

Changing Your Name

One thing you may consider if you are serious about not being found is changing your name. Of course, with the same birth date and social security number this is not foolproof, but it may stymie those who do not have this information and are just checking for your name.

In most states you cannot change your name if you have an illegal or ulterior purpose. In your request to change your name you will probably be required to list any judgments against you, any bankruptcies, and other information. Failure to answer truthfully will most likely be considered perjury.

This may not be useful for those who have already had problems, but for those with no pending claims who want to make a fresh start without worrying about events in the past which may come back to haunt them, this may work.

Each state has its own laws for changing names and some may be more useful than others. If the state in which you intend to relocate has laws that will not help you, you may wish to go to another state to change your name. To compare the name change laws of the different states you can check the name change statutes of each state in a large law library. Most law schools have statutes of all the states.

Criminal Laws

Anyone who wishes to protect his privacy should be aware of the numerous criminal laws regarding money laundering and bank secrecy. Due to their frustration in being unable to catch drug dealers, our government has passed numerous laws making different types of financial secrecy a criminal offense.

These laws are very tough and there are few loopholes. Our government does not care that they catch many innocent Americans. They just want to be sure they can catch the drug dealers. Many innocent Americans have faced criminal penalties and the loss of their savings for honest mistakes. For example, an elderly doctor who kept his savings in cash because he learned to fear banks during the Depression lost his life savings when he made a cash deposit improperly in a friend's bank.

Even local law enforcement agencies are going after Americans who innocently have cash in their possession. Cars travelling on Interstate-95 between Miami and New York which "look suspicious" are being stopped. If cash is found in the car, the cash is seized for no other reason than that it was "suspicious." Sums of $1,000, $3,000 and more are being lost simply because it is too costly to hire a lawyer to retrieve them.

Even such innocent acts as paying cash for an airline ticket or travelling without checking luggage are being used to target people for search.

Some of the laws which may affect your efforts to protect your privacy are:

The Bank Secrecy Act of 1970

- Must report cash transactions of over $10,000.

- Must report carrying cash of over $10,000 in or out of the country.

- Must report foreign bank accounts of over $10,000.

- Banks must microfilm all checks over $100 (but most banks copy all checks since it is too much work to sort them).

- Banks must request social security number or Federal Employer Identification Number for all accounts.

The Money Laundering Control Act of 1986

- Dealing in the proceeds of certain crimes is illegal and the penalty is up to 20 years in prison and a fine of $500,000 or double the amount involved. One congressman stated that if a grocer knowingly accepts payment for groceries from a drug dealer he may be guilty under this law.

- Knowingly attempting to engage in transactions involving $10,000 or more of money from certain criminal sources is illegal and the penalty is up to 10 years in prison and a fine of $250,000 or double the amount involved.

- Illegally concealing legitimately-earned money can also be a violation of the act.

- Attempting to cause a financial institution to not file a currency transaction report or to file an incorrect one is also a violation.

- It is illegal to engage in several smaller transactions to avoid financial reporting requirements. This is called "structuring." Depositing $5500 in cash into your bank account two days in a row (from the same source) is a felony. The punishment is a mandatory five-year sentence, $250,000 fine, and forfeiture of the funds involved. (A rapist may have to be released to make room for you.)

- If you violate any of the last three of these while violating any other law, or in a pattern involving over $100,000 during a one-year period, then the penalty is $500,000 and 10 years in prison.

The Anti-Drug Abuse Act of 1988

- Banks must keep logs of money orders, traveller's checks and cashier's checks of more than $3,000.

- Banks in some areas must keep logs of *all* cash transactions.

- The Treasury Secretary is authorized to negotiate with foreign countries to start cash reporting systems.

The Annunzio-Wylie Act of 1992

- Creates a new felony and forfeiture of assets for operating an "illegal money transmitter business" without a state license.

The Money Laundering Suppression Act of 1994

- Requires registration and reporting by non-bank financial institutions, such as currency exchanges, money transmitters (i.e. Western Union), travelers check issuers, money order sellers, and casinos.

- Encourages state regulation of these businesses.

As you can see, violation of these laws can have serious consequences. Don't do anything that might be illegal to protect yourself from a possible unknown future creditor. Worry about our present out-of-control government.

Part Three
Protecting Property in Your Name

Chapter 15
How Exemptions Work

Every state and the federal government provides that certain property is exempt from the claims of creditors. This is a public policy decision. It is felt that allowing a debtor keep certain property is more important than letting the creditor take everything.

The rationale is that if persons could lose everything they own to creditors, including their home and car and tools of their trade, they would be a burden on society, which would then have to support them. Allowing them to keep some property allows them to get a fresh start.

Luckily for those wanting to protect their assets, the exemptions in some states are quite generous. In some states a person can file bankruptcy and still keep millions of dollars in assets. So the fresh start can be quite a nice one. Former governor John Connolly of Texas used his state's generous bankruptcy laws to shield many of his assets when he got into financial difficulties years after he accompanied President Kennedy through Dallas.

The following chapters discuss the various types of exempt property. Laws vary greatly from state to state so this material is general and discusses the different types of systems. A comparison of the important exemptions is found in Appendix 2, and a detailed list of exemptions for each state is in Appendix 3. But these laws often change. For a final determination of what is exempt in your state be sure to consult a specialist as discussed in Chapter 46.

There are two sets of federal exemptions and a set for each state. Which ones you may use depends upon the state in which you live. In 16 states you may choose between the federal exemptions and your state's exemptions. These states are Arkansas, Connecticut, District of Columbia, Hawaii, Massachusetts, Michigan, Minnesota, New Jersey, New Mexico, Pennsylvania, Rhode Island, South Carolina, Texas, Vermont, Washington and Wisconsin.

In the other states you must use the state exemptions. In these states, and if you choose the state exemptions in any of the above states, you may also use the federal non-bankruptcy exemptions.

Therefore, you should compare the federal exemptions (page 194 of Appendix 3) against the exemptions for your state (listed in Appendix 3) together with the federal non-bankruptcy exemptions (page 195 of Appendix 3).

It is clear in the Congressional Record that people are allowed to convert their nonexempt assets into exempt assets prior to filing for bankruptcy.

> As under current law, the debtor will be permitted to convert nonexempt property into exempt property before filing a bankruptcy petition. The practice is not fraudulent as to creditors, and permits the debtor to make full use of the exemptions to which he is entitled under the law. H.R.Rep. No. 595, 95th Cong., 1st Sess. 361 (1977); S.Rep. No. 989, 95th Cong., 2nd Sess. 76 (1978).

Shifting of property can even be done on the "eve of bankruptcy." However, some courts have decided that certain types of shifting does constitute a fraud of creditors. Therefore a person must be careful in his pre-bankruptcy planning not to do anything which may be interpreted as fraud. One thing a court looks at is dealings with creditors. If a person takes actions to deceive his creditors or engages in any clandestine activities, this will look bad to the court.

In a California case, a woman was required as part of her divorce settlement to reimburse her husband for marital debts of nearly $17,000. Two years later when she failed to pay, her husband set a hearing for a writ of execution. She asked for a continuance so that she could get an attorney. It was granted and she then went out and mortgaged the available equity in her house, spent the money and filed bankruptcy.

The bankruptcy court admitted that she had the right to convert nonexempt property into exempt property, but found that she had an *intent to defraud* her husband and denied her discharge under § 727(a)(2) of the Bankruptcy Code.*

Another court explained that minor actions will be overlooked, but that "when a pig becomes a hog it is slaughtered... wholesale slaughtering of assets which otherwise would go to creditors is not permissible."

However, a Minnesota court which weighed the rights of the debtor to convert assets into exempt property against the rule that creditors not be hindered or delayed held that only if a criminal level of wrongdoing was found would discharge be denied.**

In the states in the 5th and 10th Circuits (Louisiana, Mississippi, Texas, Colorado, Kansas, New Mexico, Oklahoma, Utah and Wyoming) merely having a large amount of exempt assets can be considered a sign that creditors are being defrauded. The 2nd and 7th Circuits (Connecticut, Illinois, Indiana, New York, Vermont and Wisconsin) do not hold to this view. Because such rules are subject to change each time new cases are decided, the best way to find out your state's position will be discussed in Chapter 46.

Planning, done years before any claims arise, is the main focus of this book. If this planning is done there will be no worry of any allegations that creditors were defrauded. Buying only exempt assets should become a long-term way of life.

One thing which is definitely forbidden is borrowing money with which to buy exempt assets prior to bankruptcy. This is always considered an abuse of the system and a fraud upon the creditor from whom the money was borrowed.

The unfortunate thing about using exemptions is that they do not protect you from all types of claims. Some debts, such as alimony and child support, environmental fines, and other debts which are nondischargeable in bankruptcy may be a claim against your exempt property.

In re Oberst, 91 B.R. 97 (Bkrtcy.C.D.Cal. 1988)
**In re Johnson*, 80 B.R. 953 (Bankr.Minn. 1987)

Chapter 16
Homestead

Nearly all states offer an exemption of a person's homestead from the claims of creditors. Unfortunately, in many states it has a very small dollar limit. For example, in Arkansas it is only $2,500 and in Michigan, only $3,500. In a few states it is a lot higher, such as $100,000 in Massachusetts and $90,000 in Nevada. But in most states it ranges from $5,000 to $10,000.

In Florida, Iowa, Kansas, Minnesota, Oklahoma, South Dakota and Texas the amount of homestead exemption can be unlimited! This means that you can own a large expensive home in these states and your creditors cannot touch it no matter how big your debts. Some people have even put gold fixtures in their houses in order to shield their wealth! People who expect financial problems move to these states to protect their wealth.

Of course, the homestead exemption does not protect you from losing your home if you do not pay the mortgage or trust deed on the property itself.

The following text describes the possible protections, requirements and exceptions to protection. But these laws often change and are subject to different judicial interpretations. To be sure of the exact protection in your state you should consult with a specialist as explained in Chapter 46.

What Is Protected

The laws vary greatly from state to state as to what type and amount of homestead is protected. In some states only traditional homes are protected, but in many others condominiums, co-op apartments and mobile homes (with or without land) are protected. Some states limit the physical size of the homestead, and often a homestead outside of a city can be larger than one within city limits.

In some states the dollar limit is based upon the person's interest in the property and in others it is based upon the entire property. For example, suppose a person owned a $100,000 home in a state with a $30,000 exemption, and deeded the property to his children reserving a life estate for himself. In a state which only counted the value of the interest, the life estate might be safe from creditors if its value were determined to be less than $30,000. However, in a state which values the entire property, the creditors could reach part of the value.

If the value of the homestead is greater than the exemption, then the homestead can be sold with the amount of the exemption paid to the owner and the balance to the creditor. In some cases, if the homestead is divisible, such as a farm, part of it can be sold off to reduce the homestead to the amount allowed by law.

In most states, upon the death of the owner, the homestead passes to the spouse and/or children free of the claims of the decedent's creditors.

If the homestead burns down, the insurance money to replace the dwelling usually is exempt from creditors' claims also. In some states the homestead may be sold and the proceeds are exempt from creditors' claims for a reasonable length of time so that the person can purchase another homestead.

In many cases homestead rights have been liberally construed and people have been allowed to keep oil and gas rights, crops growing on the property and expensive additions to the property.

Requirements to Protect Homestead

In most states a person does not need to make any special declaration to obtain homestead protection. However, in some states this is necessary; if there is any doubt then a declaration of homestead should be filed in the appropriate records. This is especially true if a judgment is imminent. If a declaration is required you must be sure to strictly comply with the exact requirements of the law. Any error could cause loss of the homestead exemption.

In some states the protection of a homestead applies to any person, but in others only the head of a household is entitled to protection. This means that the person must support a spouse or child.

In most states a person must actually occupy the homestead for protection to apply. However, there are some exceptions if there is evidence that the person has a bona fide intent to make the property his or her homestead.

Usually, though, you must be domiciled in the homestead most of the time during the 180 days preceding your filing for bankruptcy to insure the exemption.

Exceptions to Homestead Protection

There are various exceptions to the protection afforded by homestead laws and they, of course, also vary by state. The following are some of the exceptions which apply in some of the states. If you have any of these types of debts you should check your state's rules before you attempt to use the homestead exemption to protect equity.

- debts incurred before the homestead is purchased
- debts incurred in purchasing the homestead
- debts incurred before establishment of the homestead
- debts incurred in improving the homestead
- debts owed for taxes
- debts owed for torts committed by the owner
- debts for alimony
- criminal penalties
- claims of parties who have a prior interest in the homestead
- judgments filed before the homestead is purchased

Note that in some states, such as Maine, the homestead is not protected against tort claims. These would include claims for malpractice and accidents. In these states the homestead is not of much value for asset protection.

In at least one case a person who filed a Chapter 11 bankruptcy (to reorganize debts) and then switched to a Chapter 7 (to discharge debts), a lien which attached to the homestead in the Chapter 11 case could not be discharged.

Not all of these exceptions apply in all states. If you have any of these types of debts and they are exceptions to homestead in your state, you would be wise to pay those debts before paying other debts (provided, of course, that you do not violate any bankruptcy rules against preferring one creditor over another; see Chapter 41).

Loss of Homestead Status

The protection of the homestead can be lost in some states if certain requirements are not complied with. For example, if the owner abandons the property or begins using it for a business instead of a home, the protection may be lost. However, some states allow the homestead to be used for a business as well as a residence. In states which only grant homestead status to the head of a household, the status may be lost if the parties divorce or if child custody changes.

Going into a nursing home, or temporarily moving in with relatives due to an illness, should not cause loss of homestead as long as the person has the intent to return to the homestead eventually.

Homestead Planning

Whatever state you live in, you should carefully plan the equity in your home to protect it from creditors.

If you live in a state with a low homestead exemption you should keep very little equity in your home. If you have a small mortgage or you own your home free and clear, you should refinance it and put the money in an investment that is free from the claims of creditors. You can also get an equity line against your home which allows you to withdraw equity at any time. However, you are limited in what you can do once a claim has been made or if you are contemplating bankruptcy. See Chapter 29 about shifting assets.

If you live in a state with a large homestead exemption you can protect your estate from creditors by having most or all of your net worth in your home. However, you must also consider the chance of divorce as a risk against your assets.

For a couple with joint funds in a state with a large homestead exemption, it is a good idea to pay off the home as quickly as possible. For an individual with the risk of marital problems in the future, other exempt property and offshore (foreign) trusts are better.

Tenancy by the Entireties

In states with low or no homestead exemption, the law of tenancy by the entireties property may protect the homestead from creditors. See the next chapter and the exemption page for your state in Appendix 3.

Creative Planning

There are some very creative ways to protect the homestead in states with low exemptions. For example, the homestead can be split into different interests and only a portion up to the homestead exemption can be left in the name of the person wishing to be protected. This can be done with life estates or a split interest trust. In a GRIT, a Grantor Retained Interest Trust, the grantor can keep the right to live in the property, and other interests can be owned by the spouse, children or other family members.

Another possibility where the exemption is low is to put the homestead into a partnership, since partnership property cannot be partitioned.

All of these methods require expertise in the field of estate planning, and should not be attempted without consulting an expert.

Your State's Exemptions

The homestead limits for each state are listed in Appendix 3. However, for the special rules and limitations you should check with a local attorney who specializes in bankruptcy law to see exactly what is protected in your area.

Further Research

A very thorough analysis of the homestead exemption is contained in the article, *Estates Arising from the Marital Relationship and Their Characteristics*, by George L. Haskins in 1 American Law of Property (A. James Crasner ed., 1952 & Supp. 1977)

Chapter 17
Joint Tenancy/
Tenancy by the Entireties

Joint Tenancy

Contrary to the belief of some, property in joint names is not safe from creditors. In most states joint property may be seized by creditors at least to the extent of the debtor's interest. If both parties are on the debt the entire property can be seized.

Joint tenancy with right of survivorship is ownership of property where the survivor owns the entire property upon the death of the other owner. **Tenancy in common** is ownership in which the death of one owner results in that person's interest going to his or her heirs.

In the rare instance where a creditor makes a claim and a debtor dies before the creditor seizes his joint property, the property would pass safely to the other owner. However, in most cases joint ownership of property is not a safe way to own property. In fact it could be more risky than individual ownership because it is subject to both parties' debts.

Some people put their property into joint ownership with their children to avoid probate. This works fine in avoiding probate, but it puts the property at risk of the children's creditors. If your children are involved in an accident or divorce after you put property jointly into their names you may lose part of it.

Community Property

In states which have adopted the community property system (Arizona, California, Idaho, Louisiana, Nevada, New Mexico, Texas, Washington and Wisconsin), there is a special problem with asset protection. Under community property principles, each spouse is considered to own an interest in community property, which is all property acquired during the marriage (other than gifts and inheritances). It does not matter in whose name the property is titled, the interest of both spouses exists the moment the property is acquired.

Because the spouses have an interest in all community property, certain creditors of either spouse can make claims against all such property. As an example, all personal property bought by a wife with her own earnings can be seized by someone who has a claim against her husband. In addition, when one spouse in a community property state files for bankruptcy, all community property comes under the control of the bankruptcy trustee.

To avoid this problem, the parties can enter into a marital agreement stating that they agree to abandon the community property system and hold their property separately. While many spouses would strongly object to signing such an agreement with a highly successful spouse, the risks to their own assets should make it worthwhile. To make the arrangement more desirable, regular gifts can be made by the wealthy spouse to equalize the assets.

A marital agreement is a complicated document and must comply with state laws in order to be valid. To have one drafted you should consult a specialist in family law.

Tenancy by the Entireties

In about half of the states the concept of "tenancy by the entireties" is recognized. Under this arrangement property owned by a married couple is considered to be owned by the couple as a unit and not as individuals. Neither party individually has the right to sell the property or any interest in it. Consequently, in some of the states that recognize this concept creditors of one spouse cannot reach the property.

Tenancy by the entireties property can always be real estate but in some states it also includes personal property. Therefore, in those states which protect it from creditors, it can be used to shield numerous items of property from creditors.

The first problem people have in protecting their entireties property from creditors is convincing a court that the property is actually held in a tenancy by the entireties. In some states joint ownership by spouses is assumed to be ownership by the entireties but in others it is not.

The classic requirement for a tenancy by the entirety is that it must be created with five "unities": unity of possession (each party is entitled to possess the property), unity of interest (each party has an equal interest in the property), unity of title (each party must have acquired ownership from the same conveyance), unity of time (the interest of each party must have been created at the same time), and unity of person (the parties must be married which makes them legally one person). In some states a spouse cannot create a tenancy by the entireties by signing property over to himself and a spouse, but in others it is allowed by law.

The only way to be sure your property is protected (if you live in a state which has tenancy by the entireties) is to execute documents which legally create a tenancy by the entirety in the property you want protected. This is done by conveying the property first to another person (a "strawman") who conveys it back to you and your spouse in an estate by the entireties. The forms for doing this are included in this book. The strawman can be your parent, sibling or child, but be sure that the person you choose is over 18 years of age and does not have any judgments against him or her.

Any property which was acquired before marriage, even if it was acquired in the names of both spouses, must be retitled in the parties names after marriage. The reason for this is that before marriage it is impossible to own property in a tenancy by the entireties, and it does not change into entireties ownership at marriage. So it must be reconveyed after marriage.

When buying a new piece of property you can be sure that it is held in a tenancy by the entireties by having it so stated on the bill of sale or invoice. If you plan to use the protection of tenancy by the entireties you should have the salesperson put language similar to the following on the paperwork whenever you buy furniture, appliances, electronics or similar items:

```
John Smith and Mary Smith, husband and wife in a tenancy
by the entireties
```

The second possible problem arises when a person converts property into entireties property within a year prior to filing bankruptcy. Transfers during this time period are often considered frauds against creditors. For this reason it is important to properly set up your property as soon as possible, or to delay bankruptcy for the necessary year.

It should be noted that entireties property is only protected against claims against one spouse. If there are any debts which are joint, those creditors can seize the property and it can be brought into bankruptcy. For this reason spouses should avoid cosigning on each others' debts whenever possible.

Of course, putting property into tenancy by the entireties will not protect it from claims by your spouse. In fact it may make it easier for your spouse to take it. A doctor in San Antonio put numerous assets in the name of his wife to protect them from creditors' claims and the next week she filed for divorce. If avoiding potential spousal claims is of concern to you, you should avoid this arrangement and use a family limited partnership as discussed in Chapter 32.

In some states the placing of property in the name of both spouses as assumed by law to be a gift unless there is written evidence to the contrary. To avoid this you should put a statement on any deeds or other transfer papers that the spouse's name is being added "for estate planning purposes only and not as a present gift."

One possible problem with entireties property is that if one party files bankruptcy and there is a loan on the property, the trustee may bring the property into the bankruptcy. Therefore it is important that no loans in the debtor's name are on the property at the time of bankruptcy. Also, if the entire interest in the property is acquired by the debtor within 6 months of bankruptcy, the bankruptcy case may be reopened.

In states which do not recognize tenancies by the entireties, it mat be possible to obtain similar protection through husband and wife A-B living trusts. See Chapter 33.

On the following page is a table of all states indicating which ones recognize tenancies by the entireties, which ones apply it to personal property and which of those have held that the property is exempt from creditors. A case is cited if available, so that you or your attorney may do periodic research to keep abreast of changes in the law.

Tenancy by the Entireties Property Laws

State	T. by E. Allowed	Personal Property	Exempt	Citation
Alabama	Unclear			
Alaska	Yes	Yes	No	
Arizona	Unclear			
Arkansas	Yes	Yes	No	
California	No			
Colorado	Unclear			
Connecticut	No			
Delaware	Yes	Yes	Yes	Citizens Sav. Bank v. Astrin, 44 Del. 451, 61 A.2d 419 (1948)
Dist. of Col.	Yes	Yes	Yes	Est. of Wall, 440 F.2d 215 (D.C.Cir. 1971)
Florida	Yes	Yes	Yes	Hunt v. Covington, 145 Fla. 406, 200 So. 76 (1941)
Georgia	Unclear			
Hawaii	Yes	Yes	Yes?	Sawada v. Endo, 57 Hawaii 608, 561 P.2d 1291 (1977)
Idaho	Unclear			
Illinois	Unclear			
Indiana	Yes	No	Yes	Myler v. Myler, 137 Ind. App. 605, 210 N.E.2d 446 (1965)
Iowa	Unclear			
Kansas	Unclear			
Kentucky	Unclear			
Louisiana	No			
Maine	No			
Maryland	Yes	Yes	Yes?	Watterson v. Edgerly, 40 Md. App. 230, 388 A.2d 934 (1978)
Massachusetts	Yes	Yes		
Michigan	Yes	No	Yes	Cole v. Cardoza, 441 F.2d 1337 (6 Cir. 1971)
Minnesota	No			
Mississippi	Yes	Yes		
Missouri	Yes	Yes	Yes	Hanebrink v. Tower Grove Bk., 321 S.W.2d 524 (Mo.Ct.App. 1959)
Montana	Unclear			
Nebraska	Unclear			
Nevada	No			
New Hamp.	No			
New Jersey	Yes	No	No	
New Mexico	No			
New York	Yes	No	No	
North Carolina	Yes	No	Yes	Hodge v. Hodge, 12 N.C.App. 574, 183 S.E.2d 800 (1971)
North Dakota	No			
Ohio	Yes	Yes		
Oklahoma	Yes	Yes		
Oregon	Yes	Yes	Part	Brownley v. Lincoln Co., 218 Or. 7, 343 P.2d 529 (1959)
Pennsylvania	Yes	Yes	Yes	Stauffer v. Stauffer, 465 Pa. 558, 351 A.2d 236 (1976)
Rhode Island	Yes	Yes	Yes	Bloomfield v. Brown, 67 R.I. 452, 25 A.2d 354 (1942)
South Carolina	Unclear			
South Dakota	No			
Tennessee	Yes	Yes	Part	C & S Nat'l. Bank v. Aver, 640 F.2d 837 (6 Cir. 1981)
Texas	Unclear			
Utah	Yes	Yes		
Vermont	Yes	Yes	Yes	Lowell v. Lowell, 138 Vt. 514, 419 A.2d 321 (1980)
Virginia	Yes	Yes	Yes	In re Bishop, 482 F.2d 381 (4 Cir. 1973)
Washington	No			
West Virginia	No			
Wisconsin	No			
Wyoming	Yes	Yes	Yes	Ward Terry & Co. v. Hensen, 75 Wyo. 444, 297 P.2d 213 (1956)

Chapter 18
Pensions and
Retirement Accounts

A pension plan can be one of the best parts of an asset protection plan. Because the public policy is to not allow people to enter old age destitute, most retirement plans are exempt from creditors' claims. In one case even a convicted embezzler was allowed to keep his pension plan.

However, pension plans do not provide protection against all types of creditors. They are not safe from such things as spouse or child support obligations and environmental fines. If you expect liabilities of these types you should avoid using pension plans for protection. If you are not yet married and expect to be able to use a premarital agreement to protect yourself from alimony, be sure to protect your pension in the agreement. In negotiating a premarital agreement, asking for a waiver of claims against a pension plan should be one of the easiest points. "You wouldn't ever take my pension plan would you???" (Use that sad puppy dog look!)

ERISA Plans

Prior to 1992 there was a split between the different courts in this country as to whether ERISA plans were exempt in bankruptcy. (ERISA plans are those covered by the federal Employee Retirement Income Security Act.) But in an important case* the

---

*Patterson v. Shumate, 112 S.Ct. 2242 (1992)

United States Supreme Court held that they were excluded from the bankruptcy estate under 11 U.S.C. §541(c)(2). ERISA plans are also exempt from creditors' claims outside of bankruptcy. This means that they cannot be seized or garnished.

ERISA plans include pension plans (defined benefit plans), voluntary plans (401(k) plans), and profit sharing plans (defined contribution plans). However, not all plans are ERISA-qualified so you should consult the director of your plan or an attorney who specializes in ERISA law to see if your plan is qualified.

One problem which can disqualify a plan is if it only benefits the owner of a business. Such plans do not qualify. To solve this problem you might be able to add an employee to the plan to make it qualify. A dentist in New York had nearly $400,000 in his Keogh plan when he filed bankruptcy, expecting to keep it all. But because he did not make the minimum contributions for his employees, the money in his plan went to his creditors.

If you have a plan in your own company you should be sure to have it designed or examined by an expert. Pension plan laws are among the most complex devised by man. Specific documentation is required, actuarial figures must be calculated correctly, and status reports must be timely filed. Mistakes could disqualify your plan for both asset protection and favorable tax treatment.

IRAs and Non-Qualified Plans

IRAs and non-qualified plans do not contain the important language which makes them non-transferable, so they must be turned over to the bankruptcy trustee unless the state has a specific provision making them exempt. Most states exempt pensions for public employees such as teachers and police, but some exempt all IRAs. In some states you can roll over a nonexempt IRA into an exempt pension plan.

In some states only amounts "needed for support" are exempt, but in others all IRA money is exempt, no matter how much there is. What is needed for support usually depends upon the age of the debtor. A 65-year-old might need his entire pension plan, whereas a 45-year-old could be considered young enough to start saving anew and lose his entire amount.

States that have laws that exempt many pension plans include California, Georgia, Idaho, Indiana, Iowa, Pennsylvania, Texas and Washington. States that exempt IRAs include California, Florida, Massachusetts and Texas. To find out what is exempt in your state check the listing in Appendix 3 of this book.

In 1994 Congress was debating the possibility of allowing a "Super IRA" which would be more flexible and could hold rare coins and bullion among other things. With the Republican majority in 1995 passage appears more likely. This will make the IRA even more valuable.

Divorce

There are rules for pension plans that can have unexpected results in divorce. Because of spousal rights a spouse cannot be eliminated as beneficiary without a signed consent. For example, one man changed his beneficiary to his brother during divorce, but when he died after the divorce the assets went to his ex-wife. Why? Because the change was ineffective while he was married. He should have waited until after the divorce to make the change.

Chapter 19
Wages

Every state has an exemption for some types of income. These may include wages, salary, social security, welfare, or unemployment compensation. Some exemptions apply only to heads of households (you must have at least one dependent) but many apply to anyone. In some states earnings of independent contractors or sole owners of corporations are not considered exempt wages.

In addition to the state laws, there is a federal exemption for certain wages. In most states at least a portion of unpaid wages are exempt, and in some states, such as Florida, even wages which have been received and placed in a bank account are exempt.

In a state with this rule, even if you have several thousand dollars in wages in the bank, you creditors cannot touch it. However, states which exempt wages often have rules that, to be exempt, the wages must not be commingled with other funds. If you have any other income in the account, such as a spouse's income, or even interest earned on the account, the court could take away the exemption for the entire account. In one case, because a person's paycheck included reimbursement for expenses, the exemption was denied.

Courts have held that income which is received by independent contractors is not exempt because it is not technically wages. If you are an independent contractor, you can get around this problem by incorporating your business and hiring yourself as an employee. Your salary from the corporation would then be considered wages. Incorporation could also offer other benefits.

If wages are exempt in your state you should put them in a separate account and not deposit any other funds in that account. You cannot even let interest on the wages be mixed with them. If the account pays interest, see if it can be credited to another account or issued as a check each month or each quarter. If you have other sources of income, such as rents, royalties, dividends or interest, you should live on that money and let your wages accumulate.

The same situation applies to social security payments. If they are deposited in a separate account they can be exempt from creditors' claims. The rationale for the exemption is that such funds provide needed support, but creditors have argued that if a person has other support social security funds should not be exempt. However, in a 1988 case the U. S. Supreme Court held that these funds are exempt even if a person has other support.

There are cases, though, which hold that the exemption is not absolute. In one case in which a person commingled social security funds with other money and fled to Switzerland with millions of dollars, the court held the funds not exempt. The lesson is to keep the funds in a separate account (and to spend nonexempt funds).

The Consumer Credit Protection Act (15 U.S.C. §§ 1601-1692r) also provides an exemption for wages.

Chapter 20
Life Insurance

Life insurance can be used for asset protection as well as estate planning. Both federal law and the laws of each state include some exemptions for the cash value or the proceeds of life insurance. Like with other exemptions, the amount protected from creditors varies from state to state.

When you pay for a life insurance policy it typically builds up a cash value (unless it is a "term" policy). Exemptions in most states protect at least some of this value from creditors' claims. Upon your death, in most states, the proceeds can pass to your beneficiaries free of any claims of your creditors.

The bankruptcy code exempts life insurance in §522(d)(7) and (8). Subsection 7 exempts any unmatured policy and subsection 8 exempts any policy with a cash value of less than $4,000. States have their own laws regarding what is exempt and some have limits while others do not.

In some states property which is purchased with the proceeds of a life insurance policy are exempt.

In tax planning, life insurance offers a way either to avoid estate taxes or to provide the funds to pay them. For persons whose estates are large but who have little cash, the insurance can make sure that the property will not have to be sold at death. And as discussed later in this chapter, giving away the ownership of a policy takes it out of your estate for tax purposes.

Exceptions to Protections

In some states a life insurance policy is exempt from creditors claims only if the beneficiaries are the spouse, children or other dependent. In some states the owner of the policy can have the power to change the beneficiary, but in others such a policy would not be protected.

Even if a policy is originally exempt, there are ways that the protections can be lost. One simple way is if you assign your policy to a creditor. While you might not think you would do such a thing, often loan papers prepared by banks contain language which can give them a right to your policies. Never sign loan documents without reading them carefully or having your attorney review them.

If you buy a policy or pay the premium at a time when you are insolvent, or use funds which would constitute a fraudulent conveyance, your life insurance policy could be challenged and found to be nonexempt. Changing the beneficiary while insolvent could also cause loss of protection.

Insurance Owned By Another

In states where the amount of insurance protected is small, it is still possible to protect your policy from creditors.

If an insurance policy against your life is owned by another person it cannot be reached by your creditors because it is not your property. It is also excluded from your estate at death for tax purposes.

If you presently have a life insurance policy, you could make a gift of it to your spouse or children. Or if you plan to purchase one in the future you could set it up with them as the owners. However, the transaction should be set up carefully to avoid liability for a gift tax. Since a person is allowed to make gifts of $10,000 per person per year tax free, it is best to structure the transaction to make a gift of $10,000 in value each year.

In order for this protection to work the gift must be absolute. If you retain any control over the policy you may lose both the asset protection and the tax benefits. Also, if you die within three years of transfer of the policy, the amount of insurance may be included in your estate. It is sometimes possible to get around this by using corporations or trusts to supply the funds to the person to purchase the insurance.

Irrevocable Life Insurance Trust

Using an irrevocable life insurance trust can provide both extra asset protection and tax savings. This is because a policy in a trust is not part of a person's assets or estate at death. However, setting up the trust may constitute a taxable gift.

To use such a trust, a person transfers to an irrevocable trust either an existing policy or the funds with which to buy a policy. If additional premiums must be paid, the funds for these can be also paid to the trust. By giving the beneficiaries certain powers to make withdrawals, the payments can qualify for the annual gift tax exclusion of $10,000 per year.

The three-year rule mentioned above also applies to policies transferred to trusts. Again, if the trust purchases the policy with its own funds the three-year rule may not apply.

In community property states there is another complication. If the insurance is purchased with community funds, the surviving spouse may be considered a half owner of the policy. This can be avoided if the policy is purchased with separate funds of the insured spouse.

Chapter 21
Annuities

In states which protect them from creditors, annuities can seem too good to be true. They offer the flexibility of a mutual fund with the tax advantages of an unlimited IRA. Even in states that allow creditors to reach annuities, setting them up out of the country may provide the needed protection.

An annuity is an agreement whereby a person is to get a sum of money regularly over a period of years. There are fixed annuities where the amounts are determined in the beginning, and variable annuities where the amount to be paid out depends upon the return on investment.

Annuities can be set up in several ways. You can pay a lump sum to a company for regular payments which will begin either immediately or at a date in the future. Or you can make periodic payments for a number of years, at which time payments will begin to come to you.

Annuities are useful in asset protection planning because they are exempt from claims in several states. The exemption ranges from $350 (in Arkansas) to an unlimited amount (in Florida). In some states all annuities are exempt, while in others only annuities payable to the spouse, children or other dependents of the debtor are exempt. Under bankruptcy law in every state annuities are exempt up to the amount "needed for support" of the debtor and his or her spouse and dependents.

In different states and in different courts of a state, annuities are offered different protection. In one state a bankruptcy court held that lottery winnings would be exempt because they were structured as an annuity. At about the same time another bankruptcy court in the same state held that lottery winnings were not exempt because the annuity was set up to benefit the state paying the winnings, not to benefit the winner.

In some states annuities are only protected if they are "unmatured," that is, if the payments to the debtor have not yet started. In other states this factor does not matter.

In recent years large mutual fund companies such as Fidelity, Vanguard, Dreyfus and Scudder have begun to offer variable annuities. These investments are similar to their other mutual funds, and offer an array of investment choices, but charge slightly higher fees to cover the insurance component. (You are guaranteed that your heirs will get at least what you invested if you die before your payments begin.) Today there are dozens of varieties to choose from and if you choose one in a family of funds then you can switch investments whenever the economy warrants it.

One of the best benefits currently available with annuities is the tax-free compounding of the investment, since the interest is not taxable until it is paid out. In effect it is like an IRA with no limit to the amount you can contribute!

Articles in the press about annuities point out that the returns are a bit lower than a regular mutual fund, and claim that you must be in a high tax bracket to benefit. However, they rarely mention that annuities can be safe from creditors' claims. This benefit more than makes up for the slightly lower return.

Offshore Annuities

An especially useful annuity is one issued by insurance companies in Switzerland. Besides the protection some states offer for annuities, Swiss law provides that if the beneficiary is one's spouse or children, of if the beneficiary is made irrevocable, the annuity cannot be reached by creditors. Even if a U.S. court ordered you to cash it in, Swiss law would protect it.

Additionally, with the U.S. national debt looming as a possible source of economic problems, the Swiss annuity offers the opportunity to keep your assets in a currency other than the dollar. Some companies offer the choice of having your investment in U.S. dollars, Swiss francs, German marks British pounds, or ECUs (European Currency Units). For a small fee you can switch currencies at any time.

An added benefit of a foreign annuity is that it is not considered a foreign bank account, it is considered an insurance policy. Therefore, you do not have to report your annuity on your income tax return in the place where you are asked if you have any foreign bank accounts.

At the time of publication there was a proposal in Congress to begin taxing the income on foreign annuities. However, the value of currency diversification and offshore asset protection would probably outweigh the cost of the tax on the income.

As for safety, the Swiss franc is backed by gold at a mere fraction of its market value and the Swiss insurance companies are among the most solvent in the world, with reserves far higher than the best U.S. companies.

Private Annuities

It is possible to set up an annuity with a private party, such as a relative. One woman transferred property to her daughter as trustee in exchange for an annuity. Later she filed bankruptcy. Because there was no fraudulent intent at the time she set up the arrangement, it was held by the bankruptcy court to be free from her creditor's claims.

A transfer of property in exchange for an annuity of the same value would not normally be considered a fraudulent transfer because it is an equal exchange. In most cases it would be a legal conversion of nonexempt property for exempt property. Of course you must have trust in the person to whom you transfer your property.

Protecting Receivables

Besides purchasing an annuity as an investment, annuities can be used to structure receivables. A woman who was in an auto accident and won a large settlement asked that it be set up as an annuity. Later when she caused an accident herself the victim could not reach her annuity because it was exempt under her state's laws.

If you expect to receive an inheritance or other large sum of money in the future, you can ask that it be set up as an annuity rather than a straight cash payment.

Resources:

Each issue of *Barron's* includes listings of annuities.
Morningstar offers a rating service on annuities. A sample copy is about $15 800-876-5005.
The VARDS Report tracks variable annuities and offers a free sample copy 404-998-5186.

Vanguard offers some of the lowest fees on variable annuities 800-522-5555.
Other high-rated annuities are offered by:

> Wellington Management Co. 800-862-6667
> Fidelity Management & Research 800-544-2442
> Scudder Horizon 800-242-4402
> Connecticut Mutual Panorama 800-234-5606

Swiss annuities are available from the following sources:

JML Jürg M. Lattmann AG
Baarerstrasse 53
CH-6304 Zug, Switzerland
Tel. 011-41-42-265500
Fax: 011-41-42-265590

B.F.I. Consulting AG
Lohwisstrasse 48
CH-8123 Ebmatingen, Switzerland
Tel. 011-41-1-9804254
Fax: 011-41-1-9804255

References:

Geer, "Safe Haven," *Forbes*, June, 1994
Schriffres, "Best of the Variable Annuities," *Kiplinger's Personal Finance Magazine*, May, 1994
Updegrave, "The Best Variable Annuities," *Money*, January, 1994
Sherrid, "A Rich Path to Retirement?," *U.S. News and World Report*, October 11, 1993
Laderman, "An Annuity for Folks of All Ages," *Business Week*, August 2, 1993
Laderman, "This Hybrid May Thrive in High-Tax Soil, *Business Week*, July 19, 1993

Chapter 22
Tools of Trade

Most states exempt some "tools of trade" from the claims of creditors. In some states only military uniforms are exempt but in others thousands of dollars in tools are free from claims. The following is a list of states and the value of the tools of trade that are exempt. In some states there are special rules for certain occupations such as farming. Some states offer no specific exemption for tools of trade, but such items could be exempt from creditors' claims if they are included in the general personal property exemption. For more specific rules see your state's page in Appendix 3.

If you need more equipment in your business than your state's exemption allows, you should lease it and limit your equity to the amount allowed as exempt. One possibility is to set up a trust for your children (see Chapter 34) which can purchase the property and lease it to your business. This also allows you to shift income to the children for education or other purposes. The value of tools of trade exempt for each state are as follows:

	Amount	Special rules for:
Federal	$750	
Alabama		Military personnel
Alaska	$2,800	
Arizona	$2,500	Military personnel
Arkansas	$750	
California sys. 1	$2,500	Spouse, vehicles
California sys. 2	$750	

State	Amount	Notes
Colorado	$1,500	Farmers, livestock
Connecticut	No limit	
Delaware		New Castle, Sussex and Kent Counties
District of Columbia	$200	Notaries, vehicles ($500), professionals ($300)
Florida	None	
Georgia	$500	
Hawaii	No limit	
Idaho	$1,000	Military
Illinois	$750	
Indiana		Military
Iowa	$10,000	Car
Kansas	$7,500	
Kentucky	$300	Farmers, motor vehicles, professionals
Louisiana	No limit	
Maine	$1,000	Farmers, boats
Maryland	No limit	No car
Massachusetts	$500	Fishing, military
Michigan	$1,000	Military
Minnesota	$7,500	Farmers, teachers
Mississippi	No special allowance	
Missouri	$2,000	
Montana	$3,000	Military, govt. employees
Nebraska	$1,500	
Nevada	$4,500	Farmers, miners, military
New Hampshire	$1,200	Farmers, military
New Jersey	No special allowance	
New Mexico	$1,500	
New York	$600	Military
North Carolina	$750	
North Dakota	No special allowance	
Ohio	$750	Notaries public
Oklahoma	$5,000	
Oregon	$3,000	
Pennsylvania	No special allowance	
Rhode Island	$500	Professionals
South Carolina	$750	
South Dakota	No special allowance	
Tennessee	$750	
Texas	No limit	
Utah	$1,500	Vehicles, military
Virginia	$5,000	
Vermont	$10,000	Nonhouseholders, farmers, military
Washington	$5,000	Professionals, farmers
West Virginia	$750	
Wisconsin	$7,500	
Wyoming	$2,000	Professionals

Chapter 23
Personal Property

All states and the federal exemptions allow people to keep certain personal property. In most states the amount ranges from $1,000 to a few thousand dollars. This property typically includes clothes, furniture, appliances, burial plots, a wedding ring, a Bible, and other similar items supposedly needed to get a fresh start in life. In some states the laws are specific (Iowa includes one cow and silverware which is not sterling) but in others there is simply a dollar amount which may not be exceeded, but may be made up of any property.

In most cases this exemption is too small to be of much help in asset protection. However, there are some exceptions, such as a $20,000 car in Kansas. And in some states the value of certain items is not limited. Thus a person could exempt new and expensive furniture, appliances, wedding rings, etc.

The laws regarding personal property are too detailed to be put into a simple table. For details of what your state allows please see Appendix 3.

Chapter 24
Alimony and Child Support

In keeping with the policy of protecting income necessary for support, funds received as alimony or child support are exempt from claims of creditors in many states. Like social security and other exempt income, they should be set aside and preserved whenever possible.

If you are receiving alimony or child support you do not have to worry that a creditor could garnish or seize the payments.

What exactly constitutes exempt alimony is an issue that has occasionally reached the courts. One woman who had received over half a million dollars in her divorce settlement filed bankruptcy with her new husband claiming the money as exempt lump sum alimony. Unfortunately for her, the court decided that this money was a division of mutual assets and not the type of alimony which would be exempt. Therefore it was available to pay her creditors' claims. One would expect that the attorney who advised her to file bankruptcy was embarrassed the court's ruling, though her ex-husband probably received the news with far less sadness in his heart.

Chapter 25
Public Benefits

In nearly all states public benefits such as unemployment compensation, workers' compensation, veterans' benefits, crime victims' compensation, Aid to Families with Dependent Children (AFDC), aid to the blind and disabled, occupational disease compensation, POWs' benefits, welfare, student aid, relocation benefits, public assistance, or some combination of these is exempt from creditors' claims.

This means that these funds cannot be assigned by a debtor to a creditor. Since these benefits are intended as a safety net for those with no other support, making them available to creditors would defeat the purpose.

Most people using this book will not be concerned with these exemptions. However, if disaster strikes, they may offer useful support while other assets are tied up in a homestead or other exempt property.

Chapter 26
Other Exemptions

There are a few other exemptions which do not fall into the previous categories. In some cases they can prove quite valuable. A short summary is as follows.

- Business partnerships (these are discussed in detail in Chapters 31 and 32)

- 75% of earned but unpaid wages

- Military deposits to savings accounts while on permanent duty outside U.S.

- Seamen's wages and clothing

- Liquor licenses in Alaska, Iowa, Kansas, Oregon and Wyoming

- $7,900 in any property (less homestead and burial plot) in California

- Unused homestead to $6,000 in Maine

- Ownership in unincorporated association in New Mexico

For more details see the state-by-state listings in Appendix 3.

Chapter 27
State Shopping

Not everyone can pack up and leave their home state. If you have lived your whole life in one town or have long-term business relationships, leaving may be the last thing you want to do. But if you face the possibility of losing everything you own, you should consider at least a temporary relocation.

In some states you can lose nearly everything, while in others you can keep millions of dollars in assets. Isn't it worth a year or two away, to keep from losing your life's earnings? You don't even have to stay full time in a new state. You can take up residency there, but only reside there part of the year.

Fortunately, two of the best states for asset protection are both popular destinations for people leaving their own states: Florida and Texas. In both of these states you can keep a home of unlimited value and also hundreds of thousands of dollars in other assets. Many people who had financial problems elsewhere moved to these states to protect their fortunes.

For those who don't like warm weather and beaches, the states of Iowa, Kansas, Minnesota, Oklahoma and South Dakota also offer generous exemptions and a wider variety of climate. Surely there is one to suit your tastes.

One thing to keep in mind is that you must be a resident of a state for six months in order to take advantage of that state's exemptions. For the homestead exemption, some states require you to reside in the property for that six month period.

As will be discussed in Chapter 46, you should consult a specialist in state exemption law before arranging your assets. If you plan to move to another state be sure to consult a specialist before you start moving assets to be sure that you understand the laws and that they haven't changed.

Chapter 28
Future Acquisitions

When doing any financial planning, you must keep in mind any possibilities of future receipts of money or property. For example, if you file bankruptcy and within the next 180 days a relative dies leaving you a large inheritance, your bankruptcy creditors are entitled to that inheritance. Or if someone dies leaving you money while you have an outstanding judgment creditors may be able to attach your inheritance.

You cannot control the timing of death, but you can suggest that your relatives set up your inheritance to avoid your creditors. For example, a trust can be set up which does not allow you to reach the property for a number of years. Or you can be given an annuity if it is exempt in your jurisdiction.

If you are protecting your assets by putting them in your spouse's name, keep in mind that your spouse may die just before, or during, some financial crisis you face. If this results in all marital assets being in your name, your protection plan may be ruined.

Asset protection for yourself may mean asset protection for relatives. Check with your parents and other relatives. If you expect any inheritances, ask that they be put into an irrevocable trust or other device which will protect them from your creditors. If they hesitate, offer to pay for the trust. It may save your inheritance.

Part Four
Taking Property Out of Your Name

Chapter 29
Shifting Property:
What's Legal/What's Not

Unlike shifting assets from nonexempt to exempt property, transferring property out of your name is not sanctioned by law or by the legislative history. But you do have the freedom to make any transfers you want as long as they are not "fraudulent." As discussed in Chapter 5, certain transfers of property to avoid creditors' claims are considered "fraudulent conveyances" and can be set aside by a court.

One big problem for people with immediate problems is that all transfers within one year of filing a bankruptcy petition must be disclosed and can be set aside by the court. Also, any payments to creditors within 90 days of filing bankruptcy can be set aside. But if you have no immediate financial problems, you are free to transfer your assets in almost any way which will protect them. The main limitation is that you cannot transfer assets out of your name if to do so will make you insolvent. In states governed by the UFCA rather than the UFTA (see Chapter 5), converting all assets out of your name or to exempt forms can be considered fraudulent.

The common law rule which dates back to the year 1571 is that you cannot transfer property if your intent is to hinder and delay creditors. One big legal issue in asset protection law is whether an asset protection plan falls under this rule, since it is clearly an attempt to defeat future creditors. Fortunately, so far most courts have ruled that if you are not trying to defeat a *specific* creditor at the time of your transfer, the transfer is not fraudulent.

Future creditors can make a successful claim if it appears that a person transferred his assets with plans to do something which might result in liability. For example, there have been cases where people transferred property out of their names and then slandered a partner, killed a girlfriend, or began a hazardous business. In these cases the transfers were found to be fraudulent because the person involved was believed to have already formulated the plan when he or she transferred the property.

Future creditors can also make a successful claim if your transfer of assets left you with an unreasonably small amount of capital for the business you are in. For example, if you borrow against all your assets and transfer the funds out of your name so that you have no equity in your business, the transfer can be ruled fraudulent.

The most important factor in deciding whether a transfer was fraudulent is **intent**. The laws usually use the phrase, "intent to defraud." But intent is something which is in your brain and cannot be seen or proven. A court can only look at the evidence and make its judgment based upon what your intent appeared to be.

A question arises when you have no known creditors at the time you make transfers, but later a claim is made for some act (such as malpractice) which you committed many years earlier. Since the person had a "contingent, unliquidated, or unmatured" claim, he or she would come under some definitions of creditor, so it is possible that a court could rule that that creditor was defrauded by a transfer.

One protection against such a possibility is to make all transfers as part of a general estate planning scheme. If you go to an estate planner and say that you want to arrange your affairs to provide for your heirs and your retirement, it will not look like you are intending to defraud any creditors, but are merely doing what is prudent with your estate.

After reading this manual you can go to an attorney and will not have to specifically ask him or her to protect your estate from future creditors. You can simply say you want to provide for your heirs, but then guide the attorney into a plan which you know protects your assets. If a future creditor ever tries to prove you were trying to protect your assets from creditors, your attorney can take the stand and honestly testify that creditors were never mentioned, you only asked for normal estate planning.

This section of the manual discusses several ways of protecting your property from creditors. The ones in which you give up all rights to your property (such as a children's trust) are the safest, but they require that you give up control and future enjoyment of the property. The limited partnership and the offshore trust are the best ways available today to protect your assets from creditors but retain control.

Probably the best protection from future creditors, even if they have claims from the past, is an offshore trust. Because of the liability crisis in America today several countries have passed laws which permit asset protection trusts. These laws usually provide that all challenges to the trust must be made within a year or two of when it was established. That means that if a client or patient from the past does not challenge the trust (by filing an action in the country in which it is established) he has no recourse.

However, such trusts usually require setup fees ranging from $3,000 to $15,000 and annual fees as well. So they are not advantageous unless you have substantial assets to protect. As more Americans seek out these trusts, companies which cater to smaller trusts will likely spring up.

Reference

Wetherington, R. Wade, "Eleventh-Hour Conversions: A Journey Into the Labyrinth of Prebankruptcy Planning," *Florida Bar Journal*, Jan. 1995

Chapter 30
Gifts

As mentioned previously, making a gift is one of the most common means people use to take property out of their names. If done after a creditor has made a claim, it is also one of the least effective and involves the greatest risk of violation of fraudulent transfer laws (Chapter 5). If not given properly, a gift can be seized by a court and sold to pay a creditor.

As usual, the best way to be sure that a gift will be valid is for it to be made before any financial problem arises. It is also possible that a gift made during financial problems can be valid if it is part of a gift-giving plan which was formulated earlier.

For example, if a person gives his children a certain sum each year, then similar sums given during financial problems may be safe from creditors. Estate planning often involves transfers to trusts for life insurance, children or charities. When a program for such giving is set up before problems arise, the gifts are usually safe.

If property is given to fulfill an obligation it is technically not a gift. It is transferred for a valid consideration. Marriage and divorce are times at which this can be done. For example, a gift given to someone in exchange for a promise to marry is considered valid. Also, property given to a spouse in a divorce is not considered a gift, but fulfillment of a valid obligation of support. Such transfers are not fraudulent.

Validity

In order for a gift to be valid, certain legal requirements must be met:

- A gift must be intended
- The person making the gift must be mentally competent
- The property must be delivered
- The property must be accepted
- The gift must be complete (no retained interest)

If you "give" your Rolex watch to your son but then continue to wear it and treat it as your own, it may not be legally considered to have been made a gift. In some states, when a gift is made but the property is not transferred, the gift is presumed to be fraudulent. Another rule of making gifts is that if property is transferred to a "natural object of a person's bounty," such as a child or spouse, then it is presumed to be a gift.

Of course, as in most areas of law, there are no black and white rules as to when a gift fails to meet legal requirements. Each case stands or falls on its own circumstances and perhaps who the judge has the most sympathy for. Some exceptions to the above rules have been made when minor children were involved, when the property was loaned back, when there was a trust, or when a life estate had been created.

Taxes

When making gifts, tax aspects must be kept in mind. Under federal gift tax law a person is allowed to give $10,000 per year tax free to any person, but any amount over that may be taxed. In addition to the $10,000 exemption, gifts of $600,000 are allowed over a lifetime and subtracted from the exclusion at death. If you are contemplating gifts of over $10,000 per person per year you should consult a competent tax advisor.

Spouses

Probably the most common practice of people attempting to avoid creditors is to put property into a spouse's name. This practice has two problems. The first problem is that since 50% of marriages end in divorce, putting your property in your spouse's name may cost you all of the property in the end anyway. If your divorce is nasty you would probably rather have your property go to your creditor than to your spouse.

Many people who think their marriages are perfectly stable find to their dismay that their spouse has gotten bored and found someone new. This is especially common for the successful male. As Dr. Warren Farrell points out in his book, *Why Men Are the*

Way They Are, women are most interested in men who are extremely successful, but then aren't happy because those men devote so much time to their professions. They then divorce the successful one, taking half the assets, and find a more nurturing man.

If you put property in the name of your spouse to protect it from creditors, be sure that in case of divorce you have evidence to prove that you were not making a gift. This could be a statement on a deed or other writing stating that a transfer is being made "not as a gift, but for estate planning purposes only."

In some states, if a piece of property owned by one party is put in joint names it is presumed to be a gift to the other party. If you transfer property to your spouse be sure you have some paperwork to show that it was done for "estate planning" purposes and not as a gift.

The second problem with putting property in the name of a spouse is that the transfer can be challenged by creditors. Under bankruptcy and fraudulent conveyance laws property transferred without fair payment after a creditor has appeared can be set aside.

In some states you can title property in the names of both a husband and wife and it will be untouchable by creditors. As explained is Chapter 17 tenancy by the entireties is a legal concept in which the title to the property is considered to be owned by the married couple as a couple and the claims of just one of them cannot touch it. Only 26 states clearly recognize the concept of tenancy by the entireties property and not all of those protect the property from creditors. But if you are lucky enough to live in a state which does, then anything you title this way can be protected from the creditors of one spouse (but not creditors of both spouses). See Chapter 17, especially the table of laws.

When using tenancy by the entireties you must be careful to be sure that all property you intend to be titled this way actually is. Unless property is clearly titled this way a court may rule that creditors can take it. You should have written documentation for all property indicating that it is so titled.

Some banks have signature cards which do not adequately provide for tenancy by the entireties and such accounts could be seized by creditors. You should review the account agreement for each of your bank accounts and be sure that it is an entireties account. If not, you should instruct your bank in writing to change your account and to acknowledge that they have done so. If they refuse to you can switch to a more knowledgeable bank.

Children

Putting property into the names of your children is an excellent way to protect it from the claims of your creditors as long as you realize that this property becomes an irrevocable gift to the children. If you have property that you intend for their education or that you are sure that you will never need again then you can transfer it permanently into their names or into a trust for them and it will be unreachable by your creditors. However, if you are afraid they will not be able to handle the money themselves, or if you think that you might need the property in the future, this is not a good idea.

To put property in the names of children who are still minors you can set up bank accounts or other investments under the Uniform Gifts to Minors Act which can protect assets from creditors and also reduce your income taxes. Keep in mind, however, that at the age of 18 (21 in some states) a minor has the right to full control of the funds to set aside and you have only whatever power of persuasion you have managed to retain over the child.

When considering putting property into your children's names, you must also consider the risk that the children themselves may have creditor problems. Even if their occupations are not as risky as yours, they may be involved in an auto accident or other incident which would result in liability. Fortunately, there is an easy solution to this. If you make the gift in the form of a spendthrift trust, the funds can be used to benefit the children and still be out of reach of their creditors. See Chapter 34 on children's trusts for more information.

Chapter 31
General Partnerships

General Partnerships

In all states, property of business partnerships is exempt from creditors. If you file for bankruptcy owning an interest in a general partnership, the property of the partnership cannot be used to pay your debts. However, for asset protection purposes, general partnerships are not a good idea, and in fact are very dangerous.

The biggest problem with general partnerships is that each partner is liable for acts of all other partners done in the scope of the business. If you are in a general partnership with other professionals, you can be personally liable if one of them gets into an auto accident while on business, defrauds someone through the business, sexually harasses an employee, or injures a client or patient.

One way to protect against liability for other partners' acts is for each partner to form a corporation and then have the corporations form a partnership. This is done by many attorneys and medical professionals. This protects the partner's personal assets from partnership claims. However, all of the assets of the corporation are subject to claims against the partnership, and the stock in the corporation itself may be seized by your personal creditors.

This is not a problem if the corporation has few assets. However, if a lot of assets are necessary for the business other devices must be used to protect them.

The best way to protect them is to have them owned by a separate corporation or trust and then to lease them. This can have tax advantages such as when the assets are owned by a children's' trust. Money which would have been given to the children anyway for education expenses can be deducted as a lease payment for equipment of the business!

Another way to protect the corporation which is the partner in the business is to have its stock owned by one's children or spouse. Of course the usefulness of this setup depends upon the potential for problems within the family. Also, in some states stockholders of some professional corporations must be licensed in the profession.

Chapter 32
Limited Partnerships

The limited partnership is one of the most important methods of protecting assets. Limited partnerships have been called the diamond among the gems of asset protection. This is because the laws in all 50 states protect partnership assets from the claims (unrelated to the business) against one partner. This protection is available because it would be unfair to other partners to have the partnership dissolved, or property seized, for acts over which they had no control.

For a serious and successful asset protection program you will need a limited partnership. When used for asset protection purposes, a limited partnership is usually called a **family limited partnership**. This and the offshore trust are the two most successful asset protection devices available today.

In recent years, some promoters of asset protection trusts have claimed there are potential risks of limited partnerships and have predicted that courts would start letting creditors reach their assets. However, so far no courts have clearly abandoned the protections offered by limited partnerships, and any judicial abandonment would probably take many years to accomplish. The few cases which ruled against limited partnerships applied to very narrow, unusual situations. At present, limited partnerships are very successful in protecting assets from creditors' claims. Even Federal Deposit Insurance Corporation claims against bank directors have been abandoned when it was discovered that all their assets were in limited partnerships.

Limited partnerships have a long history of being untouchable. Lawyers make money getting quick settlements, not litigating for years in hope of changing the law. Therefore, a limited partnership would be a successful roadblock to most claims. Even if the lawyer thought he had a chance to win in the end, few would invest the time or money involved in the appeals necessary to change the law.

What a Limited Partnership Is

A limited partnership is a partnership agreement between two or more persons in which at least one of them (the limited partner) has no right to control the business and no liability for debts of the partnership. The general partner (or partners) control the business or assets and are liable for the partnership debts. The limited partners own a share but have no say in the operation. They can share in the profits according to their percentage ownership if the general partner decides to distribute profits.

Why the Limited Partnership Works

The reason that a limited partnership works is that a creditor of a person who owns an interest in a limited partnership cannot seize the interest or the property owned by the partnership. All he can do is obtain a "charging order" which is a lien against the limited partnership interest. The charging order only entitles the creditor to any profits distributed to the partner. But in a family limited partnership, the general partner can decide not to distribute any profits.

But the biggest drawback to the creditor is that if he obtains a charging lien he has to pay a share of the taxes on the profits of the limited partnership even if no profits are distributed! This means he can go for years paying taxes but receiving nothing. Needless to say, few creditors want to obtain charging liens against limited partnerships.

Besides owning part of the limited partnership interests, you could also own a 1% interest as the sole general partner, which would give you complete control over the assets of the partnership. While some lawyers feel that this ownership could be a problem in bankruptcy, most partnerships are set up so that if you, as the general partner, face a financial problem you can resign or be automatically replaced as general partner.

Tax Advantage

The family limited partnership also offers a terrific estate tax advantage. When a business or other asset is put in a limited partnership, it is worth less than it would be if it were not in a limited partnership. This is because none of the partners has complete control. This lower value can mean lower estate taxes and the ability to give greater gifts each year under the $10,000 exclusion.

Some estates may even avoid estate taxes. If an assets valued at $800,000 are put in a limited partnership and the value is then discounted 30%, the $560,000 value would be under the $600,000 threshold for filing an estate tax return. Discounts can go as high as 40% depending on how the ownership is set up.

Small limited partnerships may not even have to file returns. Under IRC sections 6033 and 6698 a partnership return need not be filed if the individual partners fully report their shares of the income. This only applies if there are 10 or less partners and if they received income proportional to their shares.

Ways to Use a Limited Partnership

There are several ways a limited partnership can be used to protect assets. A person can have one partnership or several. Here are several examples of how limited partnerships can be used:

• A couple could put all of their investments into a limited partnership and then give $10,000 worth of shares to each family member each year. This would transfer interests tax-free to the family before death, but the husband or wife or both could keep complete control of the assets until their deaths and decide whether or not to distribute actual cash.

• A person could put his business, his investments and his apartment building each in a separate limited partnership. That way, if the business or apartment building had any liability problem it would not affect other assets. In some cases it would be better to make one partnership a subsidiary of the other, in others it would not.

• A single person could put his antiques collection into a limited partnership in which he owned the 1% general partnership interest and 94% of the limited partnership interest. His children or parents could own the other 5% limited partnership interest. If he were sued for some reason his partnership interest could be made subject to a charging lien, but the antiques could not be seized by his creditor.

• The limited partnership interests can be put into a living trust to avoid probate. For large estates, a trust could be set up for each spouse (A-B trusts) which would allow the children to inherit $1,200,000 tax-free ($600,000 from each spouse).

•For extra protection the limited partnership interest could be put into an offshore trust.

Necessary Provisions

To set up a limited partnership a certificate of limited partnership must be filed with the Secretary of State in the state in which it will be located. When setting up a limited partnership for asset protection purposes, the following provisions are important:

- •The interests should be nontransferable
- •A person obtaining an interest through foreclosure or bankruptcy should not be able to become a partner without the unanimous consent of other partners
- •The partnership should not be able to liquidate without the consent of all partners
- •The right of a partner to withdraw should be limited
- •The general partner should be replaced immediately by a named successor if he ever files bankruptcy
- •Death, bankruptcy or disability of a partner should not cause liquidation of the partnership
- •Distributions to partners should be limited
- •Redemption of a partner's interest should be provided for
- •The partnership should be set up for a set term of years (which can be extended)
- •The partnership should be properly set up so that it is not taxed as a corporation

Operation

To be sure not to lose the protections of the partnership, it should always be operated as a separate entity.

- •Partnership funds should be kept separate from personal funds
- •All dealings with the partnership should be formal and at arm's length
- •Separate books and records should be kept for the partnership
- •File partnership tax returns

Drawbacks

Nothing in life is free and there is a cost for everything, including limited partnerships. The biggest drawback to the limited partnership is the cost. There are attorney fees for formation, annual registration fees, and accounting fees for the limited partnership tax return. However, in most cases the tax savings and advantages will outweigh the costs. In researching asset protection, the author was hoping to find something easier than the limited partnership for his own use, but for some assets nothing offered the same protection.

In states which have high annual fees for limited partnerships, it may be possible to use a limited partnership registered in another state. If that state does not require a registered office your fees there could be minimal. And if the partnership holds investments, rather than conducting an active business, you might not have to pay the fees in your state.

References

Family Limited Partnerships, General American Life Insurance Co., P. O. Box 396, St. Louis, MO 63166; Telephone: (800) 835-2711; Includes book, video and forms on diskette, $75 plus $4.50 shipping

Chapter 33
Living Trusts

Living trusts are used by millions of Americans to keep their assets from going through probate. However, most living trusts are not good for protecting assets from creditors because they are revocable. This means that the person setting up the trust can revoke or change the terms of the trust at any time. If a trust is revocable, and a person can get control of the assets in the trust at any time, the courts have consistently held that that person's creditors can also get control of the assets.

There are ways to incorporate living trusts into an asset protection scheme, and some asset protection planners use them. But these are usually used in conjunction with limited partnerships or offshore trusts.

One situation in which living trusts could be useful for asset protection is where a couple in a stable marriage wished to divide their property equally to avoid claims against one spouse who is in a risky profession. In such a scenario each spouse sets up a living trust providing lifetime income to him- or herself, with the remainder to the children. The exempt property is put in the trust of the at-risk spouse and the non-exempt property is put in the other spouse's trust. This arrangement can provide protection which is similar to tenancy by the entireties property in states which do not recognize the concept.

Husband-wife living trusts, also known as A-B trusts, can also avoid estate taxes by allowing both spouses to take advantage of the $600,000 lifetime exclusion. In this arrangement each spouse has a separate trust which allows both spouses to pass $600,000 to the next generation (or other beneficiaries) tax-free.

Trusts can be more successfully used to protect assets if they are irrevocable. This means that once you set them up you cannot change the terms. Since you cannot revoke them or change the terms, your creditors cannot either, and the property in them is safe. These types of trusts are discussed in the following chapters.

Reference

Turner, George M., *Revocable Trusts, 2/e*, Shepard's/McGraw Hill 1994; 950 pages $115 (Available through Sphinx Publishing)

Chapter 34
Children's Trusts

If you have children to whom you wish to give part of your assets, a children's trust can offer both tax savings and asset protection. If you have young children, such a trust can offer three benefits. Once your property is transferred to such a trust it can no longer be reached by your creditors, it is no longer part of your estate, and at least some of the income can be taxed at the children's lower rates. This trust is usually called a "2503C" trust, after the tax code provision which covers it.

Such a trust is a good way to set aside funds which will be used for a child's education. If you plan on paying those expenses anyway, you can allow the funds to accumulate interest at a lower tax rate and keep them safe from your creditors.

A creative way to use the trust is to use the funds in the trust to purchase equipment which you need in your business. The trust can then lease these items to your business and the lease payments (which you would have given to your children for education expenses anyway) are tax deductible!

However, one aspect of the children's trust which must be stressed is that once property has been transferred to the trust it cannot be taken back. Absolute control must be surrendered and once the children reach legal age they can do what they want with the assets. While you may have intended the funds to go for education expenses your children may be more interested in clothes, cars, or drugs. One parent got a call from his daughter at a commune in California demanding to receive $50,000 from her trust on her upcoming 21st birthday. He was told that if it was not sent, he would hear from the commune's lawyer.

Legal age depends on state law and can range from 18 to 25. Parents can choose between setting up the trust in the state where the trustee is located, or the state where the donor or the child resides. Choosing the state with the highest legal age allows the parents to maintain control of the trust until the child is more mature. This does not guarantee the child will be ready to make financial decisions when the time comes, but a few years delay may help.

When a child reaches legal age it is possible to extend the trust until a later age with the child's written consent. However, not all children are cooperative at this age and some may be tempted to take the money immediately. One possibility is to threaten to cut off all future financial connections, but even this may not sway a child at that age.

Setting up the trust when a child is young allows a greater period of interest accumulation. However, at this time it is too early to tell if the child will be able to make the right decisions at the age of majority. For this reason some parents wait until a later age to set up the trust. When the child reaches fourteen, the tax law allows all income of the trust to be taxed to the child, which is another advantage because the child's tax rate is lower.

Income from the trust cannot be used to pay for necessities of the child, but can be used for other items such as vacations, uniforms, music lessons and summer camp. If the tax law is not carefully followed there could be penalties; however, this item is not one which is carefully scrutinized by the IRS.

Some other aspects of the children's trust are as follows:
- The trustee should not be you, your employee, or a close relative.
- Assets you give to the trust cannot be sold within the first two years.
- Until the age of 14, the first $1,200 in income in the trust is taxed at the child's rate and any above that at the parent's rate.
- At age 14, the income is all taxed at the child's rate.

To set up a children's trust you should check with your tax advisor and an attorney who specializes in this area. Some advisors feel that one can obtain similar benefits more easily with a family limited partnership set up for the children's benefit.

Chapter 35
Charitable Remainder Trusts

While giving your assets to charity may not sound like a way to protect them for yourself, under the amazing American system of taxation you can give away your property and enjoy it too. Americans give about five times as much to charities as the French and about three times as much as the British. The reason is our tax code.

The most useful device is the Charitable Remainder Trust or CRT. Using a CRT you can give away property but retain an income stream for life and have the value of the property go to your heirs. Sound too good to be true? It works best for those in the highest tax brackets, but it also works for others. Here is how:

Suppose you have stock worth $100,000 which you bought years ago for $30,000. If you sold it to invest in treasury bonds for retirement income, you would pay about $21,000 income tax on the profit, and upon your death (if you are in the highest tax bracket) another $44,000 in tax would be due, leaving your heirs with only $36,000 from the original $100,000 value.

Instead of selling the stock, you could give it to a CRT. As part of the deal you could require that you receive the same income that you would have gotten on Treasury bonds for the rest of your life. You not only get to deduct the donation as a gift, but with the tax savings can buy life insurance which will give your heirs more than the $36,000 they would have received if you had followed the above example. This way you get the same income, your heirs get an even better inheritance than they would have, and you get a tax deduction.

This is a simplification of the issues. There are formulas for figuring the deductions and how much income may be received. But the CRT works quite well, especially with property which has appreciated in value since you bought it.

A charitable trust can be set up as either a Charitable Remainder Annuity Trust (CRAT) or a Charitable Remainder Unitrust (CRU).

Internal Revenue Code §664 provides the rules for setting up charitable trusts. Sample forms are contained in Revenue Rulings 89-20, 89-21, 90-30 and 90-32. However, these laws are quite complicated so it is advisable to work with a qualified tax advisor or attorney.

Chapter 36
Asset Protection Trusts

Along with the limited partnership, the asset protection trust is one of the most successful methods of protecting your estate from creditors. While it is a must for larger estates, the offshore trust can also be useful for smaller estates.

A **trust** is an arrangement by which one person, the **trustee**, holds property for the benefit of another person, the **beneficiary**. The trust is set up by the **grantor** or **settlor** who conveys property to the trust. The grantor may or may not be a beneficiary. The trustee has no personal rights to the property but is legally obligated to hold it solely for the beneficiary. It is said that the trustee has a **fiduciary** duty to take care of the property and protect it for the beneficiary. Of course, the trustee is usually paid a fee to perform this duty.

The **asset protection trust** is a trust which can hold your property and keep your creditors from getting it. After your property has been transferred to an asset protection trust you no longer own it, so your creditors cannot reach it. Of course, once it is transferred, the property no longer appears on your balance sheet.

Spendthrift Trusts

Spendthrift trusts are trusts that contain clauses which prevent the beneficiaries or their creditors from getting to the assets of the trust. They have been used for many years and have been very successful. Most states recognize and enforce spendthrift trusts.

An example would be a trust that is set up for a child who cannot control his spending. If the trust is set up to pay him a certain amount each month, with no right to get any more or to assign the payments to anyone, it would be a spendthrift trust and could not be reached by the child's creditors. However, once payments were made to the child the creditor could reach them. For further protection, the trust could be set up to make payments for the benefit of the beneficiary, for example to pay his rent, food bills, etc. directly to the providers instead of to the beneficiary.

One problem with spendthrift trusts for asset protection planning is that American courts have ruled that a person cannot set up a spendthrift trust for his own benefit. Also, two people cannot set up spendthrift trusts for each other. Therefore, if you wish to set up a spendthrift trust you must make it for the benefit of someone else and forever give up control of the property.

If you wish to provide for your spouse, parents, children or other person dear to you this may be a useful way to insure that gifts to them are not taken by your creditors. Children's trusts are discussed in the previous chapter and similar trusts can be set up for other persons' benefit.

There is a way to set up a trust in which you can retain some benefit. If you set up an irrevocable trust in which you will receive the income for life and the remainder will go to others, such as your spouse and children, the property in the trust will be safe from your creditors (though it will still be considered part of your estate for tax purposes). However, if the income is paid directly to you, it can be reached by your creditors. To avoid this it can be paid directly to those who provide you with food, shelter or other items.

One way which might protect the income from your creditors would be to make it solely for your health, support and maintenance, solely at the discretion of the trustee, and only if it did not jeopardize the amounts payable to the other beneficiaries. Such an arrangement requiring loss of control of one's assets is usually not desirable. If you wish to set up a trust for your own benefit you must set it up under the jurisdiction of another country.

Foreign Trusts

The foreign, or offshore, trust is one of the most advanced techniques for protecting assets. The liability crisis in this country has been noted around the world and several countries have passed special laws that allow Americans to protect their wealth from the kinds of lawsuits we have today. Many of the banks handling these trusts are well established and some are safer than American banks.

Because of the reputation of foreign havens which have been used to hide ill-gotten funds from drug operations, most legitimate asset protection companies today are extremely careful in their dealing with Americans. They require references and clear evidence that their clients are not involved in illegal activities. Many require a personal interview.

In previous years, foreign trusts were used by the wealthy to avoid paying U. S. income tax. However, recent laws have eliminated the tax savings from foreign trusts. As explained later in this chapter, these trusts are now tax-neutral. Yet in the last few years countless Americans have begun using foreign trusts in several jurisdictions.

The two main reasons today for using foreign trusts are asset protection and the fear of economic problems due to the government spending hundreds of billions of dollars each year which it does not have. If ever the day of reckoning comes and this country experiences an economic crisis, moving funds abroad will likely be made illegal. But those who already have their funds abroad will be safe.

Years ago most people setting up offshore trusts were residents of countries that ran the risk of political strife and coup d'etat, such as Third World dictatorships. Many of them set up their trusts in the United States. It is a sad commentary on the state of our nation that it is now Americans who must send their assets abroad for protection!

Foreign trusts offer many benefits, some of which are traditional trust benefits and others of which are only available overseas. Among these are:

- Privacy
- Diversification of assets
- Avoidance of probate
- Qualification for entitlements such as Medicaid
- Avoidance of the need for a premarital agreement
- Avoidance of forced heirship laws
- Protection from seizure by creditors

To understand the asset protection benefits of a foreign trust over a U. S. trust, consider the following. In the U. S. a person suing you has a certain period of time (i.e. two or four years, depending on the state and the court) from the time *he finds out you set up a trust* to try to set it aside. In some countries the person has two years from the date you *set up the trust*. If the person does not have a claim against you until five years after you set up the foreign trust there is nothing he can do.

Next, suppose the person has filed suit against you in the U.S., and after three years of litigation has won a judgment. Most likely he won't find out about your foreign trust until after he has obtained his judgment. If he then wants to try to seize your foreign trust he must file his suit all over again in the country where your trust is located. To do so he must hire a lawyer in that country. Unlike in the U.S., the lawyers in the country where you set up your trust cannot work on a percentage basis, but must charge by the hour. Then, in the unlikely event he could win the same case under the laws of that country he would have to file another suit to try to set aside your trust. In that case the burden would be on the creditor to prove that you specifically intended to defraud *him* years ago when you set up the trust. Meanwhile, your trustee has resigned and transferred the trust to another country. So your creditor has to start all over in the new country! If not foolproof, this adventure is more than most American lawyers would like to pursue.

While this can be a drawback for other reasons, one of the best things about the foreign trust is that there is so much uncertainty and few lawyers know much about them. While a collections lawyer might be eager to seize your bank account and your car, he may have no idea how to begin collecting from a foreign trust. When he considers the cost of hiring another lawyer to help him, especially in a foreign country, and the fact that he must pay in advance, win or lose, he may settle for pennies on the dollar or just give up.

Important Characteristics

The following are the characteristics usually used in a successful offshore asset protection trust:

•**Independent Foreign Trustee.** The grantor of the trust should never be the trustee, and the trustee should not have any offices or branches in the United States. In some cases it may be advisable to have a U.S. co-trustee (mostly for tax reasons), but he should resign or be removed in the event of financial trouble of the grantor.

•**Beneficiaries.** Attorneys are divided on whether a person setting up a trust may be a beneficiary. Some suggest that a creditor might be able to reach the trust if the person was beneficiary. Others say that foreign laws would bar creditors from making claims and that the whole point of the trust is to protect assets while keeping the benefits. The best position seems to be that the person setting up the trust can be a "discretionary" beneficiary and a "contingent remainder" beneficiary as explained in the next two paragraphs.

• **All Disbursements Discretionary.** The money paid out of the trust by the trustee should be solely at the trustee's discretion. No one can force the trustee to distribute any funds except as provided for in the trust document. This is because if you could demand distribution, your creditor could also demand distributions. You may be afraid to give a trustee total discretion over what to disburse to you. However, as one trust officer explained to the author, "We have total discretion over what to disburse, however, we take your wishes into consideration." In other words, if you phone the trustee and say that you need a disbursement, it will be done.

• **Remainder.** The trust provides that it will dissolve either upon the death of the grantor or after a set number of years. The term of years could be extended by the grantor, and if the grantor were in financial trouble, the trust would be extended automatically. If the grantor were alive at the termination of the trust, the assets could go to him, or if the trust terminated upon his death, they would go to remainder beneficiaries whom he named. Since the grantor might get the assets back if he lives longer than the term of the trust, he is a "contingent beneficiary."

• **Right to Change Beneficiaries.** The grantor of the trust can retain the right to change the beneficiaries who are to get the property upon his death.

• **Jurisdiction.** The country chosen for the trust must be one which has laws specifically protecting such trusts. Such countries have recently passed laws which make it difficult for creditors to attack such a trust. Some of the best countries are the Bahamas, Cayman Islands, Cook Islands, Gibraltar and Isle of Man. In many of these it may be difficult to enforce a U.S. judgment, and in the Cook Islands it appears to be impossible.

• **Foreign law.** The trust must state that the law of the foreign jurisdiction governs interpretation of the trust.

• **Irrevocability.** The trust is irrevocable either until the grantor's death or for a set number of years. If the grantor is in financial trouble at the end of the term of years, the trust may be extended by the trustee.

• **Anti-Duress Clause.** If a court orders the grantor to attempt to obtain assets from the trust, the trustee would be compelled to refuse.

• **Flight Clause.** If there were any risk to the assets of the trust, either from a creditor or from some sort of government instability or new tax law, the trust would be transferred to another country.

• **Trust Protector.** An independent person, committee, or entity chosen by the grantor could have the power to change the trustee or the terms of the trust as necessary. This protector must be someone you trust absolutely. If the protector resides in the U.S., he must resign in the event of possible financial trouble of the grantor.

• **Insolvency.** Transfers to the trust should not be made while the grantor is insolvent, and the transfers should not make the grantor insolvent. He or she must always have other assets after the transfer.

Optional Arrangements

There are several ways of setting up an asset protection trust. Some attorneys advise putting virtually all of one's assets in such a trust while others advise only placing a small percentage. The following are some of the ways of setting up the trust.

• **Liquid Assets out of the U. S.** Putting cash into an offshore trust and having the trustee invest it in non-U.S. investments would offer protection both from U.S. economic problems and from seizure by creditors.

• **Liquid Assets in a U. S. Brokerage Account.** Using a U.S. brokerage account and having the assets titled in the offshore trust would not be as safe from creditors because assets in the U.S. may be seized by a U.S. court. But it would allow you to control them and they would not be as easy for a creditor to find as other arrangements.

• **U. S. Limited Partnership Owned by a Trust.** For a double layer of protection, a limited partnership can be used to hold assets (as described in Chapter 32) and the interests in the partnership can be owned by an offshore trust. This ought to stop even the most determined creditor. However, if the physical assets are in the U.S. a court which felt that you defrauded someone might decide to ignore the technical law and seize the assets anyway.

• **U. S. Corporation Owned by a Trust.** If you wish to keep personal control of your business or property, you could put it in a U.S. corporation of which you are an officer, and have the stock owned by your offshore trust.

• **Foreign Corporation Owned by a Trust.** Some countries, such as the Bahamas, allow the formation of International Business Corporations (IBCs). Such a corporation can hold your assets and be owned by your offshore trust.

• **Real Estate Owned by Trust.** Because real estate cannot be moved offshore, it is more difficult than liquid assets to protect with a trust. If a judge thinks your creditor should have it, he may allow it to be seized. However, if you have a substantial mortgage against the property the value to the creditor will be less and the cash can be put into the trust.

• **Blind Trust Arrangement.** A blind trust is one in which the beneficiary does not know what assets are owned by the trust. The benefit of this is that if a court orders you to disclose what assets are owned by the trust, you can honestly say that you do not know. You can be given general information, such as what types of securities or real estate is owned, but no specifics which would allow you to disclose the location.

• **U.S. Co-Trustee**. To insure the trust is treated as a domestic trust for tax purposes (see following section) and to maintain additional control, some prefer a trust with both a foreign trustee and a U.S. co-trustee. The problem with this is that the U.S. trustee would be subject to U.S. law. To avoid this the U.S. co-trustee should resign at the first sign of trouble.

Tax Status

As mentioned previously, a foreign asset protection trust is tax-neutral, which means it does not result in either higher or lower taxes. For tax purposes you still own the property in the offshore trust. The following is the tax status of such a trust:

• **Income Tax.** As long as you retain some power over the ultimate disposition of the trust assets, this would be considered a grantor-type trust. Under section 679 of the Internal Revenue Code (IRC), the grantor of such a trust is taxed on the income of the trust. This means the trust does not have to file its own tax returns; instead you put the income on your own return, just like with a living trust.

• **Gift Tax.** Because the grantor retains the right to change the beneficiary at death, the gift to the trust is not complete and under IRC §2511 no gift tax is owed.

• **Estate Taxes.** Assets in the trust would be considered part of the grantor's estate at death.

• **Excise Tax.** Again, because the transfer is not considered complete in a grantor-type trust, the 35% tax for transfer to a foreign entity does not apply to this type of trust. (Rev. Rul. 87-61.)

• **Non-U.S. Trust.** One matter which is not completely clear in the tax law is the effect of the classification of the trust as a U. S. or foreign trust. This determination is made based upon the following factors:

- where the trust was created
- where the trust assets are located
- where the trust is administered
- the nationality and residence of the trustee
- the nationality and residence of the person setting up the trust
- the nationality and residence of the beneficiaries of the trust

If a U.S. co-trustee is used the factors above would be about equal. However, whether the trust is U. S. or foreign the tax consequences would remain the same. The only difference is that with a foreign trust, extra tax forms would need to be filed. Because the law in uncertain in this area, some tax specialists advise that the trust be treated like a U.S. trust, but that it file the forms applicable to foreign trusts. These are:

- Form 3520—Creation of or Transfers to Certain Foreign Trusts
- Form 3520A—Annual Return of a Foreign Trust with U.S. Beneficiaries
- Form 926—Return of a Transferor of Property to a Foreign Corporation, Foreign Estate or Trust, or Foreign Partnership
- Form 1040NR—U.S. Nonresident Alien Income Tax Return
- Form 1041—U.S. Fiduciary Income Tax Return

When setting up your foreign trust you should rely on the opinion of an expert as to which forms to file. This will be based upon the terms of your trust.

A Possible Problem

The main problem with a foreign asset protection trust is that it is so obviously useful to defeat creditors' claims that a court could say it was set up with the "intent to defraud creditors." Intent is, of course, subjective, and you could argue that you wanted to do normal estate planning, but using such a trust looks so obviously like a way to hinder creditors that a judge might rule against you just because you have such a trust. However, if your trust is set up right, even if the creditor wins in a U.S. court, he may be physically unable to get your offshore assets. Although some high profile criminal cases have resulted in foreign banks obeying U.S. court orders, a case based upon a civil judgment would be less likely to merit the same cooperation.

To make your offshore trust more secure, consider the following:

- If you only put a portion of your assets in the trust it would look less like you were trying to defraud creditors. (Put the rest of your assets in exempt assets at a much later time.)

•If the trust had been set up for four years when a creditor attacked it, it might be too late to attack it under the UFTA §9(b).

•If you enter into a new business or incur new debts, be sure that you have enough remaining capital so that your transfer to the trust will not be considered fraudulent.

•If you vocalize to your friends and acquaintances your fears of an economic collapse due to the national debt, your reason for setting up a foreign trust might seem more influenced by that.

You should also consider that just having the trust might protect you. As explained in the chapter on limited partnerships, the years of legal work required to win such a case may scare most attorneys away, or at lease convince them to settle for less.

The Bahamas

In the Bahamas, one of the closest countries to the United States, there are hundreds of banks specializing in trusts for Americans and the government recently passed a law which makes the protections even stronger. The most important key to protection is that the trust must be set up *before* a creditor has a claim against you. Bahamian law holds that two years after the trust has been set up it cannot be touched by creditors.

You may be concerned about irrevocably turning a considerable portion of your assets over to a stranger in a foreign country. But even though the transfer is irrevocable, you should realize that you are paying the trustee for a service and he or she will "take your wishes into consideration." In other words you can't legally force trustees to take particular actions, but like any other business, their interest is in keeping their clients happy.

To set up a trust of this type you must personally visit the Bahamas and meet with an agent of the bank at least once. However, there are several "weekend excursions" and 2-day "gambling holidays" available, especially in the off-season, that offer the opportunity for a quick meeting with a trustee. Bring the spouse for a few days of relaxation, then sneak away for a couple of hours and return with a gift for your spouse and your trust attended to.

The Cook Islands

The asset protection trust laws of the Cook Islands were instigated by two lawyers from Colorado. Barry Engle and Ronald Rudman worked with the government of the Cook Islands to insure that the law offered strong protections to Americans. The Cook Islands are possibly the only country in which a U.S. judgment would not be enforceable. The Cook Islands law also allows a person setting up a trust to be a beneficiary without losing the asset protection benefits.

The laws of the Cook Islands governing trusts are the International Trusts Act 1984 and the International Trusts Amendment Act 1989.

However, the cost of this protection does not come cheap. The typical fee to set up such a trust is $15,000 to $20,000 and it can go higher.

References:

Articles:

Roush and Kirkland, "Spendthrift Trusts Not Limited To Protection of Immature Dependents," *Estate Planning*, January/February, 1991

Bruce, Gray and Luria, "Exploring the Protection Of Assets Trusts," *Trusts & Estates*, November, 1991 (Part I) and December, 1991 (Part II)

Button, "Pulling Up the Drawbridge," *Forbes*, April 27, 1992

Osborne, "The Offshore Trust: A Friendly Alien," 18 *ACTEC Notes* 19 (1992)

Korn, "Out of Harm's Way, *Worth*, April/May, 1992

Lanchner, "Keeping It By Signing It Away," *International Herald Tribune*, May 2-3, 1992

Bove, "Send assets on an island vacation if you've really got a lot to protect," *The Boston Globe*, July 23, 1992

Amari, "Asset Protection Trusts: Nuclear Bombshelter, *The Florida Bar Journal*, July/August, 1992

Janssen, "Endangered Assets? Try an Island Strongbox," *Business Week*, August 24, 1992

Slater, "Safe Harbors," *ABA Journal*, September, 1992

Osborne, "New Age Estate Planning: Offshore trusts," *1993 Institute on Estate Planning*, Matthew Bender & Co., Inc.

Engle, "Dodging the Litigation Explosion," *Chief Executive*, May, 1993

Engle, "Using Foreign Situs Trusts for Asset Protection Planning," *Estate Planning*, July/August, 1993

Book:

Turner, George M., *Revocable Trusts*, 2/e, Shepard's/McGraw Hill 1994; 900 pages $115 (Available through Sphinx Publishing)

Much additional information on asset protection trusts is contained in the general asset protection books listed in Appendix 4.

Chapter 37
Business Trusts

The business trust is one of the least understood of all legal entities. There are very few used in this country, and very few lawyers know anything about them. For this reason they make excellent asset protection devices.

As an example of how limited their use is, in one large state in which nearly a hundred thousand corporations register each year, only about two dozen business trusts are formed. Because the business trust is used so infrequently, there is little information as to the legal rights of persons who deal with them. Therefore, they may serve as a successful roadblock to creditors seeking your property.

Because of the time involved in researching a new area of law, and the fact that an attorney would not want to admit to not knowing what he was doing, a creditor's attorney would probably be very willing to settle a case dealing with a business trust.

Even if he did decide to sue, every issue would probably be a new area of law which could be appealed to a higher court, dragging the case on for years and years. In the meantime, the trust could slowly wind down its business and let its assets get old.

Business trusts originated because there was a hostility in some states to corporations. For example, in some states special taxes were levied on corporations and they were forbidden from owning real estate. To gain the benefits of a corporation without these problems, lawyers devised business trusts. Because these were most prevalent in Massachusetts, they are often called "Massachusetts trusts."

Like any other type of trust, a business trust is an arrangement whereby the trustee(s) hold property for the benefit of others. To use a business trust for asset protection purposes, you could set up your business in the form of a business trust. You could be the trustee who controls the business and the beneficiaries could be your spouse or your children. This is similar to using a corporation in the same way, but more confusing to your creditors.

A business trust can be taxed either as a trust or as a corporation. If it is a passive entity and merely holds assets for investment, it will be taxed as a trust and file IRS form 1041. If it actively runs a business then it files the corporate tax return, form 1120.

While some states require that business trusts be registered, most have no such laws. Therefore, there is no record of any of the persons in control of the business. Even where they must be registered, changes in the trustees and beneficiary may not be required.

To set up a business trust you will need to locate an attorney who is willing to do some research and learn a new area of law. This may be expensive, but some attorneys may be willing to learn on their own time and only charge you for work done on your particular case.

Chapter 38
Nonprofit Corporations
& Foundations

One often overlooked device for both asset protection and tax savings is the nonprofit corporation. Surely you have read the stories in the media about officers of such organizations as United Way and the Red Cross receiving salaries of hundreds of thousands of dollars. It is perfectly legal for a nonprofit corporation to pay a reasonable salary to its officers and employees.

Nonprofit Corporation

Suppose you set up an enterprise as a nonprofit corporation rather than a for-profit corporation. Your creditors could not reach the assets and you could have numerous benefits such as no sales or income tax, lower postage rates and exemption from such things as labor laws and customs duties. It is almost too good to be true.

For those in the medical profession, it is not unusual at all to have a nonprofit hospital or clinic and such an organization would not encounter much scrutiny. However, for those interested in setting up other types of businesses, the rules may require careful planning.

A nonprofit corporation is very similar to a regular corporation, except it does not have shareholders and does not distribute its profits. However, the profits can be paid to the officers and employees of the organization, as long as the amounts are reasonable.

To qualify for non-taxable status an application must be approved by the IRS. While this is a somewhat complicated form, many have been able to complete it without professional help. However, if you are setting up a corporation to protect your wealth, you may want the insurance that it is done right by hiring a professional.

Because nonprofit corporations are fairly common, it should be easy to find an attorney to set up one to suit your needs. It is possible to do it yourself, but to ensure following the laws precisely, you should use the advice of a specialist. Tax planning is also important, so if your attorney is not a tax specialist you should also consult an accountant.

Foundations

For those who do not wish to set up a business, but merely to set aside part of their estate to avoid estate tax and creditors, there is the private foundation. These are primarily for wealthy individuals who plan to leave part of their estate to charity upon their deaths.

Prior to 1995 large tax deductions could be taken for donations of appreciated property, but Congress put an end to that tax loophole. Still, the foundation can be useful to wealthy individuals who wish to leave their wealth to charity.

Much information is available on setting up a foundation:

• The Council on Foundations offers publications, seminars and even free consultations with their lawyers to those contemplating setting up private foundations. Their book, *First Steps in Starting a Foundation* explains how to set up a foundation and includes sample forms. It is available for $45 for nonmembers and $25 to members. For more information contact the Council on Foundations at (202) 466-6512.

• The Indiana University Center on Philanthropy includes information on foundations in their catalog of books, tapes and reports on charitable giving. For a copy call (317) 274-4200.

• The Foundation Center has information on starting a foundation. Call (800) 424-9836.

Part Five
When Disaster Strikes

Chapter 39
The Rules Change

Once you have a creditor, what you may and may not do with your property changes. A person who has a judgment against you is a creditor, even if you have filed an appeal. And as explained on page 23, the definition of a creditor is very broad and may even include people who have not yet filed suit. Those who have filed suit but not yet gotten a judgment can be considered creditors when it comes to determining if your transfers of property are fraudulent.

Your first impulse on learning of a claim that may result in the loss of a great amount of your property may be to sell, hide, or give away your property or to hide yourself. Depending on exactly what you do, some of these things can be legal or illegal, and others may be clearly illegal.

Keep in mind that you are not the first person who has been sued by a creditor. Thousands of persons over hundreds of years have been in the same situation. They have already tried every trick in the book. No matter what scheme you devise to protect your assets, someone has tried it before and some court has scrutinized it. As one court in Illinois explained in 1967,

> Every lawyer has had the experience of being importuned at one time or another by frantic clients who wish to be stripped of their

properties and have them shed in favor of spouses, relatives or friends. Such generosity is rightly suspect for largess is not the way of the world. A little friendly cross examination to plumb the depths of motive quite often brings forth the intelligence that the client has been sued, or rather, is about to be sued. He may not know it, but the law expects men to be just, before they are generous—and not the other way around. The trouble with their wish is that their intent is not really donative but rather one to thwart the oncoming creditor. Now, even the least sophisticated debtor or debtor to be, on reflection, has some hazy notion that this subterfuge won't work. More sophisticated is the approach of preferring one creditor over another, or effecting transfers to favorites where the consideration may be deemed adequate in law and doesn't involve hard cash. Of course, the *ne plus ultra* is to sell everything to innocent purchasers for value and dissipate the proceeds. Understandably, few debtors take this tack, rather, they attempt to make other "arrangements," and such arrangements are as varied and ingenious and disingenuous as people are varied, ingenious and disingenuous. *Wilkey v. Wax*, 225 N.E.2d 813 (Ill. 4 D.C.A. 1967)

In this case a man had murdered another man and was sent to prison. The wife of the decedent sued him but he had transferred all his property to his own wife in a divorce settlement. The court went on to rule that people cannot use a contrived divorce settlement to avoid paying a creditor.

So, don't think that you can easily fool the system, or that no one will investigate why your net worth is suddenly zero. There are numerous records of your financial dealings and all of these can be subpoenaed.

The following chapters explore some of the options you may be considering and how useful each one may or may not be.

Chapter 40
Settling a Claim

While you may naturally not want to pay dime one to most people who make claims against you, you must realize that in most cases a small settlement payment is far better than taking a chance with our judicial system.

One of lawyers' favorite lines is "millions for defense, but not one cent for tribute." With numerous frivolous suits being filed, this may be a good practice. If you have a record of fighting and winning cases, less people will be inclined to sue you. If more people did this, there might be less unfair lawsuits filed.

However, the cost of defending even a frivolous suit is horrendous. When Paula Jones filed her sexual harassment suit against President Clinton, it was estimated that his legal bills could amount to over a million dollars even if there was little basis to the suit. Fighting a frivolous suit is a good and noble thing to do, but as a practical matter it is sometimes better to pay a small amount in tribute than five times as much to win.

In our court system even an iron-clad case can be lost. A cunning lawyer, lost evidence, or a confused jury can result in a verdict which is contrary to the clear facts. Appeals are very expensive and are not available in many cases.

When you do not have a clearly winning case there is even more reason to settle. Juries today do not seem to have a grasp of what a million dollars is and they have given away defendants' money as if it were water. Whatever settlement you are offered, consider that a jury could come in with the same amount, one-tenth that amount or ten times that amount.

If you have adopted asset protection techniques, you should be in much better position to negotiate a settlement with a claimant. If a claimant sees that you have little or no available property, he will be much more willing to settle for your insurance limits or for a smaller cash amount from you.

You usually do not have to disclose your assets to a claimant until after he has won a judgment against you. (The exceptions are if he seeks punitive damages or claims you are making fraudulent transfers.) But if your attorney provides a financial statement showing that you have few available assets, the claimant's lawyer may lose interest in pursuing the case.

Of course, you do not tell them that all your former assets are in a children's trust or in your spouse's trust. If those were set up years ago they are no longer your property and do not have to be mentioned at all.

Chapter 41
Bankruptcy

Bankruptcy is a procedure in which a person turns over all of his (nonexempt) property to a court and is discharged from his debts and obligations. The purpose of bankruptcy is to give a fresh start to people who have gotten over their heads in debt. Once someone reaches a point where he cannot possibly catch up on his debts, there is no use in trying.

Years ago there was a real stigma attached to filing bankruptcy and people were ashamed to use the procedure. Today, with about a million Americans filing bankruptcy each year, most people have no qualms about it.

Whatever your feelings about it, if you are hit with an excessive judgment, bankruptcy may be your only option. Even if you hand over everything you own, your entire life's earnings may not be enough to satisfy the kind of judgments which are common today.

Some have said that bankruptcy is too easy and that people with millions of dollars in exempt assets are abusing the system. I dare say that people who are being awarded millions of dollars for such things as "emotional damages" by using psychological profiles of jurors are no less guilty of abusing the system. Your use of bankruptcy can cure the abuse of a creditor's misuse of the courts.

Bankruptcy is thousands of years old. In the Judeo-Christian Bible it states, "At the end of every seven years you shall grant a release and this is the manner of the release: every creditor shall release what he has lent to his neighbor..." Bankruptcy is also authorized by Article I of the United States Constitution, so it has noble roots. If you find it necessary to use it yourself to protect what you have spent a lifetime attaining, you should not hesitate to do so.

Stopping Creditors

One effect of filing a bankruptcy petition is that all creditors must immediately stop all actions against you. They cannot seize your property, pursue their court action, or even harass you for payment. If creditors are about to foreclose on your house or seize your car or office equipment, filing can give you some breathing time.

If the creditor has a mortgage on your home or a lien on your personal property, he can usually get that property released from the bankruptcy eventually so that he can foreclose. But the mere filing of the bankruptcy petition will stop the foreclosure and possibly give you time to catch up the payments.

Giving Security to a Creditor

Because secured creditors can get the property released from bankruptcy to foreclose on it, you should **never give a creditor a lien against your exempt property**. Suppose you get behind on a loan and a bank says it will sue you unless you give the bank a mortgage on your house or an assignment of your insurance policies. *Don't do it!* Those assets may be the only property you have that is exempt, and if you sign you could then lose everything you own. What you should be doing instead is selling your nonexempt property and paying down the mortgage on your home or buying more insurance. See Chapter 15.

Paying Preferred Creditors

Any creditors you pay within 90 days of filing can be made to pay the money back to be shared with other creditors. (Thus you cannot use all your money to pay that loan back to your dad and then file bankruptcy.)

Payments Within One Year

Any payments you have made or property you have transferred within a year of filing bankruptcy can be examined by the court and set aside if determined to be unfair. For example, if you sell your car to your son or give it back to the bank in a repossession, the bankruptcy trustee can bring it back into your bankruptcy estate. Even if your house has been foreclosed on the foreclosure can be set aside if the price was not fair.

Paying off debts and purchasing exempt property may cause a problem for you if you do it just before filing a bankruptcy petition, but if you have set up your affairs that way throughout your life there should be no problems.

Types of Bankruptcy

There are two types of bankruptcy for individuals, Chapter 7 and Chapter 13. If you are just temporarily behind on your debts and can catch up if given more time, Chapter 13 bankruptcy lets you reorganize your affairs and do so. If your debts are out of control, Chapter 7 bankruptcy can discharge you from your obligations. As mentioned in a previous chapter, not every debt can be discharged. Some things like taxes, child support and student loans will follow you for your entire life. See Chapter 5 for a complete list of debts that cannot be wiped out in bankruptcy.

Filing for Bankruptcy

Filing for bankruptcy consists of preparing a list of those to whom you owe money, and numerous pages of details about your financial affairs. The purpose of these details is to find out if you have hidden or disposed of any property which should be turned over to your creditors.

If you must file immediately to protect your property from being seized, you don't have much flexibility. But if bankruptcy is just something you are learning about for future contingencies, it can be helpful to know what will be asked of you should filing bankruptcy become necessary.

To help you plan ahead, the following is information which must be provided in a bankruptcy petition:

- All names you have used in the last 6 years
- Prior bankruptcies filed in the last 6 years
- Pending bankruptcies of any spouse, partner or affiliate
- List of all real estate owned
- List of all personal property owned
- Current income
- Current expenditures
- Income from employment or business

- Income from other than employment or business
- All payments of over $600 made to creditors within 90 days of filing bankruptcy
- All payments made to creditors who were insiders within 12 months of filing bankruptcy
- All suits to which you were a party within 12 months of filing bankruptcy
- All property which has been garnished or seized within 12 months of filing bankruptcy
- All property which has been repossessed, foreclosed or returned to seller within 12 months of filing bankruptcy
- All assignments made for benefit of creditors made within 120 days of filing bankruptcy
- All property which has been in the hands of a custodian, receiver or court official within one year of filing bankruptcy
- All gifts made within one year of filing bankruptcy except usual gifts to family members of under $200
- All charitable contributions of $100 or more made within one year of filing bankruptcy
- All losses to fire, theft, other casualty or gambling within one year of filing bankruptcy
- All fees paid for consultations for debt counseling within one year of filing bankruptcy
- All transfers of property other than in ordinary business within one year of filing bankruptcy
- All financial accounts closed or transferred to another person within one year of filing bankruptcy
- All safe deposit boxes in which you had any valuables within one year of filing bankruptcy
- All setoffs made by any creditor within 90 days of filing bankruptcy
- All property which other persons are holding for you
- All addresses used by you in the last 2 years
- All businesses in which you were involved in the last two years
- All bookkeepers and accountants you have used in the last 6 years
- All persons or firms which have audited your books or prepared your financial statements within the last 2 years
- All persons who are in possession of your books of account and records
- All financial institutions to whom you have given a financial statement within the last two years
- The last 2 inventories of your property and who took them
- All withdrawals of funds from your business in the last year

As you can see, any gifts to family, gambling losses, or other transfers of property will be closely scrutinized. However, if it happened several years before filing for bankruptcy, the issue might not even come up.

Knowing that some debts may not be discharged and that some assets may be kept after bankruptcy, you can arrange your affairs so that you always pay your nondischargeable debts first and that the only property you own is property which is exempt from creditors. (The bankruptcy system is meant to examine your affairs after you have gotten into trouble. Some may say you have an unfair advantage in learning these rules far in advance.)

Denial of Discharge

Under section 727(a) of the Bankruptcy Act a debtor's discharge is automatic unless one or more of the following circumstances is present:

(1) the debtor is not an individual
(2) the debtor made a fraudulent conveyance within a year of filing bankruptcy
(3) the debtor has no financial records
(4) the debtor made a false oath, false claim, paid someone to affect the outcome, or withheld records
(5) the debtor lied about his or her assets
(6) the debtor failed to testify after being given immunity
(7) the debtor did (2) thru (6) in a related bankruptcy case
(8) the debtor has been discharged within the last six years
(9) the debtor waived the right to discharge in writing

As you can see, you cannot destroy your records or take the Fifth Amendment to try to protect your assets. By planning early, you can be sure your affairs are arranged so that you can go through bankruptcy honestly and painlessly.

Chapter 42
Hiding Yourself

One reaction some people have to the threat of litigation is to run and hide. This is not a criminal offense, but it may not be a successful way to avoid liability, either.

Under the legal principle of **due process** a person cannot be made subject to a court order unless he has been notified of the pending action and given a chance to respond. Originally this meant that the papers had to be personally handed to him by a sheriff. This is called **service of process**.

However, as transportation and communication have improved, states have passed laws making it easier to subject people to lawsuits. Because people travel so often across state lines by automobile, all states have laws which allow victims of auto accidents to sue nonresidents where the accident took place, and to serve them easily.

The laws say that anyone who makes use of a state's roads automatically consents to **constructive service** of process. This service against nonresidents or residents who conceal themselves can be made by sending one copy of the court papers to the secretary of state and a copy by mail to the defendant.

The same principle used for automobile drivers also applies to those who do business in the state and to other categories of persons as listed in each state's laws.

Therefore, if you have conducted a business such as a medical or dental practice in a state you cannot avoid liability by closing up shop and hiding. In fact, hiding may hurt you. Former patients with claims against you could file suits and serve you by constructive service and then place judgment liens on any property of yours they can locate. In this case, even if you had a good defense to the suit you could not present it because you would be unaware of the suit. Once a judgment is rendered and a creditor has tracked you down to seize your assets, it is often too late to assert your defense.

If you remain in the state and just hide from the process server, that usually won't help you. If the sheriff finds you at home, but you do not open the door, the papers can be left on your doorstep or they can be read to you through the door.

Also, if you move to another state you can be served by a sheriff in that state. If the lawyer knows your address he can have the summons mailed to the sheriff in the county in which you live, and have it served upon you there. The fact that you are hundreds or thousands of miles from the trial makes it a lot more difficult for you to defend yourself and you may be required to return for depositions and for trial.

The Practical Side

While a plaintiff could pursue you if you were not locatable, as a practical matter your absence would make it a lot less likely that a case would be pursued, especially if you did not leave property behind. Lawyers like easy cases. They don't like cases that will take years to fight with unsure results. Therefore, if you do conceal yourself it may help you avoid suits. This is especially true if you have been private about your wealth (see the next chapter).

Not all lawyers are familiar with suing missing persons and some may not even want to take on such a case. Unless your claimant can find a specialist you may be safe.

If you are nearing retirement, and have always wanted to move to somewhere like Florida, Arizona, or Montana, doing so without leaving forwarding addresses may help you avoid litigation. You don't have to be secretive about it and disappear. You could buy a motor home or a houseboat and tell everyone you are going to travel around for a few years.

If you choose this option, be sure you cannot be located. Don't tell anyone your new address and don't put in a change of address order with the post office. (Anyone can get your new address from the post office.)

Obviously, moving without leaving an address will take some planning. You will need to start months ahead of time closing accounts and opening new ones. For your new accounts you should use a post office box.

If you have a dear and trusted friend in another city you could get a post office box there and ask him or her to forward your mail every month. Or, if you will be moving to somewhere near a state line, you could rent a box across the line. This way, if creditors tried to trace you in that state's records (driver license, tax records, etc.) you would not be listed.

If you are travelling around the country you could have your mail sent to a motel by overnight air once a month.

After you have moved away you might want to return to your former home in order to attend weddings, funerals or other important events. Before you do, you should check to see if any suits have been filed against you. Lawyers have been known to use such events to catch people they are looking for. By calling the state and federal courts in the area you can find out if any lawsuits have been filed in your absence. Usually the clerk can also tell you where the case stands. For example, if the clerk says "waiting for return of service" you know someone is trying to serve you.

Even if no case has yet been filed, you still might get caught if you return. A lawyer who didn't want to file a case while you were away might file it the morning of your arrival and serve you the same day.

Divorce, Alimony and Child Support

The rules explained previously for constructive service of process only apply to certain types of cases such as using an automobile in a state and doing business in the state. They do not apply to other cases, such as divorce and child support actions. For these kinds of cases the plaintiff has to actually find you and serve the papers on you in order to get a money judgment.

A court can grant a divorce against you in your absence by publishing a notice in the newspaper, but it may not deal in financial matters without personal service.

If you are ever found, however, you can be held liable for alimony and/or child support for the years you were missing. Therefore, if you plan to disappear it must be permanent.

Leaving the Country

A surprising number of Americans, scared by litigation, crime and the national deficit, and tired of high taxes and government over-regulation, are moving abroad. While no Americans gave up their citizenship in 1982, hundreds did in 1993. A Ford Motor Company director, a Campbell's Soup Co. heir, and the founder of Carnival Cruise Lines, all have left in recent years.

Merely leaving the U.S. will not lower your taxes, however. The United States is one of the few countries which significantly taxes the worldwide income of citizens overseas. To avoid U.S. income and estate taxes you would have to renounce your citizenship. Even then, if it suspects that your reason for leaving is to save on taxes, the U.S. government demands you continue to pay taxes for ten years after you leave! Of course, finding you, assessing the tax and collecting it once you are gone would be difficult. But if you plan to return periodically you may have problems.

Once your U.S. income tax liability ceases you may be free of income tax forever. Several countries have no income or estate taxes whatsoever, saving millions for those who take up residency there.

If moving out of state sounds like a big decision, becoming an expatriate is immeasurably bigger. For patriotic, practical and emotional reasons, Americans agonize over the decision. Many cannot do it. We have known this is the greatest country in the world from earliest childhood.

Before renouncing your citizenship you need to find a new country which will have you. Ireland and Israel grant citizenship quickly based on ancestry. Canada will grant citizenship after three years. St. Kitts-Nevis in the Caribbean requires the purchase of $150,000 in real estate and a $50,000 fee. However, before deciding on a new country you should investigate its tax system and other restrictions on freedom. After a few months there you may find life to be less desirable than you imagined.

If you do renounce your citizenship you will be limited in your ability to visit the U.S. The first year you can only stay 30 days. In future years you can stay 100 to 120 days. However, with computers, fax machines, cable TVs and cellular phones the U.S. may not seem as far as you actually are.

Less drastic than renouncing your citizenship is merely moving abroad. While this will not affect your taxes it may protect you from lawsuits. Many Americans have retired to such places as Costa Rica, Mexico and Poland where their social security check goes farther.

Your biggest concern if moving abroad should be the value of the dollar. While it is strong now, there is a very real risk of devaluation in the future. If you plan to live only on social security, your monthly check may slowly become worthless in the local currency. If you have other assets you should place some of them into hard assets and diversify the rest among a few different currencies.

If you leave the country just to avoid lawsuits, you still should keep your exact whereabouts a secret. It is possible to serve a summons on a person in another country. If you are served personally in another country a personal judgment can be entered against you.

References:
A Handbook for Citizens Living Abroad, American Citizens Abroad, Doubleday 1990
International Living (monthly newsletter, $39/year)
Langer, *Exile Report: Citizenship, Second Passports and Escaping Confiscatory Taxes*, Scope International, Ltd., Waterlooville, U.K.
Lenzner and Mao, "The new refugees," *Forbes*, November 21, 1994
Moving and Living Abroad, Hippocrene Books, $14.95 Tel: 718-454-2366
McMenamin, "Flight Capital," *Forbes*, February 28, 1994
O'Nes, *The Guide to Legally Obtaining a Foreign Passport*,Shapolsky Publishers, Inc., New York
Richmond, *How to Disappear Completely and Never be Found*, Carol Publishing Group, Secaucus, N.J.
Tips for Americans Residing Abroad, Superintendent of Documents, Government Printing Office, Washington, DC 20402 ($1.00)

Chapter 43
Hiding Your Assets

People commonly try to protect assets from creditors by simply hiding them. However, this method can be both illegal and unsuccessful.

Everyone is free to hide his or her assets anywhere they deem safe. This can mean burying them in the yard or storing them in the basement at mother's house. Nothing is illegal about that. The problem arises when a person must answer questions at a deposition or file a bankruptcy petition. If you own an asset but have hidden it or given it to someone else to hold and you lie under oath, you have committed perjury, which is a crime. If you are caught you may go to jail.

And you can't usually get by with tricky answers. If you try to evade an answer a good lawyer will continue asking questions to get to the truth. You will be asked what happened to property you owned and what happened to the proceeds if you sold it. You will be asked if any of your property is in the possession of another person. You are legally required to answer truthfully under oath.

If your entire financial future is at stake and you feel that a judgment against you is unjust or the system is corrupt, you may feel that it is your moral right to protect what you have earned by lying, even under oath. If you decide to ignore the legal system, you must realize what the potential consequences are and what you are up against.

There are many ways of discovering your assets. Your tax returns may be subpoenaed from the IRS. If you think you can keep a bank account or a piece of property secret, you will probably be given away by your tax return. If you listed interest or deductions or depreciation on your tax return, the property will be discovered.

Most people do not realize the sophisticated ways assets or income can be found. For example, you may think there is no way for anyone to find out about cash received in your business. However, if an audit were made of the number of products you purchased and compared to the number you claimed to have sold, a discrepancy would indicate unreported income.

Gold, jewelry, gems and other collectibles do not show up on your tax return, and often these can be easily hidden. During World War II some people who left Nazi areas first bought rare stamps and stuck them on family letters which were not even checked at customs. But there are ways these things can be discovered. A creditor can subpoena your checking account and charge card records. If you bought your collectibles by check or credit card there is a permanent record. If you insured them there is probably a cancelled check for the insurance. If you kept them in a safe deposit box there is probably a cancelled check for the box rental.

Some people erroneously believe that the Fifth Amendment to the Constitution protects them from being required to disclose their assets. But this right only applies to criminal matters. In a civil suit you cannot use the Fifth Amendment to protect yourself.

If you plan to protect your assets by hiding them you must be aware of how they can be found and what the penalties are for lying under oath.

Further Research

Roark, Dominique, "Should You Lie to Protect Your Assets?," Galt Press

Chapter 44
Your Last Resort:
Enjoying Your Assets

If you find yourself in a situation where you know you will be liable for a large claim, and you know you cannot legally shift or give away your assets, you have another alternative. You can spend your money on yourself.

Perhaps you have been frugal all your life. You rarely went to restaurants, always bought a used car, clipped coupons to save a few dollars here and there. Now someone wants a million dollars from you because they tripped over their own feet on your property?

There is no law forbidding you from spending your own money on yourself. You cannot give it away, or sell your property for less than it is worth, but you can buy things at a fair price and enjoy them. Perhaps its time to start going to good restaurants, buying a new car, taking a trip you have always wanted?

Lawsuits can take a long time. If they are appealed and reversed and retried, they can last many years. If you buy a new Jaguar today, you will at least have a year or two of enjoyment out of it. If you know you will lose, you might even prefer to spend your money on your lawyer than to give it to your creditor.

There are rules that you cannot borrow money just before filing bankruptcy, and then discharge the debt. But if you have the cash, you have the right to spend it on yourself. You can sell property you own at a fair price and spend the money on things you have always wanted.

But like anything else in law, you cannot look like a hog. You cannot be too greedy or too obvious. But if you merely improve your standard of living, you should be able to get away with it.

Keep in mind that while personal property like a boat or jewelry can be taken by a creditor, things like cruises, ski trips, operas, ballets, manicures, exotic spas, massages, and great dinners cannot be taken away. Buy a hundred pizzas for the foster children in your town.

If you are brought before a judge in bankruptcy court and accused of wasting your assets, be humble. Don't say you'd rather burn the money than see the creditor get a penny of it. Explain to the judge how hard you've worked all your life, talk about the money you gave to charity. Tell him how many years you skipped taking a vacation, and fixed your old car rather than splurge on a new one. Explain that you only have a limited number of years left and that you thought your wife deserved to see Europe with you just once.

If you have a medical condition, be sure to mention it!

Part Six
Your Immediate
Action Plan

Chapter 45
Evaluate Your Exposure

The first thing to do in setting up your asset protection plan is to evaluate which property you own can be seized by your creditors and who your possible creditors are. Sit down with your financial statement and the page listing your state's exemptions in Appendix 3 of this book and determine what property might be exposed and what is exempt from creditors' claims.

Next, go through Chapter 2 and note which risks you might face in the coming years. Do you own a boat? Do you have a teenager who drives? Are you in a partnership with other professionals? Do you own rental properties in your own name?

Do you have liabilities which cannot be protected by exempting your assets? Remember that such things as environmental claims, taxes, alimony and child support can never be discharged. They can even be claims against exempt property. The only way to protect against them is to have no property in your name. This requires using a trust.

How much insurance do you have? Do you have an umbrella policy? What would it cost to increase it to $2 million? $5 million? Is your professional insurance enough to cover you for a serious loss?

Make lists of your risks, your insurance, your assets and assets you expect to acquire in the future both through your earnings and inheritance.

Have an insolvency analysis done on your situation. This will determine, under your state's laws, how much property you can shield and still be considered solvent.

If you live in one of the states with favorable exemptions you may be in good shape and not need to make many changes. In other states you may find yourself totally exposed. Possibly everything you own could be lost if a lawsuit were filed against you tomorrow.

If your main risks are those which can be protected against with exempt assets your next step is to find out more details on your state's exemptions from a specialist as discussed in the next chapter.

If you are more concerned about liabilities such as alimony, taxes and environmental claims you will need an offshore trust as described in Chapter 36.

Chapter 46
Get an Exemption Analysis

Once you have evaluated your exposure, you need to have accurate, up-to-date information on the exemption laws of your state and the only place to get that information is from an attorney who specializes in that area of law.

I know, you hate to go to attorneys. They overcharge, they're arrogant and they're condescending. People don't like to go to doctors or dentists either, but these are unfortunate necessities of life.

Begin by finding a good attorney who specializes in bankruptcy and ask for a consultation. Some bankruptcy attorneys give free consultations, but those are intended for people who are actually contemplating bankruptcy and are for the purpose of signing up the client. Because you want valuable information from the attorney, you should expect to pay for the attorney's time. You will need half an hour or an hour and should expect to pay $100 or $200 per hour.

The purpose of your consultation is to find out exactly what assets are exempt from creditors in your state at the time. Appendix 5 of this manual includes a State Exemption Worksheet to use in talking with the attorney. You should use this form to obtain the detailed information you will need to protect your assets.

If you wish to protect yourself further and have more accurate information, you should ask the attorney for an opinion letter listing exactly what the exemptions are. A legal opinion put on paper will be more thoroughly researched than one given to you orally at a consultation. If he puts his opinion on paper and you rely on it and lose your property, you can sue him for giving erroneous advice. However, he will probably charge a few hundred dollars or more for such a letter.

You must realize that law is more like an art than a science. There are often no exact answers. In one case a trial court ruled one way but was reversed by the appellate court. Then the state supreme court looked at the case and reversed the appellate court. Was that the final answer? No, the losing party appealed to the United States Supreme Court and they reversed the state supreme court.

Now, if a state supreme court does not know what the law is, how can you expect a lowly lawyer to know? You can't. Therefore, you should get a second, or even a third opinion. If you are protecting a half-million or a million dollar estate, surely it is worth two or three $100 consultations to get the best advice on how to best protect your estate.

When meeting with your lawyer you must realize that the process of going to law school is what made him or her so arrogant. Law students are among the brightest out of college, but in their first days of law school they are made to feel incompetent and inadequate in the face of the body of law with which they are presented.

The new law student is given a series of judges' opinions to read which may consist of a 1957 New York case followed by an 1830 English case and then a 1983 California case. The cases use legal terms never before seen by the students. The logic is sometimes excellent and sometimes flawed, and the students are not told which is which. Soon the students realize how inadequate they are compared to the professors, judges and lawyers. But three years later when they graduate, they figure they have reached the exalted state which had previously held them in awe, and are amazed at their own intellectual abilities.

Keep this in mind when meeting with your lawyer. The fact that you are attempting to understand the legal system and take action to use it to your benefit may intimidate your lawyer. He or she would prefer that you throw yourself at his or her mercy and ask for advice. He or she may denigrate a manual like this which can help a layman understand the law. Act impressed but get the information you are paying for.

Chapter 47
Arrange Your Affairs

If you have read through this manual to this point you have a good understanding of how to protect yourself from claims, what property is safe from creditors and how to protect the rest of what you own. If you want to be sure not to lose what you have worked so hard for, you should start immediately arranging your affairs to protect what you own.

Throughout this manual the same message keeps coming up: If the planning had taken place sooner the asset would be safe. Once a problem arises it is too late to take most steps which would be effective.

After you have analyzed your exposure (Chapter 45) and conferred with an attorney (Chapter 46) you can sit down and plan your strategy. Compare the equity in your home with your state's exemption. Should you pay off your mortgage or get a bigger mortgage?

If pension plans or IRAs are exempt in your state, have you invested as much as you possibly can in one? Should you set up another type of plan which would allow greater contributions?

If annuities are protected in your state, have you sold your nonexempt assets and put the proceeds into an annuity? Have you considered a Swiss annuity? These may protect you even if annuities are not exempt in your state.

In planning your asset protection strategy, you have several levels of protection to choose from. These range from the most basic level in which you can merely avoid risk and invest in protected assets, to the most advanced level, in which you set up several legal devices including several limited partnerships and an offshore trust.

Basic Asset Protection   Cost: Under $500

If you don't want to put any extra effort into protecting your estate, but are still concerned about your potential losses, you can do four things which will give you basic protection:

1.   **Buy insurance.** Don't settle for 100/300 limits on your liability policies. You should have at least $1 million in coverage, preferably more. If you are in a risky profession, look into higher limits on your professional liability coverage.

2.   **Avoid risk.** In your professional life avoid cases and situations which involve higher risk. Don't volunteer for or participate in anything which could result in liability. Don't buy risky investments like real estate without a careful contract and a corporate shield against liability.

3.   **Know and use your exemptions.** Contribute as much as possible to a qualified pension plan. Check the exemptions in Appendix 3 for your state and keep them in mind when buying assets.

4.   **Keep your finances private.** You may not ever want to lie under oath, but by keeping your wealth private you will be less likely to be a target for lawsuits.

Intermediate Asset Protection   Cost: $500 to $2,000

If you are willing to take some action to protect your assets, but do not want to spend a lot of time or money, you can do some basic things which will provide protection far beyond their expense:

1.   **Incorporate.** Any business you are involved in should be incorporated. Be sure that you follow the formalities for corporations and keep your minutes up to date.

2.   **Obtain contracts.** Have a lawyer prepare contracts for your employees and clients or patients. Make the use of them routine. Don't deal with anyone who refuses to sign one. Use protective contracts in every venture which involves risk.

3.   **Shift assets.** Have an attorney who specializes in bankruptcy law prepare a list for you of what assets are exempt in your state. Ask him to review the most recent cases of people who converted nonexempt assets into exempt assets. Find out what is allowed and what is forbidden.

Advanced Asset Protection   Cost: $1,000 to $5,000

If you wish to take additional steps to protect your assets you should consult with an attorney who will be able to set up trusts and partnerships which give stronger protections than simpler arrangements.

1.   **Trusts.** Depending upon whom you wish your assets to eventually go to, you can set up trusts for your spouse, your children or a charity. You can also set up a business trust to protect part of your assets while retaining control of them.

2.   **Limited partnerships.** A limited partnership can protect your property from both creditors and spousal claims in the event of divorce. For extra protection you should set up two or more partnerships and divide your assets among them.

3.   **Nonprofit corporation or foundation.** If you can convert all or part of your business into a nonprofit corporation, you can both protect it from creditors and pay less taxes.

Total Asset Protection   Cost: $7,000 to $20,000

If you have a large estate and want to do whatever it takes to protect it, you will need to make arrangements outside the country to put the highest available protection around your property.

The Bahamas, Cayman Islands, Cook Islands, Isle of Man, Gibraltar and Turks and Caicos have trust companies which offer asset protection trusts. You can deal directly, but are well advised to be represented by an American attorney who can protect your interests.

Chapter 48
A Final Word

One unfortunate aspect of American law is that in many situations there are no black and white answers. In some cases converting assets may have been allowed while in other cases which appear identical, the same actions may have been disallowed. It is with this uncertainty that you must create your asset protection program. The reason for this is that our legal system gives judges flexibility to do what they think is fair under the circumstances.

Even the most experienced attorney can be wrong. Trial judges are overruled by appellate judges, and appellate judges are overruled by supreme court judges. State supreme court judges are overruled by the U. S. Supreme Court. How can you expect your local attorney to know how the law will be interpreted? You can't.

Therefore, you should never "put all of your eggs in one basket." You should diversify your assets and use several of the asset protection techniques found in this manual.

If you do end up in court, you must under all circumstances look like the "good guy." If you look like you are hiding something or are not telling the truth or are trying to trick the court, the law will be interpreted against you.

When appearing in court you must at all times be respectful, even reverent. If you are arrogant and display an attitude of disrespect for the judge or the system, then you will be more likely to lose your case. But if you appear honest and forthright and seem to be doing everything to comply with the law, the judge may have some sympathy for your plight and interpret the law in your favor.

Also keep in mind that for every case that turned out poorly for the debtor, there were hundreds of cases which didn't even get to court. Only a small percentage of people ever have million dollar claims against them, and only a percentage of claimants seek more than the insurance available. Of those, few have attorneys who are willing to contest each type of asset protection device. So if you have set up several devices to protect your estate, each one will make it less likely that someone will pursue the case further and get to all of your assets.

You can protect that for which you have worked your whole life. If you take control and use the laws that are available to you, you will be way ahead of those who let life happen to them. The information is in this manual. It is up to you to use it.

I wish you the best.

Appendixes

Appendix 1
Glossary

The following definitions explain the common meanings of the words as used in this book and in colloquial speech. Such use may not be the same as the technical definition of a legal dictionary.

Bankruptcy A court proceeding whereby a person or business can restructure or wipe out debts. See "Chapter 7," "Chapter 11," and "Chapter 13."

Beneficiary A person who owns the underlying interest in the property placed in a trust.

C-corporation Any corporation which has not elected to be treated as an s-corporation. (See s-corporation) A c-corporation pays taxes at the corporate tax rate on all of its profits. When a c-corporation pay a dividend to shareholders the money is taxed twice, once as a corporate profit, next as a dividend to a shareholder.

Chapter 7 A bankruptcy proceeding in which a debtor seeks to be discharged from all of his debts.

Chapter 11 A bankruptcy proceeding in which a debtor seeks to restructure his debts and pay them off over a longer period of time. Used by corporations and by individuals with over $1,000,000 in debts.

Chapter 13 A bankruptcy proceeding in which a debtor seeks to restructure his debts and pay them off over a longer period of time. Used by individuals with under $1,000,000 in debts.

Claim An assertion by a person that some amount of money is owed by another.

Claimant Someone who believes he has a claim against another.

Constructive service of process The act of notifying a person he is being sued by placing an ad in the newspaper and mailing him a copy.

Contempt of court An act which hinders a court in its attempt to carry out the laws.

Corporation An artificial "person" which can conduct business and which is created by the execution and filing of a document with the secretary of state of any state in the union.

Creditor A creditor is someone who is owed money. The debt may be based upon an agreement to pay or upon a court order to pay.

Debtor A person who owes money to another.

Defendant A person against whom a lawsuit is filed.

Deposition A series of questions under oath. Usually a creditor sets a deposition of a debtor to ask about assets. Lying under oath is perjury which is a crime.

Director A person elected by the shareholders of a corporation who is in charge of electing the officers and making the major decisions for the corporation.

Docket To register a judgment with a sheriff for future levy or seizure of property.

Due process A concept that each person must be treated fairly by the government. The interpretation of this concept changes depending upon the interpretation of the judge. Ultimately the United States Supreme Court decides what process is due, but this, also, can change from term to term.

Equitable title The actual or underlying ownership of the property.

Exempt assets Property which is by law free from the claims of creditors.

Fraudulent conveyance A transfer of property which violates the rights of creditors and which may be cancelled by a judge.

Garnish To order a party to turn over to a creditor any property which is being held for a debtor.

General partners All of the partners of a general partnership. Also, the partners of a limited partnership who control the venture and whose liability is not limited.

Grantor A person who transfers property to another (such as to a trustee).

Homestead Property which is the primary residence of a debtor and which is protected by law

Joint Tenancy with Right of Survivorship A form of owning property in which the death of one party results in the property automatically passing to the other party.

Judgment A court document determining the outcome of a case, often declaring that a sum of money is owed.

Judgment debtor A person who owes money, the amount of which has been decided by the court in the form of a judgment.

Land trust Also known as an "Illinois-type land trust." A trust which is used to hold interests in real estate in which the trustee holds both legal and equitable title and the beneficiary only hold a right to an interest in the trust which is personal property. In a normal trust which owns real estate the trustee will hold legal title, but he beneficiaries will hold equitable title.

Legal title The legal owner of the property as recorded in public records.

Levy A seizure of property by a sheriff. The property may be physically taken or left in place with a notice posted on or near it.

Limited partners The members of a limited partnership who have no control over the business and whose liability is limited to the contribution which they have made.

Limited partnership An agreement between two or more persons to carry on a business in which one or more will be a general partner and one or more will be a limited partner.

Nonexempt property Property which is not protected by exemption laws and which, therefore, may be seized by creditors.

Perjury False testimony given under oath.

Pierce the corporate veil To successfully assert a claim against the owner of a corporation.

Plaintiff A person who files a lawsuit.

S-corporation A corporation which has filed form 2335 with the IRS to elect to have all profits taxed to shareholders rather than corporation. An S-corporation usually pays no taxes. It files a return which shows how much profit it made and then the shareholders each pay taxes on a proportional share of that profit. Corporations must meet certain qualifications (such as 35 or fewer shareholders ad no aliens as shareholders) to obtain S-corporation status.

Service of process The delivery of court papers to a person, notifying him that a court action has been commenced against him.

Settlor A person who places property in trust, also called a grantor.

Shareholder A person who owns one or more shares in a corporation.

Subpoena   An order by a court to appear or to produce something.

Summons   A notice by a court that an action has been filed.

Tenancy by the Entireties   Ownership of property by a married couple which is allowed in some states.

Trust   An arrangement whereby one person (the trustee) holds property for another person or persons (the beneficiary).

Trustee   A person who holds property for another under a trust arrangement.

Appendix 2
State Exemption Comparisons

This table is meant to give a quick overview of how the states compare in the three key areas of asset exemption from creditors: homestead, pensions and annuities. For example, a quick glance will make clear that although in Nebraska you would only be able to keep about $20,000 in assets, by moving to neighboring Kansas you could buy a home of unlimited value and not lose it to creditors. For specific details of your state's exemptions refer to the detailed table in the next appendix.

	Homestead	Pensions	Annuities
Federal	$7,500	Yes-ERISA	No
Alabama	$5,000	Few	Yes: $250/mo.
Alaska	$54,000	Some	Yes: $10,000
Arizona	$100,000	Yes	No
Arkansas	$2,500	Some	Yes
California sys. 1	$50,000+	Few	No
California sys. 2	$7,500	No	No
Colorado	$30,000	Yes	No
Connecticut	$75,000	Yes-ERISA	No
Delaware	None unless T/E*	Few	Yes: $350/mo.
District of Columbia	Condo deposit or T/E*	Few	No
Florida	Unlimited	Yes	Yes
Georgia	$5,000	Some	Yes
Hawaii	$20,000+	Some	Some
Idaho	$50,000	Yes	Yes: $350/mo.
Illinois	$7,500	Some	Yes
Indiana	$7,500, T/E*	Few	No
Iowa	Unlimited	Yes	No
Kansas	Unlimited	Some	No
Kentucky	$5,000	Yes	Yes:$350/mo
Louisiana	$15,000	Yes-ERISA	No
Maine	$12,500+	Some	Yes: $450/mo.
Maryland	None unless T/E*	ERISA,No IRAs	No
Massachusetts	$100,000+	Some	Yes
Michigan	$3,500 unless T/E*	Yes	Yes
Minnesota	Unlimited	Yes to $45,000	Yes
Mississippi	$75,000	Yes	No
Missouri	$8,000	Some	No
Montana	$40,000	Some	Yes: $350mo.
Nebraska	$10,000	Some	Yes: $10,000
Nevada	$95,000	Public empl.	Yes: $350/mo.

	Homestead	Pensions	Annuities
New Hampshire	$30,000	Few	No
New Jersey	None	Some	Yes: $500/mo.
New Mexico	$30,000 if dependents	Some	Yes
New York	$10,000	Yes	Yes
North Carolina	$10,000	Few	No
North Dakota	$80,000	Yes	Yes
Ohio	$5,000	Yes	Some
Oklahoma	Unlimited	Some	No
Oregon	$25,000	Some	Yes: $500/mo.
Pennsylvania	None unless T/E*	Some	Some
Rhode Island	None	Some	No
South Carolina	$5,000	Some	No
South Dakota	Unlimited	Few	Yes: $250/mo.
Tennessee	$5,000	Some	No
Texas	Unlimited	Yes	Yes
Utah	$8,000	Some	No
Vermont	$30,000 unless T/E*	Some	Yes: $350/mo.
Virginia	$5,000 unless T/E*	Few	No
Washington	$30,000	Yes	Yes: $250/mo.
West Virginia	$7,500	Some	No
Wisconsin	$40,000	Few	No
Wyoming	$10,000	Few	Yes: $350/mo.

*T/E = Tenancy by the entireties property

Appendix 3
State by State Exemptions*

This appendix lists the exempt property under each state's laws and under the federal bankruptcy laws. In some states you are allowed to choose between the state exemptions and the federal exemptions, but in most states you must use your state exemptions. On the following page are the federal exemptions and a list of the states which can use them. In states which you must use the state exemptions, you are also allowed to use the "federal non-bankruptcy exemptions." These are listed on the page following the federal exemptions. California offers its citizens a choice between two lists of exemptions, which are listed as system 1 and system 2. Both of these lists are included.

These lists are as up-to-date as possible. However, the laws change constantly and are subject to different interpretations. Therefore you should not rely on these tables in making final decisions to protect your property. You should consult an attorney who has expertise in bankruptcy law. Citations are given for each exemption so it can be researched further.

Amounts. If an amount is listed next to an exemption then that is the dollar limit. If there is no amount listed then there is no limit.

Doubling exemptions. Some states allow a husband and wife to each claim a separate exemption. For example, if an automobile is exempt up to $3,000 in equity, the husband and wife may each claim an auto up to $3,000. This is referred to as "doubling" the exemption. An asterisk (*) after an item indicates that doubling is specifically prohibited by law. Two asterisks (**) indicates that doubling is specifically approved by law. No notation indicates that the law does not state whether doubling is permitted, so you may want to list the exemption for both husband and wife, and see if the trustee accepts it.

Pension plans. In some states the exemption of a pension plan depends upon whether it is an "ERISA-qualified" plan. ERISA is the Employee Retirement Security Act. To find out whether your plan is qualified you should check with your employer or plan administrator.

*The material in this appendix is reprinted with permission from the book, *How to File Your Own Bankruptcy (or How to Avoid It)* by Edward A. Haman, attorney at law, published by Sphinx Publishing and available for $19.95.

FEDERAL BANKRUPTCY EXEMPTIONS

The following Federal Bankruptcy Exemptions are available if you live in one of the following states:

Arkansas	Massachusetts	New Mexico	Texas
Connecticut	Michigan	Pennsylvania	Washington
District of Columbia	Minnesota	Rhode Island	Wisconsin
Hawaii	New Jersey	South Carolina	Vermont

If you use these exemptions, however, you may not use the exemptions listed under your state. Be sure to compare these exemptions to those in the listing for your state, and use whichever allows you to keep more of your property.

The following section numbers relate to Title 11 of the United States Code, which is abbreviated "11 U.S.C." followed by the appropriate section ("§" is the symbol for "section" number.) An example is: "11 U.S.C. § 522(d)(1)." Only the section number is used below.

HOMESTEAD
522(d)(1)   Real property, up to $7,500. Unused portion, up to $3,750, may be used for other property.

PERSONAL PROPERTY
522(d)(2)   Motor vehicle up to $1,200.
522(d)(3)   Animals, crops, clothing, appliances and furnishings, books, household goods, and musical instruments up to $200 per item, and up to $4,000 total.
522(d)(4)   Jewelry up to $500.
522(d)(9)   Health aids.
522(d)(11)(B)   Wrongful death recovery for person you depended upon.
522(d)(11)(D)   Personal injury recovery up to $7,500, except for pain and suffering or for pecuniary loss.
522(d)(11)(E)   Lost earning payments.

PENSIONS
522(d)(10)(E)   ERISA-qualified benefits needed for support.

PUBLIC BENEFITS
522(d)(10)(A)   Public assistance, Social security, Veterans' benefits, Unemployment Compensation.
522(d)(11)(A)   Crime victims' compensation.

TOOLS OF TRADE
522(d)(6)   Implements, books and tools of trade, up to $750.

ALIMONY AND CHILD SUPPORT
522(d)(10)(D)   Alimony and child support needed for support.
522(d)(7)   Unmatured life insurance policy.
522(d)(8)   Life insurance policy with loan value up to $4,000.
522(d)(10)(C)   Disability, unemployment or illness benefits.
522(d)(11)(C)   Life insurance payments for a person you depended on, which you need for support.

MISCELLANEOUS
522(d)(5) $400 of any property, and unused portion of homestead up to $3,750.

FEDERAL NON-BANKRUPTCY EXEMPTIONS

You may only use these exemptions if you choose the exemptions listed under your state. You may not use these if you choose to use the Federal Bankruptcy Exemptions listed above.

RETIREMENT BENEFITS

50 U.S.C. §403	CIA employees.
5 U.S.C. §8346	Civil Service employees.
22 U.S.C. §4060	Foreign service employees.
10 U.S.C. §1440	Military service employees.
45 U.S.C.§.231m	Railroad workers.
42 U.S.C. §407	Social security benefits.
38 U.S.C. §3101	Veteran's benefits.

SURVIVOR'S BENEFITS

10 U.S.C. §1450	Military service.
28 U.S.C. §376	Judges, U.S. court directors.
33 U.S.C. §775	Lighthouse workers.

DEATH AND DISABILITY BENEFITS

5 U.S.C. §8130	U.S. Government employees.
33 U.S.C. §916	Longshoremen, harbor workers.
42 U.S.C. §1717	Military service.

MISCELLANEOUS

10 U.S.C. §1035	Military deposits to savings accounts (while on permanent duty outside the U.S.).
15 U.S.C. §1673	75% of earned but unpaid wages (Judge may approve more).
25 U.S.C. §543 & 545	Klamath Indians tribe benefits.
38 U.S.C. §770(g)	Military group life insurance.
45 U.S.C. §352(e)	Railroad workers' unemployment.
46 U.S.C. §11110	Seamen's clothing.
46 U.S.C. §11111	Seamen's wages (while on a voyage and pursuant to a written contract).

ALABAMA

Code of Alabama, Title 6, Chapter 10 (C.A. §6-10-2). Ignore volume numbers; look for "title" numbers.

HOMESTEAD
6-10-2   Real property or mobile home, up to $5,000. Property can't exceed 160 acres.(**) Must record homestead declaration. 6-10-20.

PERSONAL PROPERTY
6-10-5   A burial place and a church pew or seat.
6-10-6   Clothing, books and family portraits and pictures, and $3,000 of any other personal property (except life insurance).

WAGES
6-10-7   75% of earned but unpaid wages. Judge may approve more for low-income debtors.

PENSIONS
12-18-10   Judges.
16-25-23   Teachers.
36-21-77   Law enforcement officers.
36-27-28   State employees.

PUBLIC BENEFITS
15-23-15   Crime victims' compensation.
25-4-140   Unemployment compensation.
25-5-86   Workers' compensation.
25-5-179   Coal miners' pneumoconiosis benefits.
31-7-2   Southeast Asian War POW's benefits.
38-4-8   AFDC and aid to blind, aged, and disabled.

TOOLS OF TRADE
31-2-78   Arms, uniforms and equipment required to be kept by state military personnel.

INSURANCE
6-10-8;
27-14-29   Life insurance proceeds if beneficiary is spouse or child of the insured.
27-14-31   Disability proceeds up to an average of $250 per month.
27-14-32   Annuities up to $250 per month.
27-15-26   Life insurance, if policy prohibits use to pay creditors.
27-30-25   Mutual aid association benefits.
27-34-27   Fraternal benefit society benefits.

MISCELLANEOUS
10-8-72   Business partnership property.

ALASKA

Alaska Statutes, Title 9, Section 9.38.010 (A.S. §9.38.010). Ignore volume numbers; look for "title" numbers. Alternative federal exemptions are allowed according to case law, *In re McNutt*, 87 B.R. 84 (9th Cir. 1988).

HOMESTEAD
9.38-010   Up to $54,000 total, even for husband and wife filing jointly.

PERSONAL PROPERTY
9.38.015   A burial plot; needed health aids; and tuition credits under an advance college payment contract.
9.38.020   Motor vehicle up to $3,000, if market value is no more than $20,000; pets up to $1,000; jewelry up to $1,000; and household goods, clothing, books, musical instruments, and family portraits and heirlooms up to $3,000.
9.38.030   Personal injury and wrongful death recoveries, to the extent wages are exempt.
9.38.060   Proceeds from damaged exempt property.
34.35.105   Building materials.

WAGES
9.38.030;
9.38.050   Weekly net earnings up to $350, or up to $550 if sole wage earner in a household. If no regular pay, up to $1,400 paid in any month, or $2,200 if sole wage earner in household.

PENSIONS
9.38.015   Teachers, judicial & public employees, and elected officers, as to benefits accruing.
9.38.017   ERISA-qualified benefits, if deposited more than 120 days before filing.
9.38.030   Payments being received from other pensions.

PUBLIC BENEFITS
9.38.015   Alaska longevity bonus, crime victims' compensation and federally exempt public benefits.
23.20.405   Unemployment compensation.
23.30.160   Workers' compensation.
43.23.065   45% of permanent fund dividends (this is income distributed to residents from the state's natural resources).
47.25.210   General relief assistance.
47.25.395   AFDC.
47.25.550   Assistance to blind, elderly and disabled adults.

TOOLS OF TRADE
9.38.020   Implements, books or tools up to $2,800.

ALIMONY AND CHILD SUPPORT
9.38.015   Child support if received from a collection agency.
9.38.030   Alimony, to extent wages are exempt.

INSURANCE
9.38.015;
9.38.030   Medical and disability benefits.
9.38.025   Life insurance or annuity contracts up to a $10,000 loan value.
9.38.030   Life insurance proceeds to a spouse or dependent, to extent wages are exempt.
21.84.240   Fraternal benefit society benefits.

MISCELLANEOUS
9.38.015   Liquor licenses.
9.38.100   Business partnership property.

ARIZONA

Arizona Revised Statutes Annotated, Section 33-1101 (A.R.S. §33-1101). Ignore volume numbers; look for "section" numbers.

HOMESTEAD (*)
33-1101	Up to $100,000. Includes sale proceeds up to 18 months after sale, or new home purchased, whichever occurs first. Must record homestead declaration. 33-1102.

PERSONAL PROPERTY (**)
33-1123	The following items up to $4,000 total: Two beds; one bed table, dresser and lamp for each bed; bedding; kitchen table and 4 chairs; dining table and 4 chairs; living room chair for each family member; couch; 3 living room tables and lamps; living room carpet or rug; refrigerator; stove; washer and dryer; one TV, radio or stereo (not one of each); radio alarm clock; vacuum cleaner; family portraits; and any pictures, oil paintings, and drawings created by the debtor. Additional bed, and dining chair, for each additional dependent if more than 4 persons in household.
33-1124	Food and fuel for 6 months.
33-1125	Motor vehicle up to $1,500 (or $4,000 if disabled); clothing to $500; pets, horses, milk cows and poultry to $500; books to $250; wedding and engagement rings to $1,000; musical instruments to $250; watch to $100; wheelchair and prostheses; and up to $500 total for bicycle, sewing machine, typewriter, burial plot, firearm and bible (only one of each may be kept).
33-1126	Proceeds for sold or damaged exempt property; prepaid rent or security deposit to lesser of $1,000 or 1.5 times rent (only if not claiming homestead); bank deposit to $150 in one account.

WAGES
33-1126	Earnings of minor child, unless debt is for child.
33-1131	Minimum of 75% of unpaid net wages or pension payments. Judge may allow more.

PENSIONS
9-931	Police officers.
9-968	Firefighters.
15-1628	Members of board of regents.
33-1126	ERISA-qualified benefits, if deposited more than 120 days before filing [IRS's included, *In re Herrscher*, 121 B.R. 29 (D. Ariz. 1990)].
38-762	State employees.
38-811	Elected officials.
38-850	Public safety personnel.
41-955	Rangers.

PUBLIC BENEFITS
23-783	Unemployment compensation.
23-1068	Workers' compensation.
46-208	Welfare benefits.

TOOLS OF TRADE
33-1127	Teaching aids of a teacher.
33-1130 (**)	Tools, equipment and books up to $2,500; Farm machinery, utensils, instruments of husbandry, feed, seed, grain and animals up to a total value of $2,500; and arms, uniforms and equipment you are required by law to keep.

INSURANCE
20-881	Fraternal benefit society benefits.
20-1131	Life insurance cash value up to $2,000 per dependent/$10,000 total.
20-1132	Group life insurance policy or proceeds.
33-1126 (**)	Life insurance proceeds if beneficiary is spouse or child, up to $20,000; life insurance cash value to $1,000 per dependent/ $5,000 total; and health, accident or disability benefits.

MISCELLANEOUS
29-225	Business partnership property.

ARKANSAS

Arkansas Code of 1987 Annotated, Title 16, Chapter 66, Section 16-66-210 (A.C.A. §16-66-210). Ignore volume numbers; look for "title" and "chapter" numbers.

HOMESTEAD (Choose one of the following)
16-66-210 (*)	Head of family may claim: Real or personal property used as a residence; of up to 1/4 acre in a city, town, or village; or up to 80 acres elsewhere. If between 1/4 and 1 acre in city, etc., or 80 to 160 acres elsewhere, amount of exemption in limited to $2,500. No homestead may exceed 1 acre in city, etc., or 160 acres elsewhere. This exemption is also found in the State Constitution, and the reference to "Ark. Const. 9-3, 9-4, & 9-5" should also be used.
16-66-218	Real or personal property used as a residence, up to $800 if single or $1,250 if married. Also, $500 of any personal property, if married or head of household; $200 if single (cite "Ark. Const. 9-1; 9-2" also).

PERSONAL PROPERTY
16-66-218	Motor vehicle up to $1,200, and wedding bands provided that any diamonds can't exceed 1/2 carat.
16-66-207	Burial plot up to 5 acres, provided you don't use the homestead exemption in section 16-66-218.
Ark. Const.	Clothing of unlimited value; and any personal property of up to $500 if married or head of family, or $200 otherwise. Use reference to "Ark. Const. 9-1 &9-2".

WAGES
16-66-208	Earned but unpaid wages due for 60 days, but in not less than $25 per week.

PENSIONS
16-66-218	IRA deposits up to $20,000 if deposited over 1 year before filing for bankruptcy.
24-6-223	State police officers.
24-7-715	School employees.
24-10-616	Police officers and firefighters.
24-11-417	Disabled police officers.
24-11-814	Disabled firefighters.

PUBLIC BENEFITS
11-9-110	Worker's compensation.
11-10-109	Unemployment compensation.
16-90-716	Crime victims' compensation, unless you are seeking to discharge a debt for treatment of an injury incurred during the crime.
20-76-430	AFDC, and aid to blind, aged or disabled.

TOOLS OF TRADE
16-66-218	Tools, books and implements of trade to $750.

INSURANCE
16-66-209	Life, health, accident or disability proceeds, whether paid or due (case law limits to $500).
23-71-112	Stipulated insurance premiums.
23-72-114	Mutual assessment life or disability benefits up to $1,000.
23-74-119	Fraternal benefit society benefits.
23-79-131	Life insurance proceeds if beneficiary isn't the insured; life insurance proceeds if policy prohibits proceeds from being used to pay beneficiary's creditors.
23-79-132	Group life insurance.
23-79-133	Disability benefits.
23-79-134	Annuity contract.

MISCELLANEOUS
4-42-502	Business partnership property.

CALIFORNIA

West's Annotated California Codes, Civil Procedure, Section 704.710 (Cal. Code Civ. Proc. §704.710). California has two separate systems of exemptions. You must select one, and cannot mix exemptions from the two systems. References are to the California Code of Civil Procedure unless otherwise stated (look for volume marked "Civil Procedure," not just "Civil").

CALIFORNIA (SYSTEM 1)

HOMESTEAD

704.710; 704.730	Real or personal property occupied at time of filing for bankruptcy, including mobile home, boat, stock cooperative, community apartment, planned development or condominium, up to the following limits: $50,000 if single and not disabled; $75,000 if family and no other member has homestead; $100,000 if 65 or older or if physically or mentally disabled; $100,000 if creditors are seeking to force sale of your home and you are either (a) 55 or older, single and earn under $15,000 per year, or (b) 55 or older, married and earn under $20,000 per year. Sale proceeds are exempt for up to 6 months after sale. (*)

PERSONAL PROPERTY

704.010	Motor vehicle or insurance if vehicle lost, destroyed or damaged up to $1,200.
704.020	Food, clothing, appliances and furnishings.
704.030	Building materials to repair or improve home up to $1,000.
704.040	Jewelry, heirlooms and art up to $2,500 total.
704.050	Health aids.
704.080	Bank deposits from Social Security Administration up to $500 for single payee, and $750 for more than one payee; proceeds from exempt property in form of cash or bank deposits.
704.090	Inmates trust funds up to $1,000.
704.140	Personal injury causes of action, and recoveries needed for support.
704.150	Wrongful death causes of action, & recoveries needed for support.
704.200	Burial plot

WAGES

704.070	75% of wages paid within 30 days prior to filing bankruptcy.
704.113	Public employee vacation credits.

PENSIONS

704.110	Public retirement benefits.
704.115	Private retirements benefits to extent tax-deferred, including IRA & Keogh.
Gov't. 21201	Public employees.
Gov't. 31452	County employees.
Gov't. 31913	County peace officers.
Gov't. 32210	County fire fighters.

PUBLIC BENEFITS

704.120	Unemployment benefits and union benefits due to labor dispute.
704.160	Workers' compensation.
704.170	AFDC and aid to blind, aged and disabled.
704.180	Relocation benefits.
704.190	Financial aid to students.

TOOLS OF TRADE

704.060	Tools, implements, materials, books, uniforms, instruments, equipment, furnishings, motor vehicle, and vessel up to $2,500, or up to $5,000 if used by both spouses in the same occupation. Can't claim motor vehicle here if already claimed under 704.010.

INSURANCE

704.100 (**)	Matured life insurance benefits needed for support of unlimited value, unmatured life insurance policy up to $4,000 in value, and fraternal life insurance benefits to $4,000.
704.120	Fraternal unemployment benefits.
704.130	Disability or health benefits.
704.720	Homeowners' insurance proceeds for 6 months after received, up to amount of homestead limit.
Other	Fidelity bonds. Refer to as "Labor 404".
Other	Life insurance proceeds if policy prohibits use to pay creditors. Refer to as "Ins. 10132, 10170 & 10171".

MISCELLANEOUS

Corp. 15025	Business partnership property.

CALIFORNIA (SYSTEM 2)

HOMESTEAD

703.140(b)(1); 695.060	Business and professional licenses, except liquor licenses. Real or personal property used as a residence up to $7,500. Any unused portion of the $7,500 may be applied to any property.

PERSONAL PROPERTY

703.140(b)(1)	Burial plot up to $7,500, instead of homestead.
703.140(b)(2)	Motor vehicle up to $1,200.
703.140(b)(3)	Clothing, household goods, appliances, furnishings, animals, books, musical instruments and crops up to $200 per item.
703.140(b)(4)	Jewelry up to $500.
703.140(b)(5)	$400 of any property.
703.140(b)(9)	Health aids.
703.140(b)(11)	Wrongful death recoveries needed for support.
703.140(b)(11)	Personal injury recoveries up to $7,500, not to include pain, suffering or pecuniary loss.

PENSIONS

703.140(b)(10)	ERISA-qualified benefits needed for support.

PUBLIC BENEFITS

703.140(b)(10)	Unemployment compensation, social security, and public assistance.
703.140(b)(10)	Veterans' benefits.
703.140(b)(11)	Crime victims' compensation.

TOOLS OF TRADE

703.140(b)(6)	Tools, books and implements of trade up to $750.

ALIMONY AND CHILD SUPPORT

703.140(b)(10)	Alimony and child support needed for support.

INSURANCE

703.140(b)(7)	Unmatured life insurance policy, other than credit.
703.140(b)(8)	Unmatured life insurance contract accrued interest, dividends, loan, cash or surrender value up to $4,000.
703.140(b)(10)	Disability benefits.
703.140(b)(11)	Life insurance proceeds needed for support.
Other	Fidelity bonds. Refer to as "Labor 404".

MISCELLANEOUS

703.140(b)(5)	$7,900 of any property, less any claim for homestead or burial plot.

COLORADO

West's Colorado Revised Statutes Annotated, Title 13, Article 54, Section 13-54-102 (C.R.S.A. §13-54-102).

HOMESTEAD
13-54-102	Mobile home used as residence up to $6,000 value; house trailer or coach used as residence up to $3,500.
38-41-201	Real property, including mobile or manufactured home if loan incurred after 1/1/83, up to $30,000. For homestead exemption, must be occupied at time petition is filed. Sale proceeds are exempt for 1 year after sale. Spouse or child of deceased owner can also qualify.

PERSONAL PROPERTY
13-54-102	Motor vehicles to $1,000 to get to work (up to $3,000 to get medical care if elderly or disabled); clothing to $750; health aids; household goods to $1,500; food and fuel to $300; 1 burial plot per person; jewelry and articles of adornment to $500 total; pictures and books to $750; security deposit; proceeds for damaged exempt property; personal injury recoveries, unless debt related to the injury.

WAGES
13-54-104	Minimum 75% of earned but unpaid wages, and pension payments. Judge may approve more for low income debtors.

PENSIONS
13-54-102	ERISA-qualified benefits, including IRS's.
22-64-120	Teachers.
24-51-212	Public employees.
31-30-313; 31-30-616	Police officers.
31-30-412; 31-30-518	Firefighters.

PUBLIC BENEFITS
8-80-103	Unemployment compensation.
8-52-107	Workers' compensation.
13-54-102	Veterans' benefits for veteran, spouse or child if veteran served in war.
13-54-102; 24-4.1-114	Crime victims' compensation.
26-2-131	AFDC, aid to blind, aged and disabled.

TOOLS OF TRADE
13-54-102	Stock in trade, supplies, fixtures, machines, tools, maps, equipment and books to $1,500 total; library of a professional to $1,500; livestock and poultry of a farmer to $3,000; horses, mules, wagons, carts, machinery, harness and tools of farmer to $2,000 total.

INSURANCE
10-7-106	Life insurance proceeds if policy prohibits use to pay creditors.
10-7-205	Group life insurance policy or proceeds.
10-8-114	Disability benefits up to $200 per month.
10-14-122	Fraternal benefit society benefits.
13-54-102	Life insurance dividends, interest, cash or surrender value up to $5,000.
38-41-209	Homeowners' insurance proceeds for 1 year after received up to $20,000.

MISCELLANEOUS
7-60-125	Business partnership property.

CONNECTICUT

Connecticut General Statutes Annotated, Title 52, Section 52-352B (C.G.S.A. §52-352B). Ignore "chapter" numbers; look for "title" numbers. Compare federal exemptions.

HOMESTEAD
52-352b(t)	Real property or mobile or manufactured home up to $75,000.

PERSONAL PROPERTY
52-352b	Motor vehicle up to $1,500; food, clothing and health aids; appliances, furniture and bedding; wedding and engagement rings; burial plot; residential utility and security deposits for 1 residence; proceeds for damaged exempt property.

WAGES
52-361a	Minimum 75% of earned but unpaid wages. Judge may approve more for low income debtors.

PENSIONS
5-171;5-192w	State employees.
10-183q	Teachers.
52-352b	ERISA-qualified benefits, but only as to payments received and only to the extent wages are exempt.

PUBLIC BENEFITS
7-446	Municipal employees.
27-140	Vietnam veterans' death benefits.
31-272; 52-352b	Unemployment compensation.
45-48	Probate judges and employees.
52-352b	Workers' compensation; veterans' benefits; social security; wages from earnings incentive programs; AFDC; aid to blind, aged and disabled.
52-352b; 54-213	Crime victims' compensation.

TOOLS OF TRADE
52-352b	Arms, military equipment, uniforms and musical instruments of military personnel; tools, books, instruments and farm animals needed.

ALIMONY AND CHILD SUPPORT
52-352b	Alimony and child support, to extent wages are exempt.

INSURANCE
38a-380	Benefits under no-fault insurance law, to extent wages are exempt.
38a-453	Life insurance proceeds, dividends, interest, or cash or surrender value.
38a-454	Life insurance proceeds if policy prohibits use to pay creditors.
38a-636	Fraternal benefit society benefits.
52-352b	Health and disability benefits; disability benefits paid by association for it members.

MISCELLANEOUS
34-63	Business partnership property.

DELAWARE

Delaware Code Annotated, Title 10, Section 4902 (D.C.A. 10 §4902). Ignore volume numbers; look for "title" numbers.

LIMITATION:

10 §4914   Total exemptions for a single person may not exceed $5,000; and for husband and wife may not exceed $10,000.

HOMESTEAD

    Tenancies by the entirety exempt without limitation as to debts of one spouse. [*In re Hovatter*, 25 B.R. 123 (D. Del. 1982)].

PERSONAL PROPERTY

10 §4902; 10 §4903

    Clothing, including jewelry; books; family pictures; piano; leased organs and sewing machines; burial plot; church pew or any seat in public place of worship. Also $500 of any other personal property if head of family. Except tools of trade. School books & family library.

WAGES

10 §4913   85% of earned but unpaid wages.

PENSIONS

9 §4316   Kent County employees.
11 §8803   Police officers.
16 §6653   Volunteer firefighters.
29 §5503   State employees.

PUBLIC BENEFITS

19 §2355   Workers' compensation.
19 §3374   Unemployment compensation.
31 §513   General assistance; AFDC; aid to aged and disabled.
31 §2309   Aid to blind.

TOOLS OF TRADE

10 §4902   Tools, implements and fixtures, up to $75 in New Castle and Sussex counties, and up to $50 in Kent County.

INSURANCE

12 §1901   Employee life insurance benefits.
18 §2726   Health or disability benefits.
18 §2727   Group life insurance policy or proceeds.
18 §2728   Annuity contract proceeds up to $350 per month.
18 §2729   Life insurance proceeds if policy prohibits use to pay creditors.
18 §6118   Fraternal benefit society benefits.

MISCELLANEOUS

6 §1525   Business partnership property.

DISTRICT OF COLUMBIA

D.C. Code, Title 45, Section 1869 (D.C.C. §45-1869). Ignore "Chapter" number; look for "title" number. Compare federal exemptions.

HOMESTEAD

45-1869   Residential condominium deposit. Tenancies by the entirety exempt without limit as to debts of one spouse [*Estate of Wall*, 440 F.2d 215 (D.C.Cir. 1971)].

PERSONAL PROPERTY

15-501   Clothing up to $300 (also refer to 15-503); beds, bedding, radios, cooking utensils, stoves, furniture, furnishings and sewing machines up to $300 total; books to $400; family pictures; food and fuel to last 3 months.
29-1128   Cooperative association holding to $50.

WAGES

15-503   Non-wage, earnings, including pensions, for 60 days up to $200 per month for head of family, or $60 per month otherwise.
16-572   Minimum 75% of earned but unpaid wages or pension payments.

PENSIONS

11-1570   Judges.
31-1217;
31-1238   Public school teachers.

PUBLIC BENEFITS

3-215.1   General assistance; AFDC; aid to blind, aged and disabled.
3-407   Crime victims' compensation.
36-317   Workers' compensation.
46-119   Unemployment compensation.

TOOLS OF TRADE

1-806   Seal and documents of notary public.
15-501   Motor vehicle, cart, wagon or dray, horse or mule harness up to $500; stock and materials to $200; library, furniture, tools of professional or artist to $300.
15-501;15-503   Mechanic's tools, tools of trade or business to $200.

INSURANCE

15-503   Other insurance proceeds to $200 per month, for a maximum of 2 months, for head of family; up to $60 per month otherwise.
35-521   Life insurance proceeds, dividends, interest, cash or surrender value.
35-522   Disability benefits.
35-523   Group life insurance policy or proceeds.
35-525   Life insurance proceeds if policy prohibits use to pay creditors.
35-1211   Fraternal benefit society benefits.

MISCELLANEOUS

41-124   Business partnership property.

FLORIDA

Florida Statutes, Chapter 222, Section 222.05 (F.S. §222.05). Ignore volume numbers; look for "chapter" numbers.

HOMESTEAD

222.05   Real or personal property, including mobile or modular home and condominium, to unlimited value. Property cannot exceed 1/2 acre in a municipality, or 160 acres elsewhere. Spouse or child of deceased owner may claim exemption. (Also refer to Florida Constitution, as "Fla. Const. 10-4."). Also, tenancies by the entireties in real property are exempt as to debts of one spouse [*In re Avins*, 19 B.R. 736 (S.D.Fla. 1982)].

PERSONAL PROPERTY

222.25   **Motor vehicle up to $1,000; prescribed health aids.**
Other   Any personal property up to $1,000 total. (Refer to as "Fla. Const. 10-4").(**)

WAGES

222.11   Earned but unpaid wages, or wages paid and in a bank account, only if head of household.
222.21   Federal government employees pension payments needed for support and received 3 months before filing bankruptcy.

PENSIONS

112.215   Government employees' deferred compensation plans.
121.131   State officers and employees.
122.15   County officers and employees.
175.241   Firefighters.
185.25   Police officers.
222.21   Retirement plans under various sections of Internal Revenue Code. Includes pension, profit sharing and stock bonus plans under §401(a); annuity plans [§403(a)]; educational annuities [§403(b)]; IRAs [§408]; and employee stock ownership plans [§409]. Also, ERISA-qualified benefits.
238.15   Teachers.
321.22   Highway patrol officers.

PUBLIC BENEFITS

222.201   Public assistance and social security.
222.201;
443.051   Unemployment compensation.
222.201;
744.626   Veterans' benefits.
440.22   Workers' compensation.
769.05   Proceeds for job-related injuries under Chapter 769 relating to hazardous occupations.
960.14   Crime victims' compensation unless seeking to discharge debt for treatment of crime related injury.

ALIMONY AND CHILD SUPPORT

222.201   Alimony and child support needed for support.

INSURANCE

222.13   Death benefits payable to a specific beneficiary.
222.14   Annuity contract proceeds and life insurance cash surrender value.
222.18   Disability or illness benefits.
632.619   Fraternal benefit society benefits, if received before 10/1/96.

MISCELLANEOUS

222.22   Funds paid to the Prepaid Postsecondary Education Trust Fund program.
620.68   Business partnership property.

GEORGIA

Official Code of Georgia Annotated, Title 44, Chapter 13, Section 1 (C.G.A. §44-13-100). [This is not the same set as the "Georgia Code," which is a separate set of books with a completely different numbering system.] Ignore volume numbers; look for "title" and "chapter" numbers.

HOMESTEAD

44-13-100   Real or personal property, including coop, used as a residence up to $5,000. Unused portion may be applied to any other property.

PERSONAL PROPERTY

44-13-100   Motor vehicles up to $1,000; clothing, household goods, appliances, furnishings, books, musical instruments, animals and crops up to $200 per item, and $3,500 total; jewelry up to $500; health aids; lost future earnings needed for support; personal injury recoveries up to $7,500; wrongful death recoveries needed for support. Also, burial plot in lieu of homestead. Also, $400 of any property.

WAGES

18-4-20   Minimum 75% of earned but unpaid wages for private and federal government workers. Judge may approve more for low income debtors.

PENSIONS

18-4-22   ERISA-qualified benefits.
47-2-332   Public employees.
44-13-100   Other pensions needed for support, but only as to payments being received.

PUBLIC BENEFITS

44-13-100   Unemployment compensation, veterans' benefits, social security, crime victims' compensation, and local public assistance.
49-4-35   Old age assistance.
49-4-58   Aid to blind.
49-4-84   Workers' compensation; aid to disabled.

TOOLS OF TRADE

44-13-100   Tools, books and implements of trade up to $500.

ALIMONY AND CHILD SUPPORT

44-13-100   Alimony and child support needed for support.

INSURANCE

44-13-100   Unmatured life insurance contract, unmatured life insurance dividends, interest, loan value or cash value up to $2,000 if you or someone you depend on is beneficiary, life insurance proceeds if policy is owned by someone you depend on and is needed for support.
33-15-20   Fraternal benefit society benefits.
33-25-11   Life insurance proceeds, dividends, interest, loan, cash or surrender value, provided that beneficiary is not the insured.
33-28-7   Annuity and endowment contract benefits.
33-27-7   Group insurance.
33-26-5   Industrial life insurance policy owned by someone you depend on for support.
33-29-15   Disability or health benefits up to $250 per month.

HAWAII

Hawaii Revised Statutes Annotated, Chapter 36, Title 651, Section 36-651-92 (H.R.S. §36-651-92). Ignore volume numbers; look for "chapter" and "title" numbers. Compare federal exemptions.

HOMESTEAD

36-651-91;

36-651-92   Up to $30,000 if head of family or over 65; up to $20,000 otherwise. Property can't exceed 1 acre (includes long-term leased land). Sale proceeds are exempt for 6 months after sale. Tenancies by the entirety are exempt without limit as to debts of one spouse [*Hinchee v. Security Nat'l. Bank*, 624 P.2d 821 (Haw. 1981)].

PERSONAL PROPERTY

20-359-104   Down payment for home in state project.

36-651-121   Motor vehicle up to wholesale value of $1,000; clothing; appliances and furnishings needed; books; jewelry and articles of adornment up to $1,000; proceeds for sold or damaged exempt property (sale proceeds exempt for 6 months after sale); burial plot up to 250 square feet, plus on-site tombstones, monuments and fencing

WAGES

20-353-22   Prisoner's wages held by Dept. of Public Safety.

36-651-121;

36-652-1   Unpaid wages due for services of the past 31 days. If more than 31 days, 95% of first $100, 90% of second $100, and 80% of balance.

PENSIONS

7-88-91;

36-653-3   Public officers and employees.

36-651-124   ERISA-qualified benefits, if deposited more than 3 years before filing.

7-88-169   Police officers and firefighters.

PUBLIC BENEFITS

20-346-33   Public assistance paid by Dept. of Public Safety.

21-383-163   Unemployment compensation.

21-386-57   Workers' compensation.

36-653-4   Unemployment work relief up to $60 per month.

TOOLS OF TRADE

36-651-121   Tools, books, uniforms, implements, instruments, furnishings, fishing boat, nets, motor vehicle and other personal property needed for livelihood.

INSURANCE

24-431:10-231   Disability benefits.

24-431:10-232   Annuity contract or endowment policy proceeds if beneficiary is insured spouse, child or parent.

24-431:10-233   Group life insurance policy or proceeds.

24-431:10-234   Life or health insurance policy for child.

24-431:10-D:112   Life insurance proceeds if policy prohibits use to pay creditors.

24-432:2-403   Fraternal benefit society benefits.

MISCELLANEOUS

23-425-125   Business partnership property.

IDAHO

Idaho Code, Title 55, Section 55-1201 (I.C. §55-1201). Ignore volume number.

HOMESTEAD

55-1001 to $50,000. Sale proceeds are exempt for 6 months. Before filing
55-1011   for bankruptcy, you must file a homestead declaration.

PERSONAL PROPERTY

11-603   Health aids; burial plot.

11-604   Personal injury and wrongful death recoveries needed for support.

11-605   Motor vehicle up to $1,500; jewelry up to $250; clothing, pets, appliances, furnishings, books, musical instruments, 1 firearm, family portraits and sentimental heirlooms up to $500 per item, but only up to $4,000 total; crops cultivated by the debtor on up to 50 acres (including water rights up to 160 inches) to $1,000.

11-606   Proceeds for damaged exempt property, for up to 3 months after received.

45-514   Building materials.

WAGES

11-207   Minimum of 75% of earned but unpaid wages and pension payments. Judge may approve more for low income debtors.

PENSIONS

11-604   Payments being received from pensions needed for support, provided payments are not mixed with other money.

50-1517   Police officers.

55-1011   ERISA-qualified benefits.

59-1325   Public employees.

72-1417   Firefighters.

PUBLIC BENEFITS

11-603   Unemployment compensation, social security, veterans' benefits, and federal, state and local public assistance.

56-223   General assistance, AFDC, and aid to blind, aged and disabled.

72-802   Workers' compensation.

72-1020   Crime victims' compensation, unless debt related to injury sustained during the crime, and only as to benefits received before 6/30/91, as law has since been repealed.

TOOLS OF TRADE

11-605   Tools, books and implements of trade up to $1,000; arms, uniforms and accoutrements required to be kept by peace officer, national guard or military personnel.

ALIMONY AND CHILD SUPPORT

11-604   Alimony and child support needed for support.

INSURANCE

11-603   Medical or hospital care benefits

11-604;41-1833;

41-1834   Death and disability benefits; life insurance if insured in not the beneficiary.

41-1830   Life insurance policy if the beneficiary is a married woman.

41-1833   Life insurance proceeds, dividends, interest, loan, cash or surrender value if the insured is not the beneficiary.

41-1835   Group life insurance benefits.

41-1836   Annuity contract proceeds up to $350 per month.

41-1930   Life insurance proceeds if policy prohibits use to pay creditors.

41-3218   Fraternal benefit society benefits.

55-1201   Homeowners's insurance proceeds up to $25,000.

MISCELLANEOUS

53-325   Business partnership property.

ILLINOIS

Smith-Hurd Illinois Annotated Statutes, Chapter 110, Paragraph 12-901 (I.A.S. 110 ¶12-901). Look for "chapter" numbers. [This is not "West's Smith Hurd Illinois Compiled Statutes Annotated," which is a separate set of books with another numbering system.]

HOMESTEAD (**)
110 ¶12-901   Real or personal property, including a farm, lot and buildings, condominium, coop or mobile home, up to $7,500. Spouse or child of deceased owner can claim homestead. 110 ¶12-902. Proceeds up to 1 year.

PERSONAL PROPERTY
110 ¶12-1001   Motor vehicle up to $1,200; clothing needed; health aids; school books; family pictures; bible; personal injury recoveries up to $7,500; wrongful death recoveries needed for support; proceeds from sale of exempt property; any other personal property up to $2,000 (including wages).

WAGES
110 ¶12-803   Minimum 85% of earned but unpaid wages. Judge may approve more for low income debtor.

PENSIONS
108.5 ¶2-154	General assembly members.
108.5 ¶3-144.1; 108.5 ¶5-218	Police officers.
108.5 ¶4-135; 108.5 ¶6-213	Firefighters.
108.5 ¶4-135; 110 ¶12-1006	ERISA-qualified benefits.
108.5 ¶7-217; 108.5 ¶8-244	Municipal employees.
108.5 ¶9-228	County employees.
108.5 ¶11-223	Civil service employees.
108.5 ¶12-190	Park employees.
108.5 ¶13-213	Sanitation district employees.
108.5 ¶14-147	State employees.
108.5 ¶15-185	State university employees.
108.5 ¶16-190; 108.5 ¶17-151	Teachers.
108.5 ¶18-161	Judges.
108.5 ¶19-117	House of correction employees.
108.5 ¶22-230	Disabled firefighters, and widows and children of firefighters.

PUBLIC BENEFITS
23 ¶11-3	AFDC; aid to blind, aged and disabled.
48 ¶138.21	Workers' compensation.
48 ¶172.56	Workers' occupational disease compensation.
48 ¶540	Unemployment compensation.
110 ¶12-1001	Veterans' benefits; social security; crime victims' compensation.

TOOLS OF TRADE
110 ¶12-1001   Tools, books and implements of trade up to $750

ALIMONY AND CHILD SUPPORT
110 ¶12-1001   Alimony and child support needed for support.

INSURANCE
73 ¶850	Life insurance, annuity or cash value if beneficiary is spouse, child, parent, or other dependent.
73 ¶853	Life insurance proceeds if policy prohibits use to pay creditors.
73 ¶925	Fraternal benefit society benefits.
110 ¶12-907	Homeowners' insurance proceeds for destroyed home, up to $7,500.
110 ¶12-1001	Health and disability benefits, life insurance proceeds needed for support, and life insurance policy if beneficiary is spouse or child.

MISCELLANEOUS
106.5 ¶25   Business partnership property.

INDIANA

West's Annotated Indiana Code, Title 34, Article 2, Chapter 28, Section 1 (A.I.C. §34-2-28-1). Look for "title" numbers.

HOMESTEAD
34-2-28-1   Real or personal property used as a residence up to $7,500 (LIMIT: Homestead plus personal property can't exceed $10,000); tenancies by the entirety exempt without limit unless bankruptcy is seeking to discharge debts incurred by both spouses.

PERSONAL PROPERTY
34-2-28-1   Health aids; up to $4,000 of real or tangible personal property; up to $100 of intangible personal property (except for money owed to you).

WAGES
24-4.5-5-105   Minimum of 75% of earned but unpaid wages. Judge may approve more for low income debtors.

PENSIONS
5-10.3-8-9	Public employees.
10-1-2-9;	
36-8-8-17	Police officers, but only as to benefits accruing.
21-6.1-5-17	State teachers.
34-2-28-1	Public or private retirement benefits.
36-8-7-22;	
36-8-8-17	Firefighters.
36-8-10-19	Sheriffs, but only benefits accruing.

PUBLIC BENEFITS
16-7-3.6-15	Crime victims' compensation, unless seeking to discharge debt for treatment of crime-related injury.
22-3-2-17	Workers' compensation.
22-4-33-3	Unemployment compensation.

TOOLS OF TRADE
10-2-6-3   National guard arms, uniforms and equipment.

INSURANCE
27-1-12-14	Life insurance policy or proceeds if beneficiary is spouse or dependent.
27-1-12-29	Group life insurance policy.
27-2-5-1	Life insurance proceeds if policy prohibits use to pay creditors.
27-8-3-23	Mutual life or accident policy proceeds.
27-11-6-3	Fraternal benefit society benefits.

MISCELLANEOUS
23-4-1-25   Business partnership property.

IOWA

Iowa Code Annotated, Section 499A.18 (I.C.A. §449A.18). Ignore volume numbers; look for "section" numbers.

HOMESTEAD
499A.18;561.2;
561.16   Real property or apartment, unlimited in value, but cannot exceed 1/2 acre in a city or town, or 40 acres elsewhere.

PERSONAL PROPERTY
627.6   Motor vehicle, musical instruments and tax refunds up to $5,000 total (but tax refund portion limited to $1,000 of the total); clothing up to $1,000, plus receptacles to hold clothing; household goods, appliances, and furnishings up to $2,000 total; wedding and engagement rings; books, portraits, paintings and pictures up to $1,000; health aids; burial plot up to 1 acre; rifle or musket; shotgun; up to $100 of any other personal property including cash.

WAGES
642.21   Minimum of 75% of earned but unpaid wages and pension payments. Judge may approve more for low income debtors.

PENSIONS
97A-12   Peace officers.
97B-39   Public employees.
410.11   Disabled firefighters and police officers, but only for benefits being received.
411.13   Police officers and firefighters.
627.6   Other pensions needed for support, but only as to payments being received, including IRAs.
627.8   Federal government pension, but only as to payments being received.

PUBLIC BENEFITS
627.6   Unemployment compensation, veterans' benefits, social security, AFDC, and local public assistance.
627.13   Workers' compensation.
627.19   Adopted child assistance.

TOOLS OF TRADE
627.6   Non-farming equipment up to $10,000; farming equipment, including livestock and feed, up to $10,000; but not including a car.

ALIMONY AND CHILD SUPPORT
627.6   Alimony and child support needed for support.

INSURANCE
508.32   Life insurance proceeds if policy prohibits use to pay creditors.
509.12   Employee group insurance policy or proceeds.
627.6   Life insurance proceeds up to $10,000, (if acquired within 2 years prior to filing for bankruptcy); and accident, disability, health, illness or life proceeds, dividends, interest, loan, cash or surrender value; if beneficiary is spouse, child or other dependent.

MISCELLANEOUS
123.38   Liquor licenses.
544.25   Business partnership property.

KANSAS

Kansas Statutes Annotated, Section 60-2301 (K.S.A. §60-2301). Ignore volume numbers; look for "section" numbers. You may find either "Vernon's Kansas Statutes Annotated," or "Kansas Statutes Annotated, Official." The most recent law will be in the supplements, which is a pocket part in "Vernon's" and a separate soft-cover volume in the "Official." Both have a poor index.

HOMESTEAD
60-2301   Real property or mobile home of unlimited value, but can't exceed 1 acre in a city or town, or 160 acres on a farm. You must occupy or intend to occupy the property at the time you file for bankruptcy. (Also refer to "Const. 15-9").

PERSONAL PROPERTY
60-2304   Motor vehicle up to $20,000 (no limit if equipped or designed for a disabled person); clothing to last 1 year; household equipment and furnishings; food and fuel to last 1 year; jewelry and articles of adornment up to $1,000; burial plot.
16-310   Funeral plan prepayments.

WAGES
60-2310   Minimum of 75% of earned but unpaid wages. Judge may approve more for low income debtor.

PENSIONS
12-5005;
13-14a10   Police officers.
12-5005;
14-10a10   Firefighters.
13-14,102   Elected and appointed officials in cities with populations of between 120,000 and 200,000.
60-2308   Federal government pension needed for support and received within 3 months prior to filing bankruptcy; ERISA-qualified benefits.
72-5526   State school employees.
74-2618   Judges.
74-4923;
74-49,105   Public employees.
74-4989   State highway patrol officers.

PUBLIC BENEFITS
39-717   AFDC; general assistance; social welfare.
44-514   Workers' compensation.
44-718   Unemployment compensation.
74-7313   Crime victims' compensation.

TOOLS OF TRADE
48-245   National guard uniforms, arms and equipment.
60-2304   Equipment, instruments, furniture, books, documents, breeding stock, seed, stock and grain up to $7,500 total.

INSURANCE
40-258   Life insurance proceeds up to $1,000, but only if payable to the decedent's estate.
40-414   Life insurance proceeds or cash value deposited into a bank account; life insurance forfeiture value, only if policy issued over 1 year prior to filing for bankruptcy; fraternal benefit society benefits.
40-414a   Life insurance proceeds if policy prohibits use to pay creditors.

MISCELLANEOUS
41-326   Liquor licenses.
56-325   Business partnership property.

KENTUCKY

Kentucky Revised Statutes. Chapter 427, Section 060 (K.R.S. §427.060). Ignore volume numbers; look for "chapter" numbers.

HOMESTEAD
427.060   Real or personal property used as a family residence up to $5,000. Sale proceeds are also exempt up to $1,000.

PERSONAL PROPERTY
304.39-260   Reparation benefits received and medical expenses paid under motor vehicle reparation law.
427.010   Motor vehicle up to $2,500; health aids; clothing, furniture, jewelry and articles of adornment up to $3,000 total.
427.060   Burial plot up to $5,000, in lieu of homestead.
427.150   Lost earnings payments needed for support; wrongful death recoveries for person you depended upon for support; personal injury recoveries up to $7,500, but not including pain, suffering or pecuniary loss.
427.160 $1,000 of any other property.

WAGES
427.101   Minimum of 75% of earned but unpaid wages. Judge may approve more for low income debtor.

PENSIONS
61.690   State employees.
67A.350   Urban county government employees.
67A.620;95.878;
427.120;427.125   Police officers and firefighters.
161.700   Teachers.
427.150   Other pensions needed for support, including IRAs.

PUBLIC BENEFITS
205.220   AFDC; aid to blind, aged and disabled.
341.470   Unemployment compensation.
342.180   Workers' compensation.
427.110   Cooperative life or casualty insurance benefits; fraternal benefit society benefits.
427.150   Crime victims' compensation.

TOOLS OF TRADE
427.010   Farmer's tools, equipment, livestock and poultry up to $3,000.
427.030   Non-farmer's tools up to $300; motor vehicle of mechanic, mechanical or electrical equipment servicer, minister, attorney, physician, surgeon, dentist, veterinarian or chiropractor up to $2,500.
427.040   Library, office equipment, instruments and furnishings of a minister, attorney, physician, surgeon, dentist, veterinarian or chiropractor up to $1,000.

ALIMONY AND CHILD SUPPORT
427.150   Alimony and child support needed for support.

INSURANCE
304.14-300   Life insurance proceeds or cash value if beneficiary is not the insured.
304.14-310   Health or disability benefits.
304.14-320   Group life insurance proceeds.
304.14-330   Annuity contract proceeds up to $350 per month.
304.14-340   Life insurance policy if the beneficiary is a married woman.
304.14-350   Life insurance proceeds if policy prohibits use to pay creditors.

MISCELLANEOUS
362.270   Business partnership property.

LOUISIANA

West's Louisiana Revised Statutes Annotated, Section 20:1 (L.R.S.A. §20:1). Ignore volume numbers; look for "section" numbers. Also, be sure to use the volumes marked "Revised Statutes," except for the item marked "Civil 223" under personal property which will be found in a volume marked "West's LSA Civil."

HOMESTEAD
20:1   Up to $15,000, but cannot exceed 160 acres on one tract, or 160 acres on more than 1 tract if there is only a home on one of the tracts. Must occupy at time of filing bankruptcy. Spouse or child of deceased owner, or spouse obtaining home in divorce, may claim exemption.(**)

PERSONAL PROPERTY
8:313   Cemetery plot and monuments.
13:3881   Living room, dining room and bedroom furniture; clothing; chinaware, glassware, utensils, and silverware (but not sterling); refrigerator, freezer, stove, washer and dryer; bedding and linens; family portraits; musical instruments; heating and cooling equipment; pressing irons and sewing machine; arms and military accoutrements; poultry, fowl and 1 cow; engagement and wedding rings up to $5,000; and equipment needed for therapy.
13:3881;
Civil 223   Property of a minor child.

WAGES
13:3881   Minimum of 75% of earned but unpaid wages. Judge may approve more for low income debtor.

PENSIONS
13:3881   ERISA-qualified benefit contributions, if deposited more than 1 year before filing.
20:33   Gratuitous payments to employee or heirs, whenever paid.

PUBLIC BENEFITS
23:1205   Workers' compensation.
23:1693   Unemployment compensation.
46:111   AFDC; aid to blind, aged and disabled.
46:1811   Crime victims' compensation.

TOOLS OF TRADE
13:3881   Tools, books, instruments, non-luxury car, pickup truck (up to 3 tons), and utility trailer needed for work.

INSURANCE
22:558   Fraternal benefit society benefits.
22:646   Health, accident or disability proceeds, dividends, interest, loan, cash or surrender value.
22:647   Life insurance proceeds, dividends, interest, loan, cash or surrender value.
22:649   Group insurance policies or proceeds.

MAINE

Maine Revised Statutes Annotated, Title 14, Section 4422 (14 M.R.S.A. §4422). Ignore volume numbers; look for "title" numbers.

HOMESTEAD
14-4422	$12,500.(**), up to $60,000 if over 60 or disabled. Proceeds for 6 months if reinvested.

PERSONAL PROPERTY
9-A-5-103	Balance due on repossessed goods, provided total amount financed is not more than $2,000.
14-4422	Motor vehicle up to $2,500; cooking stove; furnaces and stoves for heat; food to last 6 months; fuel not to exceed 5 tons of coal, 1,000 gallons of oil, or 10 cords of wood; health aids; 1 wedding ring & 1 engagement ring; other jewelry up to $750; up to $200 per item for each of the following: household goods & furnishings, clothing, appliances, books, animals, crops, and musical instruments; lost earnings payments needed for support; feed, seed, fertilizer, tools and equipment to raise and harvest food for 1 season; wrongful death recoveries needed for support; personal injury recoveries up to $12,500, not including pain and suffering; $400 of any property. Burial plot up to $7,500, in lieu of homestead exemption.
37-B-262	Military arms, clothes and equipment.

PENSIONS
3-703	Legislators.
4-1203	Judges.
5-17054	State employees.
14-4422	ERISA-qualified benefits.

PUBLIC BENEFITS
14-4422	Unemployment compensation, veterans' benefits, social security, and crime victims' compensation.
22-3753	AFDC
39-67	Workers' compensation.

TOOLS OF TRADE
14-4422	Books, materials and stock up to $5,000; 1 of each type of farm implement necessary to raise and harvest crops; 1 boat not to exceed 5 tons used in commercial fishing.

ALIMONY AND CHILD SUPPORT
14-4422	Alimony and child support needed for support.

INSURANCE
14-4422	Unmatured life insurance policy; life insurance policy, dividends, interest, or loan value for person you depended upon up to $4,000.
24-A-2428	Life, annuity, accident or endowment policy, proceeds, dividends, interest, loan, cash or surrender value.
24-A-2429	Disability or health insurance proceeds, dividends, interest, loan, cash or surrender value.
24-A-2430	Group life or health policy or proceeds.
24-A-2431	Annuity proceeds up to $450 per month.
24-A-4118	Fraternal benefit society benefits.

MISCELLANEOUS
14-4422	Unused homestead up to $6,000 total for tools of trade, personal injury recoveries, or household goods & furnishings, clothing, appliances, books, animals, crops, and musical instruments.
31-305	Business partnership property.

MARYLAND

References with numbers only are to Annotated Code of Maryland, Article 23, Section 164 (A.C.M. §23-164). Other references are to specific volumes, which have the title on the book. Example: "A.C.M. Courts and Judicial Procedure §11-504 (Ct. & Jud. Proc. 11-504)," or "A.C.M. Corporations §9-502 (Corp. 9-502)."

HOMESTEAD:
	Tenancies by the entirety to unlimited amount as to debts of one spouse [*In re Sefren*, 41 B.R. 747 (D. Md. 1984)].

PERSONAL PROPERTY
Ct.&Jud.Proc.11-504	Clothing, household goods & furnishings, appliances, books and pets up to $500 total; health aids; cash or property up to $3,000; lost future earnings recoveries.
23-164	Burial plot.

WAGES
Comm.15-601.1	Earned but unpaid wages are exempt as follows: in Kent, Caroline and Queen Anne's of Worcester counties, the greater of 75% of actual wages or 30% of the federal minimum wage; in all other counties, the greater of 75% or $145 per week.

PENSIONS
73B-17;73B-125	State employees.
73B-49	Deceased Baltimore police officers, but only as to benefits accruing.
73B-96;73B-152	Teachers.
88B-60	State police.
Ct. & Jud. Proc. 11-504	ERISA-qualified benefits, except IRAs.

PUBLIC BENEFITS
26A-13	Crime victims' compensation.
88A-73	AFDC; general assistance.
95A-16	Unemployment compensation.
101-50	Workers' compensation.

TOOLS OF TRADE
Ct.&Jud.Proc.11-504	Tools, books, instruments, appliances and clothing needed for work (but can't include car), up to $2,500.

INSURANCE
48A-328,Estates and Trusts 8-115	Fraternal benefit society benefits.
48A-385,Estates and Trusts 8-115	Life insurance or annuity contract proceeds, dividends, interest, loan, cash or surrender value if beneficiary is a dependent of the insured.
Comm.15-601.1	Medical benefits deducted from wages.
Ct.&Jud.Proc.11-504	Disability or health benefits.

MISCELLANEOUS
Corp. 9-502	Business partnership property.

MASSACHUSETTS

Annotated Laws of Massachusetts, Chapter 188, Section 1 (A.L.M. §188-1).

HOMESTEAD
188-1;188-1A	$100,000; if over 65 or disabled then $200,000. Some tenancies by the entirety are exempt without limit. Must record homestead declaration before filing bankruptcy. Must occupy or intend to occupy the property at the time of filing for bankruptcy. Spouse or child of deceased owner may claim the exemption.(*)
209-1	Tenancies by the entirety exempt as against debts for non-necessities.

PERSONAL PROPERTY
79-6A	Moving expenses for eminent domain (that is, if the government took your property).
235-34	Motor vehicle up to $700; furniture up to $3,000; clothing needed; beds and bedding; heating unit; books up to $200 total; cash up to $200 per month for rent, in lieu of homestead; cash for fuel, heat, water or electricity up to $75 per month; bank deposits to $125; cash for food or food to $300; sewing machine to $200; burial plots and tombs; church pew; 2 cows, 2 swine, 12 sheep and 4 tons of hay. Co-op shares up to $100.
246-28A	Bank, credit union or trust company deposits up to $500 total.

WAGES
246-28	Earned but unpaid wages up to $125 per week.

PENSIONS
32-19	Public employees.
32-41	Private retirement benefits.
168-41; 168-44	Savings bank employees.
235-34A; 246-28	ERISA-qualified benefits.

PUBLIC BENEFITS
115-5	Veterans' benefits.
118-10	AFDC
151A-36	Unemployment compensation.
152-47	Workers' compensation.
235-34	Aid to aged and disabled.

TOOLS OF TRADE
235-34	Tools, implements and fixtures up to $500 total; materials you designed and procured up to $500; boats, nets and fishing tackle of fisherman up to $500; arms, uniforms and accoutrements you are required to keep.

INSURANCE
175-110A	Disability benefits up to $35 per week.
175-119A	Life insurance proceeds if policy prohibits use to pay creditors.
175-125	Life insurance annuity contract which states it is exempt; life or endowment policy, proceeds, dividends, interest, loan, cash or surrender value.
175-126	Life insurance policy if beneficiary is a married woman.
175-132C	Group annuity policy or proceeds.
175-135	Group life insurance policy.
175F-15	Medical malpractice self-insurance.
176-22	Fraternal benefit society benefits.

MISCELLANEOUS
108A-25	Business partnership property.

MICHIGAN

Michigan Compiled Laws Annotated, Section 600.6023. (M.C.L.A. §600.6023). (In addition to the Michigan Compiled Laws, there are also the Michigan Statutes Annotated, or "M.S.A." If you wish to look up these laws but can only find the M.S.A., there is a cross-reference to the M.C.L.A. number in the M.S.A. itself.)

HOMESTEAD
559.214; 600.6023; 600.6027	Real property, including condominium, up to $3,500; but not to exceed 1 lot in a city, town or village, or 40 acres elsewhere. Tenancies by the entirety are exempt without limit as to debts of one spouse [*SNB Bank & Trust v. Kensey*, 378 NW2d 594 (Mich. App. 1985)]. Spouse or child of a deceased owner may claim the exemption.

PERSONAL PROPERTY
128.112	Burial plots.
600.6023	Clothing; household goods, furniture, appliances, utensils and books up to $1,000 total; food and fuel to last 6 months if head of household; building and loan association shares up to $1,000 par value, in lieu of homestead exemption; family pictures; church pew, slip or seat; 2 cows, 5 swine, 10 sheep, 5 roosters, 100 hens, and hay and grain to last 6 months if head of household.

WAGES
600.5311	60% of earned but unpaid wages for head of household; 40% for others; subject to following minimums: $15 per week plus $2 per week for each dependent other than spouse for head of household; $10 per week for others.

PENSIONS
38.40	State employees.
38.559	Police officers and firefighters.
38.826	Judges.
38.927	Probate judges.
38.1057	Legislators.
38.1346	Public school employees.
600.6023	IRAs, to extent tax-deferred; ERISA-qualified benefits.

PUBLIC BENEFITS
18.362	Crime victims' compensation.
35.926	Veterans' benefits for WWII veterans.
35.977	Korean War veterans' benefits.
35.1027	Vietnam veterans' benefits.
330.1158a	AFDC.
400.63	Social welfare benefits.
418.821	Workers' compensation.
421.30	Unemployment compensation.

TOOLS OF TRADE
600.6023	Tools, implements, materials, stock, apparatus, motor vehicle, horse, team and harness up to $1,000 total; arms and accoutrements you are required to keep.

INSURANCE
500.2207	Life insurance proceeds, dividends, interest, loan, cash or surrender value; life or endowment proceeds if beneficiary is spouse or child of insured.
500.2209	Life insurance proceeds up to $300 per year if the beneficiary is a married woman or a husband.
500.4054	Life, annuity or endowment proceeds if policy or contract prohibits use to pay creditors.
500.8046	Fraternal benefit society benefits.
600.6023	Disability, mutual life or health benefits.

MISCELLANEOUS
449.25	Business partnership property

MINNESOTA

Minnesota Statutes Annotated, Section 510.01 (M.S.A. §510.01). Ignore volume numbers; look for "section" numbers. Be sure to see Cumulative Annual Pocket Part for current limitation amounts. NOTE: Some courts have held "unlimited" exemptions invalid as state constitution only allows for "reasonable" exemptions. *In re Tveten*, 402 NW2d 551 (Minn. 1987).

HOMESTEAD

510.01;510.02; 550.37	Real property, mobile or manufacturer home of unlimited value, but cannot exceed 1/2 acre in a city or 160 acres elsewhere.

PERSONAL PROPERTY

550.37	Motor vehicle up to $3,000; clothing, including watch; furniture, appliances, radio, TV and phonographs up to $6,750 total; food and utensils; books and musical instruments; burial plot; church pew or seat; proceeds for damaged exempt property; personal injury lost earnings and wrongful death recoveries.

WAGES

550.37	Wages deposited into bank accounts for 20 days after deposit; earned but unpaid wages paid within 6 months of returning to work if you previously received welfare; wages of released inmates paid received within 6 months of release.
571.55	Minimum of 75% of earned but unpaid wages. Judge may approve more for low income debtor.
550.37	Earnings of a minor child.

PENSIONS

181B.16	Private retirement benefits accruing.
352.15	State employees.
352B.071	State troopers.
353.15	Public employees.
354.10;354A.11	Teachers.
550.37	ERISA-qualified benefits, including IRAs, need for support, up to $45,000 present value.

PUBLIC BENEFITS

176.175	Workers' compensation.
268.17	Unemployment compensation.
550.37	AFDC, supplemental security income (SSI), general assistance, supplemental assistance.
550.38	Veterans' benefits.
611A.60	Crime victims' compensation.

TOOLS OF TRADE

550.37	Tools, library, furniture, machines, instruments, implements and stock in trade up to $7,500; Farm machines, implements, livestock, produce and crops of farmers up to $13,000. (Total of these cannot exceed $13,000.) Teaching materials of a school teacher, including books and chemical apparatus, of unlimited value and not subject to $13,000 limit.

INSURANCE

61A.04	Life insurance proceeds if policy prohibits use to pay creditors.
61A.12	Life insurance or endowment proceeds, dividends, interest, loan, cash or surrender value if the insured is not the beneficiary.
64B.18	Fraternal benefit society benefits.
550.37	Life insurance proceeds if beneficiary is spouse or child, up to $30,000 plus additional $7,500 per dependent; unmatured life insurance contract dividends, interest, loan, cash or surrender value if insured is the debtor or someone the debtor depends upon, up to $6,000; police, fire or beneficiary association benefits.
550.39	Accident or disability proceeds.

MISCELLANEOUS

323.24	Business partnership property.

MISSISSIPPI

Mississippi Code 1972 Annotated, Title 85, Section 85-3-21 (M.C. §85-3-21).

HOMESTEAD

85-3-21	$75,000, but cannot exceed 160 acres. Must occupy at time of filing bankruptcy, unless you are widowed or over 60 and married or widowed. Sale proceeds are also exempt. 85-3-23.

PERSONAL PROPERTY

85-3-1	Tangible personal property of any kind up to $10,000; proceeds from exempt property.
85-3-17	Personal injury judgments up to $10,000.

WAGES

85-3-4	Earned but unpaid wages owed for 30 days, 75% after 30 days.

PENSIONS

21-29-257	Police officers and firefighters.
25-11-129	Public employees retirement and disability benefits.
25-11-201-23	Teachers.
25-13-31	Highway patrol officers.
25-14-5	State employees.
71-1-43	Private retirement benefits.
85-3-1	IRAs, Keoghs, and ERISA-qualified benefits, if deposited more than 1 year before filing.

PUBLIC BENEFITS

25-11-129	Social security.
43-3-71	Assistance to blind.
43-9-19	Assistance to aged.
43-29-15	Assistance to disabled.
71-3-43	Workers' compensation.
71-5-539	Unemployment compensation.
99-41-23	Crime victims' compensation.

INSURANCE

83-7-5	Life insurance proceeds if policy prohibits use to pay creditors.
83-29-39	Fraternal benefit society benefits.
85-3-1	Disability benefits.
85-3-11	Life insurance policy or proceeds up to $50,000.
85-3-13	Life insurance proceeds if beneficiary is the decedent's estate, up to $5,000.
85-3-23	Homeowners' insurance proceeds up to $75,000.

MISCELLANEOUS

79-12-49	Business partnership property.

MISSOURI

Vernon's Annotated Missouri Statutes, Chapter 513, Section 513.430 (A.M.S. §513.430). Ignore volume numbers; look for "section" numbers.

HOMESTEAD
513.430;
513.475   Real property up to $8,000, or mobile home up to $1,000. Tenancies by the entirety are exempt without limit as to debts of one spouse [*In re Anderson*, 12 B.R. 483 (W.D. Mo. 1981)].(*)

PERSONAL PROPERTY
214.190   Burial grounds up to $100 or 1 acre.
513.430   Motor vehicle up to $500; clothing, household goods, appliances, furnishings, books, animals, musical instruments and crops up to $1,000 total; health aids; jewelry up to $500; wrongful death recoveries for a person you depended upon.

513.430;
513.440   Any property up to $1,250 plus $250 per child for head of family; up to $400 for others.
Other   Personal injury causes of action. Refer to as: "*In re Mitchell*, 73 B.R. 93".

WAGES
513.470   Wages of a servant or common laborer up to $90.
525.030   Minimum of 75% of earned but unpaid wages. Judge may approve more for low income debtor. 90% for head of family.

PENSIONS
70.695   Public officers and employees.
71.207   Employees of cities with more than 100,000 population.
86.190;86.353;
86.493;86.780   Police department employees.
87.090;87.365;
87.485   Firefighters.
104.250   Highway and transportation employees.
104.540   State employees.
169.090   Teachers.
513.430   ERISA-qualified benefits needed for support; life insurance dividends, loan value, or interest, up to $5,000, if bought more than 6 months before filing.

PUBLIC BENEFITS
287.260   Workers' compensation.
288.380;
513.430   Unemployment compensation.
513.430   Social security, veterans' benefits, and AFDC.

TOOLS OF TRADE
513.430   Tools, books and implements to $2,000.

ALIMONY AND CHILD SUPPORT
513.430   Alimony and child support up to $500 per month.

INSURANCE
376.530;
376.560   Life insurance proceeds if policy owned by woman insuring her husband.
376.550   Life insurance proceeds if policy owned by an unmarried woman and beneficiary is her father or brother.
377.090   Fraternal benefit society benefits, up to $5,000, if bought more than 6 months before filing.
377.330   Assessment or stipulated premium proceeds.
513.430   Death, disability or illness benefits needed for support; unmatured life insurance policy.

MISCELLANEOUS
358.250   Business partnership property.

184

MONTANA

Montana Code Annotated, Title 70, Chapter 32, Section 70-32-101 (M.C.A. §70-32-101). Ignore volume numbers; look for "title" numbers.

HOMESTEAD
70-32-101; 70-32-104; 70-32-201;
70-32-216   Real property or mobile home up to $40,000. Must occupy at time of filing for bankruptcy, and must record a homestead declaration before filing. Proceeds for 18 months.

PERSONAL PROPERTY
25-13-608   Health aids; burial plot.
25-13-609   Motor vehicle up to $1,200; clothing, household goods and furnishings, appliances, jewelry, books, animals and feed, musical instruments, firearms, sporting goods, and crops up to $600 per item and $4,500 total.
25-13-610   Proceeds for damaged or lost exempt property for 6 months after receipt.
35-15-404   Cooperative association shares up to $500 value.

WAGES
25-13-614   Minimum of 75% of earned but unpaid wages. Judge may approve more for low income debtor.

PENSIONS
19-3-105   Public employees.
19-4-706   Teachers.
19-5-704   Judges.
19-6-705   Highway patrol officers.
19-7-705   Sheriffs.
19-8-805   Game wardens.
19-9-1006;19-10-504   Police officers.
19-11-612;19-13-1004   Firefighters.
19-21-212   University system employees.
31-2-106   ERISA-qualified benefits in excess of 15% of annual income, if deposited at least 1 year before filing.

PUBLIC BENEFITS
25-13-608   Social security, veterans', & local public assistance benefits.
39-71-743   Workers' compensation.
39-73-110   Silicosis benefits.
39-51-3105   Unemployment compensation.
53-2-607   AFDC, aid to aged and disabled, vocational rehabilitation to the blind, subsidized adoption payments.
53-9-129   Crime victims' compensation.

TOOLS OF TRADE
25-13-609   Tools, books and instruments of trade up to $3,000.
25-13-613   Arms, uniforms and accoutrements needed to carry out government functions.

ALIMONY AND CHILD SUPPORT
25-13-608   Alimony and child support.

INSURANCE
25-13-608;
33-15-513   Disability or illness proceeds, benefits, dividends, interest, loan, cash or surrender value, and medical or hospital benefits.
25-13-609   Unmatured life insurance contracts up to $4,000.
33-7-511   Fraternal benefit society benefits.
33-15-511   Life insurance proceeds, dividends, interest, loan, cash or surrender value.
33-15-512   Group life insurance policy or proceeds.
33-15-514   Annuity contract proceeds up to $350 per month.
33-20-120   Life insurance proceeds if policy prohibits use to pay creditors.
80-2-245   Hail insurance benefits.

MISCELLANEOUS
35-10-502   Business partnership property.

NEBRASKA

Revised Statutes of Nebraska, Chapter 40, Section 40-101 (R.S.N. §40-101). Ignore volume numbers; look for "chapter" numbers.

HOMESTEAD
40-101	$10,000, but cannot exceed 2 lots in a city or 160 acres elsewhere. Sale proceeds are exempt for 6 months after sale.

PERSONAL PROPERTY
12-511	Perpetual care funds.
12-517	Burial plot.
12-605	Tombs, crypts, lots, niches and vaults.
25-1552	$2,500 of any property except wages, in lieu of homestead.
25-1556	Personal possessions; clothing needed; furniture and kitchen utensils up to $1,500; food and fuel to last 6 months.
25-1563	Recovery for personal injuries.

WAGES
25-1558	Minimum of 85% of earned but unpaid wages or pension payments for head of family; 75% for others. Judge may approve more for low income debtor.

PENSIONS
23-2322	County employees.
25-1559	Military disability benefits up to $2,000.
25-1563	ERISA-qualified benefits needed for support.
79-1060;	
79-1552	School employees.
84-1324	State employees.

PUBLIC BENEFITS
48-149	Workers' compensation.
48-647	Unemployment compensation.
68-1013	AFDC; aid to blind, aged and disabled.

TOOLS OF TRADE
25-1556	Tools or equipment up to $1,500. (**)

INSURANCE
44-371	Life insurance or annuity contract proceeds up to $10,000 loan value.
44-754	Disability benefits to $200 per month.
44-1089	Fraternal benefit society benefits up to loan value of $10,000.

MISCELLANEOUS
67-325	Business partnership property.

NEVADA

Nevada Revised Statutes Annotated, Chapter 21, Section 21.090 (N.R.S.A. §21.090(m)). Ignore volume numbers; look for "chapter" numbers.

HOMESTEAD
21.090(m);	
115.010;	
115.020	Real property or mobile home up to $95,000. Must record a homestead declaration before filing for bankruptcy.(*)

PERSONAL PROPERTY
21.090	Motor vehicle up to $1,500 (no limit if equipped for the disabled); household goods, furniture, home and yard equipment up to $3,000 total; books up to $1,500 total; pictures and keepsakes; health aids; 1 gun.
21.100	Metal-bearing ores, geological specimens, paleontological remains or art curiosities (must be arranged, classified, catalogued, and numbered in reference books).
452.550	Burial plot purchase money held in trust.
689.700	Funeral service contract money held in trust.

WAGES
21.090	Minimum of 75% of earned but unpaid wages. Judge may approve more for low income debtor.

PENSIONS
286.670	Public employees.

PUBLIC BENEFITS
422.291	AFDC; aid to blind, aged and disabled.
612.710	Unemployment compensation.
615.270	Vocational rehabilitation benefits.
616.550	Industrial insurance (worker's compensation).

TOOLS OF TRADE
21.090	Tools, materials, library, equipment and supplies up to $4,500; farm trucks, equipment, tools, stock and seed up to $4,500; cabin or dwelling of a miner or prospector, cars, implements and appliances for mining and a mining claim you work up to $4,500; arms, uniforms and accoutrements you are required to keep.

INSURANCE
21.090	Life insurance policy or proceeds if premiums don't exceed $1,000 per year.
687B.260	Life insurance proceeds if you are not insured.
687B.270	Health insurance proceeds, dividends, interest, loan, cash or surrender value.
687B.280	Group life or health policy or proceeds.
687B.290	Annuity contract proceeds up to $350 per month.
695A.220	Fraternal benefit society benefits.

MISCELLANEOUS
87.250	Business partnership property.

NEW HAMPSHIRE

New Hampshire Revised Statutes Annotated, Chapter 480, Section 480:1 (N.H.R.S.A. §480:1). Ignore "title" numbers; look for "chapter" numbers.

HOMESTEAD
480:1   Real property, or manufactured home if you own the land, up to $30,000.

PERSONAL PROPERTY
511:2   Automobile up to $1,000; clothing, beds, bedsteads, bedding and cooking utensils; furniture up to $2,000; refrigerator, cooking and heating stoves; food and fuel up to $400; jewelry up to $500; books up to $800; sewing machine; burial plot, lot, and church pew; 1 cow, 6 sheep or fleece, 4 tons of hay, and 1 hog, pig or pork if already slaughtered.

512:21   Proceeds for lost or destroyed exempt property.

WAGES
512:21   Earned but unpaid wages of debtor and spouse (Judge determines amount exempt based on percent of federal minimum wage, so claim all); jury and witness fees; wages of a minor child.

PENSIONS
100A:26   Public employees.
102:23   Firefighters.
103:18   Police officers.
512:21   Federally created pensions accruing.

PUBLIC BENEFITS
167:25   AFDC; aid to blind, aged and disabled.
281A:52   Workers' compensation.
282A:159   Unemployment compensation.

TOOLS OF TRADE
511:2   Tools of trade up to $1,200; arms, uniforms and equipment of a military member; 1 yoke of oxen or horse needed for farming or teaming.

ALIMONY AND CHILD SUPPORT
161C:11   Child support only.

INSURANCE
402:69   Firefighters' aid insurance.
408:1   Life insurance or endowment proceeds if beneficiary is a married woman.
408:2   Life insurance or endowment proceeds if you are not the insured.
418:24   Fraternal benefit society benefits.
512:21   Homeowners' insurance proceeds up to $5,000.

MISCELLANEOUS
304A:25   Business partnership property.

NEW JERSEY

New Jersey Statutes Annotated, Title 2A, Chapter 17, Section 2A-17-19 (N.J.S.A. §2A:17-19). The spine of these volumes will be marked "NJSA." Compare federal exemptions.

PERSONAL PROPERTY
2A:17-19   Clothing; goods, personal property and stock or interest in corporations up to $1,000 total.
2A:26-4   Household good and furniture up to $1,000.
8A:5-10   Burial plots.

WAGES
2A:17-56   90% of earned but unpaid wages if your income is less than $7,500; otherwise judge may exempt less.
38A:4-8   Military personnel wages and allowances.

PENSIONS
A:057.6   Civil defense workers.
18A:66-51   Teachers.
18A:66-116   School district employees.
43:6A-41   Judges.
43:7-13   Prison employees.
43:8A-20   Alcohol beverage control officers.
43:10-57;
43:10-105   County employees.
43-13-9   ERISA-qualified benefits.
43:13-44   Municipal employees.
43:15A-55   Public employees.
43:16-7;
43:16A-17   Police officers, firefighters and traffic officers.
43:18-12   City boards of health employees.
43:19-17   Street and water department employees.
53:5A-45   State police.

PUBLIC BENEFITS
34:15-29   Workers' compensation.
43:21-53   Unemployment compensation.
44:7-35   Old-age, permanent disability assistance.
52:4B-30   Crime victims' compensation.

INSURANCE
A:9-57.6   Civil defense workers' disability, death, medical or hospital benefits.
17:18-12
17B:24-8   Health and disability benefits.
17:44A-19   Fraternal benefit society benefits.
17B:24-6   Life insurance proceeds, dividends, interest, loan, cash or surrender value, if you are not the insured.
17B:24-7   Annuity contract proceeds up to $500 per month.
17B:24-9   Group life or health policy or proceeds.
17B:24-10   Life insurance proceeds if policy prohibits use to pay creditors.
38A:4-8   Military member disability or death benefits.

MISCELLANEOUS
42:1-25   Business partnership property.

NEW MEXICO

New Mexico Statutes 1978 Annotated, Chapter 42, Section 42-10-9 (N.M.S.A. §42-10-9). Ignore volume numbers; look for "chapter" numbers.

HOMESTEAD
42-10-9	$30,000 only if married, widowed or supporting another person.(**)

PERSONAL PROPERTY
42-10-1	Motor vehicle up to $4,000; $500 of any property.
42-10-1; 42-10-2	Clothing; jewelry up to $2,500; books, furniture, and health equipment.
42-10-10	$2,000 of any property, in lieu of homestead.
48-2-15	Building materials.
53-4-28	Minimum amount of shares needed for membership in cooperative association.
70-4-12	Tools, machinery and materials needed to dig, drill, torpedo, complete, operate or repair an oil line, gas well or pipeline.

WAGES
35-12-7	Minimum of 75% of earned but unpaid wages. Judge may approve more for low income debtor.

PENSIONS
22-11-42	Public school employees.
42-10-1; 42-10-2	Pension or retirement benefits.

PUBLIC BENEFITS
27-2-21	AFDC; general assistance.
31-22-15	Crime victims' compensation paid before July 1, 1993.
51-1-37	Unemployment compensation.
52-1-52	Workers' compensation.
52-3-37	Occupational disease disablement benefits.

TOOLS OF TRADE
42-10-1; 42-10-2	$1,500.

INSURANCE
42-10-3	Life, accident, health or annuity benefits or cash value, if beneficiary is a citizen of New Mexico.
42-10-4	Benevolent association benefits up to $5,000.
42-10-5	Life insurance proceeds.
59A-44-18	Fraternal benefit society benefits.

MISCELLANEOUS
53-10-2	Ownership in an unincorporated association.
54-1-25	Business partnership property.

NEW YORK

References of numbers only are to McKinney's Consolidated Laws of New York, Civil Practice Law and Rules, Section 5206 (C.P.L.R. §5206). Other references are to "Debtor & Creditor" (D&C); "Estates, Powers & Trusts" (Est, Pow & Tr.); "Insurance" (Insur.); "Retirement & Social Security" (Ret. & Soc. Sec.); "Partnership" (Part.); and "Unconsolidated" (Unc.).

HOMESTEAD
5206	Real property, including mobile home, condominium or coop, up to $10,000.(**)

PERSONAL PROPERTY
5205	Clothing, furniture, refrigerator, TV, radio, sewing machine, security deposits with landlord or utility company, tableware, cooking utensils and crockery, stoves with food and fuel to last 60 days, health aids (including animals with food), church pew or seat, wedding ring, bible, schoolbooks, and pictures; books up to $50; burial plot without a structure up to 1/4 acre; domestic animals with food up to $450; watch up to $35; trust fund principal; 90% of trust fund income.
D&C282	Motor vehicle up to $2,400; lost earnings recoveries needed for support; personal injury recoveries up to $7,500, not including pain and suffering; wrongful death recoveries for a person you depended upon for support.
D&C283	IN LIEU OF HOMESTEAD: Cash in the lesser amount of $2,500, or an amount when added to an annuity equals $5,000.

WAGES
5205	90% of earned but unpaid wages received within 60 days of filing for bankruptcy; 90% of earnings from milk sales to milk dealers; 100% for a few militia members.

PENSIONS
5205; D&C 282	ERISA-qualified plans, Keoghs and IRAs needed for support.
Insur. 4607	Public retirement benefits.
Ret. & Soc. Sec. 110	State employees.
Unc. 5711-o	Village police officers.

PUBLIC BENEFITS
D&C282	Unemployment benefits; veterans' benefits; social security; AFDC; aid to blind, aged and disabled; crime victims' compensation; home relief; local public assistance.

TOOLS OF TRADE
5205	Professional furniture, books, instruments, farm machinery, team and food for 60 days, up to $600 total; arms, swords, uniforms, equipment, horse, emblem and medal of a military member.

ALIMONY AND CHILD SUPPORT
D&C282	Alimony and child support needed for support.

INSURANCE
5205	Insurance proceeds for damaged exempt property.
5205; D&C283	Annuity contract benefits up to $5,000, if purchased within 6 months of filing for bankruptcy and not tax-deferred.
Est,Pow&Tr.7-1.5	Life insurance proceeds if policy prohibits use to pay creditors.
Insur.3212	Fraternal benefit society benefits; disability or illness benefits up to $400 per month; life insurance proceeds, dividends, interest, loan, cash or surrender value if beneficiary is not the insured.

MISCELLANEOUS
Part. 51	Business partnership property.

NORTH CAROLINA

General Statutes of North Carolina, Chapter 1C, Section 1C-1601 (G.S.N.C. §1C-1601). Ignore volume numbers; look for "chapter" numbers.

HOMESTEAD
1C-1601   Real or personal property used as a residence, including coop, up to $10,000. Tenancies by the entirety exempt without limit as to debts of one spouse [*In re Crouch*, 33 B.R. 271 (E.D. N.C. 1983)].

PERSONAL PROPERTY
1C-1601   Motor vehicle up to $1,500; health aids; clothing, household goods, furnishings, appliances, books, animals, musical instruments and crops up to $3,500 total, plus additional $750 per dependent up to 4 dependents; personal injury and wrongful death recoveries for a person you depended upon; $3,500 of any property, less any amount claimed for homestead or burial plot.

1C-1601   IN LIEU OF HOMESTEAD: burial plot up to $10,000.

1C-1601 $3,500 of any property, less any amount claimed for homestead or burial plot.

WAGES
1-362   Earned but unpaid wages received 60 days before filing for bankruptcy.

PENSIONS
58-86-90   Firefighters and rescue squad workers.
120-4.29   Legislators.
128-31   Municipal, city and county employees.
135-9;135-95   Teachers and state employees.
143-166.30   Law enforcement officers.

PUBLIC BENEFITS
15B-17   **Crime victims' compensation.**
96-17   Unemployment compensation.
97-21   Workers' compensation.
108A-36   AFDC; special adult assistance.
111-18   Aid to blind.

TOOLS OF TRADE
1C-1601   Tools, books and implements of trade up to $750.

INSURANCE
Const.10-5   Life insurance policy if beneficiary is insured spouse or child.
58-58-115   Life insurance proceeds, dividends, interest, loan, cash or surrender value.
58-58-165   Group life insurance policy or proceeds.
58-58-165   Employee group life policy or proceeds.
58-24-85   Fraternal benefit society benefits.

MISCELLANEOUS
59-55   Business partnership property.

NORTH DAKOTA

North Dakota Century Code Annotated, Title 28, Chapter 28-22, Section 28-22-02 (N.D.C.C. §28-22-02). Ignore volume numbers; look for "title" numbers.

HOMESTEAD
28-22-02;
47-18-01   Real property, mobile home or house trailer up to $80,000.

PERSONAL PROPERTY
The following list applies to all debtors:
28-22-02   Clothing; fuel to last 1 year; bible; books up to $100; pictures; church pew; burial plots; crops or grain raised on the debtor's tract of land, limited to 1 tract of 160 acres.
28-22-03.1   Motor vehicle up to $1,200; personal injury recoveries not including pain and suffering, up to $7,500; wrongful death recoveries up to $7,500.
28-22-03.1   IN LIEU OF HOMESTEAD: cash to $7,500.

The following list applies to the head of household, not claiming crops or grain:
28-22-03 $5,000 of any personal property; OR
28-22-04   Furniture and bedding up to $1,000; books and musical instruments up to $1,500; tools and library of a professional up to $1,000; tools of a mechanic and stock in trade up to $1,000; and farm implements and livestock up to $4,500.

The following list applied to a non-head of household not claiming crops:
28-22-05 $2,500 of any personal property.

WAGES
32-09.1-.03   Minimum of 75% of earned but unpaid wages. Judge may approve more for low income debtor.

PENSIONS
28-22-03.1   Disabled veterans' benefits (does not include military retirement pay); annuities, pensions, IRAs, Keoghs, simplified employee plans (together with the insurance exemption under this section total may not exceed $200,000, although no limit if needed for support).
28-22-19   Public employees.

PUBLIC BENEFITS
28-22-03.1   Social security.
28-22-19   AFDC; crime victims' compensation.
37-25-07   Vietnam veterans' adjustment compensation.
52-06-30   Unemployment compensation.
65-05-29   Workers' compensation.

TOOLS OF TRADE: See personal property section.

INSURANCE
26.1-15.1-18;
26.1-33-40   Fraternal benefit society benefits.
26.1-33-40   Life insurance proceeds payable to the decedent's estate.
28-22-03.1   Life insurance surrender value up to $100,000 per policy if beneficiary is relative of the insured and the policy was owned for more than 1 year before filing for bankruptcy. Together with pension exemption in this section total cannot exceed $200,000, or $100,000 per plan, although no limit if needed for support.

MISCELLANEOUS
45-08-02   Business partnership property.

OHIO

Page's Ohio Revised Code, Title 23, Section 2329.66 (O.R.C. §2329.66).

HOMESTEAD
2329.66 — Real or personal property used as a residence up to $5,000. Tenancies by the entirety are exempt without limit as to debts of one spouse [*In re Thomas*, 14 B.R. 423 (N.D. Ohio 1981)].

PERSONAL PROPERTY
517.09;2329.66 — Burial plot.
2329.66 — Motor vehicle up to $1,000; one piece of jewelry up to $400; household goods, furnishings, appliances, jewelry, books, animals, musical instruments, firearms, hunting and fishing equipment and crops up to $200 per item, $1,500 total (IN LIEU OF HOMESTEAD: $2,000 total); clothing, beds and bedding up to $200 per item; cooking unit and refrigerator up to $300 each; health aids; lost future earnings needed for support; cash, bank and security deposits, tax refund and money due within 90 days up to $400 total; personal injury recoveries not including pain and suffering up to $5,000; wrongful death recoveries for person you depended upon for support; $400 of any property.

WAGES
2329.66 — Minimum of 75% of earned but unpaid wages. Judge may approve more for low income debtor.

PENSIONS
145.56 — Public employees.
146.13 — Volunteer firefighters' dependents.
742.47 — Police officers and firefighters.
2329.66 — Police officers' and firefighters' death benefits; ERISA-qualified benefits, IRAs and Keoghs needed for support.
3307.71;3309.66 — Public school employees.
5505.22 — State highway patrol employees.

PUBLIC BENEFITS
2329.66;4123.67 — Workers' compensation.
2329.66;4141.32 — Unemployment compensation.
2329.66;5107.12 — AFDC.
2329.66; 5113.03 — General assistance.
2329.66; 5115.07 — Disability assistance.
2743.66 — Crime victims' compensation.
3304.19 — Vocational rehabilitation benefits.

TOOLS OF TRADE
147.04 — Seal and official register of a notary public.
2329.66 — Tools, books and implements of trade up to $750.

ALIMONY AND CHILD SUPPORT
2329.66 — Alimony and child support needed for support.

INSURANCE
2329.63;2329.66 — Benevolent society benefits to $5,000.
2329.66;3917.05 — Group life insurance policy or proceeds.
2329.66;3921.18 — Fraternal benefit society benefits.
2329.66;3923.19 — Disability benefits to $600 per month.
3911.10 — Life, endowment or annuity contract dividends, interest, loan, cash or surrender value for your spouse, child or other dependent.
3911.12 — Life insurance proceeds for spouse.
3911.14 — Life insurance proceeds if policy prohibits use to pay creditors.

MISCELLANEOUS
1775.24; 2329.66 — Business partnership property.

OKLAHOMA

Oklahoma Statutes Annotated. Title 31, Section 2 (31 O.S.A. §2).

HOMESTEAD
31-2 — Real property or manufactured home to unlimited value, but cannot exceed 1/4 acre. If over 1/4 acre, you may claim up to $5,000 on 1 acre in a city, town or village, or $5,000 on 160 acres elsewhere. You do not need to occupy the home as long as you don't acquire another.

PERSONAL PROPERTY
8-7 — Burial plots.
31-1 — Motor vehicle up to $3,000; clothing up to $4,000; furniture, books, portraits, pictures, gun and health aids; food to last 1 year; 2 bridles and 2 saddles; 100 chickens, 20 sheep, 10 hogs, 5 cows and calves under 6 months, 2 horses and forage for livestock to last 1 year; personal injury, workers' compensation and wrongful death recoveries (not to include punitive damages) up to $50,000 total.

WAGES
12-1171.1;31-1 — 75% of wages earned within 90 days prior to filing bankruptcy. Judge may approve more if you can show hardship.

PENSIONS
11-49-126 — Firefighters.
11-50-124 — Police officers.
19-959 — County employees.
31-1 — ERISA-qualified benefits.
31-7 — Disabled veterans.
47-2-303.3 — Law enforcement employees.
60-328 — Tax exempt benefits.
70-17-109 — Teachers.

PUBLIC BENEFITS
21-142.13 — Crime victims' compensation.
40-2-303 — Unemployment compensation.
56-173 — AFDC; social security.
85-48 — Workers' compensation.

TOOLS OF TRADE
31-1 — Tools, books, apparatus of trade, and husbandry implements to farm homestead, up to $5,000 total.

ALIMONY AND CHILD SUPPORT
31-1 — Alimony and child support.

INSURANCE
36-2410 — Assessment or mutual benefits.
36-2510 — Limited stock insurance benefits.
36-2720 — Fraternal benefit society benefits.
36-3631 — Life insurance policy or proceeds if you are not the insured.
36-3632 — Group life insurance policy or proceeds if you are not the insured.
36-6125 — Funeral benefits if pre-paid and placed in trust.

MISCELLANEOUS
54-225 — Business partnership property.

OREGON

Oregon Revised Statutes Annotated, Chapter 23, Section 23.164 (O.R.S. §23.164). Ignore volume numbers; look for "chapter" numbers.

HOMESTEAD
23.164;23.250   Real property, houseboat, or mobile home on land you own up to $25,000 ($33,000 if joint owners). Mobile home on land you don't own, $23,000 ($30,000 if joint). Property may not exceed 1 block in a city or town, or 160 acres elsewhere. Must occupy or intend to at time of filing. Sale proceeds exempt 1 year if plan to purchase another home.

PERSONAL PROPERTY
23.160   Motor vehicle to $1,700(**); clothing, jewelry, personal items to $1,800 total(**); household items, furniture, utensils, TVs and radios to $3,000 total; health aids; cash for sold exempt property; books, pictures & musical instruments to $600 total(**); food & fuel to last 60 days if debtor is householder; domestic animals & poultry with food to last 60 days to $1,000; lost earnings payments for debtor or someone debtor depended upon needed for support(**); personal injury recoveries (not pain and suffering) to $7,500(**); $400 of any personal property (can't be used to increase an existing exemption.

23.166   Bank deposits up to $7,500, and cash for sold exempt items.
23.200   Pistol; rifle or shotgun if owned by person over the age of 16.
65.870   Burial plot.

WAGES
23.185   Minimum of 75% of earned but unpaid wages. Judge may approve more for low income debtor.
292.070   Wages withheld in a state employee's bond saving account.

PENSIONS
23.170   Federal, state or local government employees. ERISA-qualified benefits, if deposited at least 1 year before filing (IRAs, but not Keoghs).
237.201   Public officers and employees.
239.261   School district employees.

PUBLIC BENEFITS
23.160;147.325   Crime victims' compensation (**).
344.580   Vocational rehabilitation.
401.405   Civil and disaster relief.
411.760   General assistance.
412.115   Aid to blind.
412.610   Aid to disabled.
413.130   Old-age assistance.
414.095   Medical assistance.
418.040   AFDC
655.530   Injured inmates benefits.
656.234   Workers' compensation.
657.855   Unemployment compensation.

TOOLS OF TRADE
23.160   Tools, implements, apparatus, team, harness, or library, up to $3,000 total (**).

ALIMONY AND CHILD SUPPORT
23.160   Alimony and child support needed to support.

INSURANCE
732.240   Life insurance proceeds if policy prohibits use to pay creditors.
743.046   Life insurance proceeds or cash value if you are not the insured.
743.047   Group life insurance policy or proceeds.
743.049   Annuity contract benefits up to $500 per month.
743.050   Health or disability insurance proceeds, dividends, interest, loan, cash or surrender value.
748.225   Fraternal benefit society benefits.

MISCELLANEOUS
68.420   Business partnership property.
471.301   Liquor licenses.

PENNSYLVANIA

Purdon's Pennsylvania Statutes Annotated, Title 42, Section 8123 (42 Pa.C.S.A. §8123). Compare federal exemptions.

HOMESTEAD:
None, but tenancies by the entirety are exempt without limit as to debts of one spouse [*In re McCormick*, 18 B.R. 911 (W.D. Pa. 1982)].

PERSONAL PROPERTY
42-8123 $300 of any property.
42-8124   Clothing, bibles, school books, sewing machines, uniform and accoutrements.
42-8125   Tangible personal property at an international exhibition sponsored by the U.S. government.

WAGES
42-8127   Earned but unpaid wages.

PENSIONS
16-4716   County employees.
24-8533   Public school employees.
42-8124   Self-employment benefits; private retirement benefits if clause prohibits use to pay creditors, to extent they are tax deferred, and limited to $15,000 per year deposited, and must be deposited at least 1 year before filing.
53-764;53-776;
 53-23666   Police officers.
53-881.115   Municipal employees.
53-13445;
53-23572;
 53-39383   City employees.
71-5953   State employees.

PUBLIC BENEFITS
42-8124   Workers' compensation.
43-863   Unemployment compensation.
51-20012   Veterans' benefits.
51-20098   Korean conflict veterans' benefits.
71-180-7.10   Crime victims' compensation.

INSURANCE
42-8124   No-fault automobile insurance proceeds; accident or disability benefits; group life insurance policy or proceeds; fraternal benefit society benefits; life insurance proceeds if policy prohibits use to pay creditors; life insurance annuity contract payments, proceeds or cash value up to $100 per month; life insurance annuity policy, proceeds or cash value if beneficiary is descendent's spouse, child or other dependent.

MISCELLANEOUS
15-8341   Business partnership property.

RHODE ISLAND

General Laws of Rhode Island, Section 7-8-25 (G.L.R.I. §7-8-25). Ignore "title" and "chapter" numbers; look for "section" numbers. Compare with federal exemptions.

PERSONAL PROPERTY

7-8-25	Consumer cooperative association holdings up to $50.
9-26-3	.Body of a deceased person.
9-26-4	Clothing needed; furniture and family stores of a housekeeper, beds and bedding up to $1,000 total; books up to $300; burial plot; debt owed to you which is secured by a promissory note or bill of exchange.

WAGES

9-26-4	Earned but unpaid wages up to $50; wages of spouse; earned but unpaid wages of a seaman, or if you have received welfare during the year prior to filing for bankruptcy; wages paid to the poor by a charitable organization; earnings of a minor child.
30-7-9	Earned but unpaid wages of a military member on active duty.

PENSIONS

9-26-4	ERISA-qualified benefits.
9-26-5	Police officers and firefighters.
28-17-4	Private employees.
36-10-34	State and municipal employees.

PUBLIC BENEFITS

28-33-27	Workers' compensation.
28-41-32	State disability benefits.
28-44-58	Unemployment compensation.
30-7-9	Veterans' disability or survivor benefits.
40-6-14	AFDC; general assistance; aid to blind, aged and disabled.

TOOLS OF TRADE

9-26-4	Working tools up to $500; library of a professional in practice.

INSURANCE

27-4-11	Life insurance proceeds, dividends; interest, loan, cash or surrender value if beneficiary is not the insured.
27-4-12	Life insurance proceeds if policy prohibits use to pay creditors.
27-18-24	Accident or illness proceeds, benefits, dividends, interest, loan, cash or surrender value.
27-25-18	Fraternal benefit society benefits.
28-41-32	Temporary disability insurance.

MISCELLANEOUS

7-12-36	Business partnership property.

SOUTH CAROLINA

Code of Laws of South Carolina, Title 15, Section 15-41-30 (C.L.S.C. §15-41-30). Ignore volume numbers; look for "title" numbers.

HOMESTEAD

15-41-30	Real property, including coop, up to $5,000.(**)

PERSONAL PROPERTY

15-41-30	Motor vehicle up to $1,200; clothing, household goods, furnishings, appliances, books, musical instruments, animals and crops up to $2,500 total; jewelry up to $500; health aids; personal injury and wrongful death recoveries.
15-41-30	IN LIEU OF HOMESTEAD: Burial plot up to $5,000.(**)
15-41-30	IN LIEU OF HOMESTEAD AND BURIAL PLOT: Cash and other liquid assets up to $1,000.

PENSIONS

9-1-1680	Public employees.
9-8-190	Judges and solicitors.
9-9-180	General assembly members.
9-11-270	Police officers.
9-13-230	Firefighters.
15-41-30	ERISA-qualified benefits.

PUBLIC BENEFITS

15-41-30	Unemployment compensation; social security; veterans' benefits.
15-41-30; 16-3-1300	Crime victims' compensation.
42-9-360	Workers' compensation.
43-5-190	AFDC; general relief; aid to blind, aged and disabled.

TOOLS OF TRADE

15-41-30	Tools, books and implements of trade up to $750 total.

ALIMONY AND CHILD SUPPORT

15-41-30	Alimony and child support.

INSURANCE

15-41-30	Unmatured life insurance contract (but a credit insurance policy is not exempt); disability or illness benefits; life insurance proceeds from a policy for a person you depended upon which is needed for support; life insurance dividends, interest, loan, cash or surrender value from a policy for a person you depended upon up to $4,000.
38-37-870	Fraternal benefit society benefits.
38-63-40	Life insurance proceeds for a spouse or child up to $25,000.
38-63-50	Life insurance proceeds if policy prohibits use to pay creditors.

MISCELLANEOUS

33-41-720	Business partnership property.

SOUTH DAKOTA

South Dakota Codified Laws, Title 43, Chapter 31, Section 43-31-1 (S.D.C.L. §43-31-1). Ignore volume numbers; look for "title" numbers.

HOMESTEAD

43-31-1; 43-31-2 Real property, including mobile home if larger than 240 square feet and registered in the State at least 6 months prior to filing bankruptcy, of unlimited value; but cannot exceed 1 acre in a town or 160 acres elsewhere. Sale proceeds are exempt for 1 year after sale up to $30,000 (of unlimited value if you are an unmarried widow or widower, or are over 70). Spouse or child of a deceased owner may also claim exemption. Can't include gold or silver mine, mill or smelter. 43-31-5.

PERSONAL PROPERTY

43-45-2 All debtors may claim clothing; food and fuel to last 1 year; bible; books up to $200; pictures; church pew; burial plot.

43-45-4 Non-head of family may also claim $2,000 of any personal property.

43-45-5 Head of family may claim either $4,000 of any personal property, OR furniture and bedding up to $200; books and musical instruments up to $200; tools and library of professional up to $300; tools of a mechanic and stock in trade up to $200; farm machinery, utensils, wagon, sleigh, 2 plows, harrow, and tackle for teams up to $1,250 total; 2 yoke of oxen or a span of horses or mules; 2 cows, 5 swine, 25 sheep with lambs under 6 months, wool, yarn or cloth of sheep, and food for all to last 1 year.

WAGES

15-20-12 Earned wages owing 60 days prior to filing for bankruptcy, needed for support.

24-8-10 Wages of prisoners in work programs.

PENSIONS

3-12-115 Public employees.

9-16-47 City employees.

PUBLIC BENEFITS

28-7-16 AFDC.

61-6-28 Unemployment compensation.

62-4-42 Workers' compensation.

TOOLS OF TRADE See Personal Property.

INSURANCE

43-45-6 Life insurance proceeds if beneficiary is surviving spouse or child up to $10,000.

58-12-4 Health benefits up to $20,000; endowment or life insurance policy, proceeds or cash value up to $20,000(*).

58-12-8 Annuity contract proceeds up to $250 per month.

58-15-70 Life insurance proceeds if policy prohibits use to pay creditors.

58-37-68 Fraternal benefit society benefits.

MISCELLANEOUS

48-4-14 Business partnership property.

TENNESSEE

Tennessee Code Annotated, Title 66, Section 66-2-301 (T.C.A. §26-2-301). Ignore volume numbers; look for "section" numbers.

HOMESTEAD

26-2-301 $5,000; $7,500 for joint owners. Tenancies by the entirety are exempt without limit as to debts of one spouse [In re Hamilton, 32 B.R. 337 (M.D. Tenn. 1983)]. Spouse or child of deceased owner may claim. May also claim a life estate or a 2 to 15 year lease.

PERSONAL PROPERTY

26-2-102 $4,000 of any personal property.

26-2-103 Clothing and storage containers; schools books, pictures, portraits, and bible.

26-2-111 Health aids; lost earnings payments for yourself or a person you depended upon; personal injury recoveries, not including pain and suffering, up to $7,500; wrongful death recoveries up to $10,000 (LIMIT: total of personal injury claims, wrongful death claims and crime victims' compensation cannot exceed $15,000).

26-2-305;
46-2-102 Burial plot up to 1 acre.

WAGES

26-2-106;

26-2-107 Minimum of 75% of earned but unpaid wages, plus $2.50 per week per child. Judge may approve more for low income debtor.

PENSIONS

8-36-111 Public employees.

26-2-104 State and local government employees.

26-2-111 ERISA-qualified benefits.

45-9-909 Teachers.

PUBLIC BENEFITS

26-2-111 Unemployment compensation; veterans' benefits; social security; local public assistance.

26-2-111;
29-13-111 Crime victims' compensation up to $5,000, but see" LIMIT" under Personal Property above.

50-6-223 Workers' compensation.

71-2-216 Old-age assistance.

71-3-121 AFDC.

71-4-117 Aid to blind.

71-4-1112 Aid to disabled.

TOOLS OF TRADE

26-2-111 Tools, books and implements of trade up to $750.

ALIMONY AND CHILD SUPPORT

26-2-111 Alimony which is owed for at least 30 days prior to filing for bankruptcy.

INSURANCE

26-2-110 Disability, accident or health benefits, for a resident and citizen of Tennessee.

26-2-111 Disability or illness benefits.

26-2-304 Homeowners' insurance proceeds up to $5,000.

56-7-201 Life insurance proceeds or cash value if beneficiary is the debtor's spouse, child or other dependent.

56-25-208 Fraternal benefit society benefits.

MISCELLANEOUS

61-1-124 Business partnership property.

TEXAS

Vernon's Texas Revised Civil Statutes, (T.R.C.S. §6228f). Other references are to other subject volumes in the Codes, such as "T.C.A. Property 41.001").

SPECIAL LIMIT:

Prop. 42.001 — Total of personal property stated in §42.002 (except burial plot, current wages, & health aids), wages, tools of trade, and cash value of insurance cannot exceed $30,000 total ($60,000 for head of family).

HOMESTEAD
Prop. 41.001;
Prop. 41.002 — Unlimited amount, but cannot exceed 1 acre in a city, town or village, or 100 acres (200 acres for family) elsewhere. Sale proceeds are exempt for 6 months after sale. You need not occupy at time of filing bankruptcy as long as you don't acquire another home.

PERSONAL PROPERTY
Prop. 41.001 — Burial plots.
Prop. 42.001;
42.002 — Clothing, including jewelry; pets; furnishings; heirlooms; food; athletic and sporting equipment; 2 firearms; 2 horses, mules, donkeys, and forage on hand; 12 head cattle; 60 head other livestock; 120 fowl; household pets; 1 motor vehicle for each adult with drivers license or who relies on another to operate a vehicle; up to $15,000 total ($30,000 for head of family).

WAGES
Prop. 42.002 — Earned but unpaid wages.

PENSIONS
110B-21.005	State employees.
110B-31.005	Teachers.
110B-41.004	Judges.
110B-51.006	County and district employees.
6228f	Law enforcement officers' survivors.
6243d-1;6243j; 6243g-1	Police officers.
6243e;6243e.1; 6243e.2	Firefighters.
6243g; 110B-61.006	Municipal employees.
Prop. 42.0021	Church benefits; ERISA-qualified retirement benefits to extent tax-deferred, including IRAs, Keoghs and simplified employee plans. Not subject to Special Limit.

PUBLIC BENEFITS
5221b-13	Unemployment compensation.
8306-3	Workers' compensation.
8309-1	Crime victims' compensation.
Hum.Res. 31.040	AFDC.
Hum.Res. 32.036	Medical assistance.

TOOLS OF TRADE
Prop. 42.002 — Tools, books, and equipment, including boat; farming or ranching vehicles and implements.

INSURANCE
Insur. 3.50-2	Texas employee uniform group insurance.
Insur. 3.50-3	Texas state college or university employee benefits.
Insur. 3.50-4	Retired public school employees group insurance.
Insur. 10.28	Fraternal benefit society benefits.
Insur. 21.22	Life, health, accident or annuity benefits; life insurance proceeds if policy prohibits use to pay creditors.
Prop. 42.002	Life insurance cash value if beneficiary is debtor or family member.

MISCELLANEOUS
6132b-25 — Business partnership property.

UTAH

Utah Code Annotated 1953, Title 78, Chapter 23, Section 78-23-3 (U.C.A. §78-23-3). Ignore volume numbers; look for "title" numbers.

HOMESTEAD
78-23-3 — Real property, mobile home or water rights up to $8,000, plus $2,000 for spouse and $500 for each other dependent. Homestead declaration must be filed before selling home.

PERSONAL PROPERTY
78-23-5 — Clothing, except furs and jewelry; refrigerator, freezer, stove, washer, dryer and sewing machine; health aids needed; food to last 3 months; beds and bedding; carpets; artwork done by, or depicting, a family member; burial plot; personal injury recoveries for yourself or a person you depend upon; wrongful death recoveries for a person you depended upon.
78-23-8 — Furnishings and appliances up to $500; books, musical instruments and animals up to $500 total; heirloom or sentimental item up to $500.
78-23-9 — Proceeds for damaged personal property.

WAGES
70C-7-103 — Minimum of 75% of earned but unpaid wages. Judge may approve more for low income debtor.

PENSIONS
49-1-609	Public employees.
78-23-5	ERISA-qualified benefits.
78-23-6	Any pension needed for support.

PUBLIC BENEFITS
35-1-80	Workers' compensation.
35-2-35	Occupational disease disability benefits.
35-4-18	Unemployment compensation.
55-15-32	AFDC; general assistance.
63-63-21	Crime victims' compensation.
78-23-5	Veterans' benefits.

TOOLS OF TRADE
39-1-47	Military property of a national guard member.
78-23-8	Motor vehicle up to $1,500; tools, books and implements of trade up to $1,500.

ALIMONY AND CHILD SUPPORT
78-23-5	Child support.
78-23-6	Alimony needed for support.

INSURANCE
31A-9-603	Fraternal benefit society benefits.
78-23-5	Disability, illness, medical or hospital benefits.
78-23-6	Life insurance proceeds if beneficiary is insured's spouse or other dependent, needed for support.
78-23-7	Life insurance policy cash surrender value up to $1,500.

MISCELLANEOUS
48-1-22 — Business partnership property.

VERMONT

Vermont Statutes Annotated, Title 27, Section 101 (27 V.S.A. §101). Look for "title" numbers.

HOMESTEAD
27-101 $30,000. Tenancies by the entirety are exempt without limit as to debts of one spouse [*In re McQueen*, 21 B.R. 736 (D. Ver. 1982)]. May include outbuildings, rents, issues and profits. Spouse of a deceased owner may claim.

PERSONAL PROPERTY
12-2740   Motor vehicles up to $2,500; clothing, goods, furnishings, appliances, books, musical instruments, animals and crops up to $2,500 total; refrigerator, stove, freezer, water heater, heating unit and sewing machines; health aids; bank deposits up to $700; wedding ring; jewelry up to $500; 500 gallons of oil, 5 tons of coal or 10 cords of firewood; 500 gallons of bottled gas; lost future earnings for yourself or a person you depended upon; personal injury and wrongful death recoveries for a person you depended upon; 1 cow, 10 sheep, 10 chickens, 3 swarms of bees, and feed to last 1 winter; 1 yoke of oxen or steers, 2 horses, 2 harnesses, 2 halters, 2 chains, 1 plow and 1 ox yoke; growing crops up to $5,000.

12-2740 $400 of any property; plus $7,000, less any amount claimed for clothing, goods, furnishings, appliances, books, musical instruments, animals, crops, motor vehicle, jewelry, tools of trade and growing crops, of any property.

WAGES
12-3170   Minimum of 75% of earned but unpaid wages (judge may approve more for low income debtor); all wages if you received welfare during the 2 months prior to filing for bankruptcy.

PENSIONS
3-476   State employees.
12-2740   Self-directed accounts, including IRAs and Keoghs, up to $10,000; other pensions.
16-1946   Teachers.
24-5066   Municipal employees.

PUBLIC BENEFITS
12-2740   Veterans' benefits, social security and crime victims' compensation needed for support.
21-681   Workers' compensation.
21-1376   Unemployment compensation.
33-2575   AFDC; general assistance; aid to blind, aged and disabled.

TOOLS OF TRADE
12-2740   Tools and books of trade up to $5,000.

ALIMONY AND CHILD SUPPORT
12-2740   Alimony and child support needed for support.

INSURANCE
8-3705   Life insurance proceeds if policy prohibits use to pay creditors.
8-3706   Life insurance proceeds if insured is not the beneficiary.
8-3708   Group life or health benefits.
8-3709   Annuity contract benefits up to $350 per month.
8-4086   Health benefits up to $200 per month.
8-4478   Fraternal benefit society benefits.
12-2740   Unmatured life insurance contract (but not credit insurance policy); disability or illness benefits needed for support; life insurance proceeds for a person you depended upon.

MISCELLANEOUS
11-1282   Business partnership property.

VIRGINIA

Code of Virginia 1950, Title 34, Section 34-4 (C.V. §34-4). Ignore "chapter" numbers; look for "title" and "section" numbers.

HOMESTEAD
34-4; 34-4.1; 34-18 $5,000 ($7,000 for veterans) plus $500 per dependent (**). Tenancies by the entirety are exempt without limitation as to debts of one spouse [*In re Costley*, 39 B.R. 585 (E.D.Va. 1984)]. Includes rents and profits. Sale proceeds are exempt up to $5,000. Must file homestead declaration prior to filing for bankruptcy. 34-6.

PERSONAL PROPERTY
34-4.1 $2,000 of any property of a disabled veteran who is a householder.
34-13   Unused homestead.
34-26   ONLY IF YOU ARE A HOUSEHOLDER YOU MAY CLAIM: Motor vehicle up to $2,000; wearing apparel up to $1,000; household furnishings up to $5,000; family portraits and heirlooms up to $5,000; burial plot; wedding and engagement rings, family Bible; animals owned as pets, provided they are not raised for sale or profit; and medically prescribed health aids.
34-13   IN LIEU OF HOMESTEAD: $5,000 of any personal property.

WAGES
34-29   Minimum of 75% of earned but unpaid wages or pension payments. Judge may approve more for low income debtor.

PENSIONS
51-111.15   State employees.
51-127.7   County employees.
51-180   Judges.

PUBLIC BENEFITS
19.2-368.12   Crime victims' compensation, unless seeking to discharge debt for treatment of crime-related injury.
60.2-600   Unemployment compensation.
63.1-88   AFDC; general relief; aid to blind, aged and disabled.
65.1-82   Workers' compensation.

TOOLS OF TRADE
IF YOU ARE A HOUSEHOLDER YOU MAY CLAIM:
34-26   Tools, books, instruments, implements, equipment, and machines, including motor vehicles, vessels, and aircraft, necessary for use in occupation or trade up to $10,000.
34-27   For farmer: tractor, wagon, cart, horses, pair of mules with gear up to $3,000; fertilizer, 2 plows, harvest cradle, 2 iron wedges, pitchfork and rake, up to $1,000.
IF NOT A HOUSEHOLDER YOU MAY CLAIM:
44-96   Arms, uniforms and equipment of a military member.

INSURANCE
38.2-3122   Life insurance proceeds, dividends, interest, loan, cash or surrender value if beneficiary is not the insured.
38.2-3123   If you are a householder, life insurance cash values up to $10,000.
38.2-3339   Group life insurance policy or proceeds.
38.2-3549   Accident, sickness or industrial sick benefits.
38.2-3811   Cooperative life insurance benefits.
38.2-4021   Burial society benefits.
38.2-4118   Fraternal benefit society benefits.
51-111.67:8   Group life or accident insurance for government officials.

MISCELLANEOUS
50-25   Business partnership property.

WASHINGTON

West's Revised Code of Washington Annotated, Title 6, Chapter 6.13, Section 6.13.010 (R.C.W.A. §6.13.010).

HOMESTEAD

6.13.010;
6.13.030   Real property or mobile home up to $30,000. If property is unimproved or unoccupied at time of filing bankruptcy, you must file a homestead declaration.

PERSONAL PROPERTY

6.15.010   2 motor vehicles up to $2,500 total; clothing, but furs, jewelry & ornaments limited to $1,000 total; household goods, furniture, appliances, food, fuel, home and yard equipment up to $2,700 total; books up to $1,000; pictures and keepsakes; private libraries up to $1,500; $1,000 of any other personal property, but not more than $100 of it in cash, bank deposits, stocks, bonds or other securities.

68.20.120   Burial plots if sold by a non-profit cemetery association.

WAGES

6.27.150   Minimum of 75% of earned but unpaid wages. Judge may approve more for low income debtor.

PENSIONS

6.15.020   Federal employees; ERISA-qualified benefits, including IRAs.
41.24.240   Volunteer firefighters.
41.28.200   City employees.
41.40.380   Public employees.
43.43.310   State patrol officers.

PUBLIC BENEFITS

7.68.070;
51.32.040   Crime victims' compensation.
50.40.020   Unemployment compensation.
51.32.040   Industrial insurance (workers' compensation).
74.04.280   General assistance.
74.08.210   Old-age assistance.
74.13.070   AFDC (child welfare).

TOOLS OF TRADE

6.15.010   Tools and materials used in another person's trade up to $5,000; library, office furniture, equipment and supplies of a physician, surgeon, attorney, clergyman or other professional up to $5,000; farm trucks, tools, equipment, supplies, stock and seed of a farmer up to $5,000.

INSURANCE

6.15.030   Fire insurance proceeds for destroyed exempt property.
46.18.400   Disability benefits, proceeds, dividends, interest, loan, cash or surrender value.
46.18.410   Life insurance proceeds, dividends, interest, loan, cash or surrender value if the insured is not the beneficiary.
46.18.420   Group life insurance policy or proceeds.
46.18.430   Annuity contract proceeds up to $250 per month.
48.36A.180   Fraternal benefit society benefits.

MISCELLANEOUS

25.04.250   Business partnership property.

WEST VIRGINIA

West Virginia Code, Chapter 38, Article 10, Section 38-10-4 (.W.V.C. §38-10-4). Ignore volume numbers; look for "chapter" numbers.

HOMESTEAD

38-10-4   Real or personal property used as a residence up to $7,500. Unused portion may be applied to any other property.

PERSONAL PROPERTY

38-10-4   Motor vehicle up to $1,200; clothing, household goods, furnishings, appliances, books, musical instruments, animals and crops up to $200 per item, and $1,000 total; jewelry up to $500; health aids; lost earnings payments needed for support; personal injury recoveries, not including pain and suffering, up to $7,500; wrongful death recoveries for a person you depended upon needed for support; $400 of any property.
38-10-4 $7,900, less amount of homestead claimed, of any property.
38-10-4   IN LIEU OF HOMESTEAD: Burial plot up to $7,500.

WAGES

38-5A-3   80% of earned but unpaid wages. Judge may approve more for low income debtor.

PENSIONS

5-10-46   Public employees.
18-7A-30   Teachers.
38-10-4   ERISA-qualified benefits needed for support.

PUBLIC BENEFITS

9-5-1   AFDC; general assistance; aid to blind, aged and disabled.
14-2A-24;
38-10-4   Crime victims' compensation.
23-4-18   Workers' compensation.
38-10-4   Unemployment compensation; veterans' benefits; social security.

TOOLS OF TRADE

38-4-10   Tools, books and implements of trade up to $750.

ALIMONY AND CHILD SUPPORT

38-10-4   Alimony and child support needed for support.

INSURANCE

33-6-27   Life insurance proceeds unless you are policy owner and beneficiary.
33-6-28   Group life insurance policy and proceeds.
33-23-21   Fraternal benefit society benefits.
38-10-4   Unmatured life insurance contract (except for credit life insurance contract); health or disability benefits; life insurance dividends, interest, loan, cash or surrender value for person you depended upon up to $4,000.
48-3-23   Life insurance proceeds or cash value if the beneficiary is a married woman.

MISCELLANEOUS

47-8A-25   Business partnership property.

WISCONSIN

West's Wisconsin Statutes Annotated, Section 815.20 (W.S.A. §815.20). Look for "section" numbers.

HOMESTEAD
815.20 $40,000. Sale proceed exempt for 2 years after sale provided you intend to acquire another home. Must occupy or intend to occupy at time of filing for bankruptcy.

PERSONAL PROPERTY
815.18   Automobile up to $1,200; household goods and furnishings; wearing apparel, keepsakes, jewelry and other articles of adornment, appliances, books, musical instruments, firearms, sporting goods, animals or other items for family use up to $5,000 total; burial plot, monument, tombstone, etc.; and bank deposits up to $1,000; wrongful death proceeds and lost earnings compensation for debtor or person on whom debtor was dependent, to extent necessary to support debtor or family; and personal injury payments for debtor or person upon whom debtor depended, up to $25,000.

WAGES
815.18   75% of net wages, but limited to amount necessary for support, and no less that 30 times the state or federal minimum wage, whichever is greater.

PENSIONS
40.08   Public employees.
66.81   Certain municipal employees in a city of more 150,000 or more in population.
815.18   Police officers, firefighters, military pensions, and public and private retirement benefits (including plans for self-employed persons).

PUBLIC BENEFITS
45.35   Veterans' benefits.
49.41   AFDC; other social service payments.
102.27   Workers' compensation.
108.13   Unemployment compensation.
949.07   Crime victims' compensation.

TOOLS OF TRADE
815.18   Equipment, inventory, farm products, and professional books used in the business of the debtor or a dependent, up to $7,500.

ALIMONY AND CHILD SUPPORT
815.18   Alimony & child support needed for support.

INSURANCE
614.96   Fraternal benefit society benefits.
632.42   Life insurance proceeds if policy prohibits use to pay creditors.
815.18   Unmatured life insurance contracts, and up to $4,000 in value in accrued dividends, interest or loan value (except for credit life contracts) if owned by debtor and insuring debtor, dependent, or person debtor is dependent upon; federal disability benefits; life insurance proceeds if debtor was dependent upon insured, to extent necessary to support debtor or family; and fire insurance proceeds received during prior 2 years for destroyed exempt property.

MISCELLANEOUS
178.21   Business partnership property.

WYOMING

Wyoming Statutes Annotated, Title 1, Chapter 20, Section 1-20-101 (.W.S.A. §1-20-101). Ignore volume numbers; look for "title" numbers.

HOMESTEAD
1-20-101;
1-20-104   Real property up to $10,000; house trailer up to $6,000. Tenancies by the entirety are exempt without limit as to debts of one spouse [In re Anselmi, 52 B.R. 479 (D. Wyo. 1985)]. Spouse or child of deceased owner may claim; Must occupy at time of filing for bankruptcy. (**)

PERSONAL PROPERTY
1-20-105   Clothing and wedding rings up to $1,000 total.
1-20-106   Household articles, furniture, bedding and food up to $2,000 per person in the home; school books, pictures and bible; motor vehicle up to $2,000.
1-20-106;
35-8-104   Burial plot.
26-32-102   Pre-paid funeral contracts.

WAGES
1-15-511   Minimum of 75% of earned but unpaid wages. Judge may approved more for low income debtor.
17-16-308   Wages of inmates on work release.
19-2-501   Earnings of national guard members.

PENSIONS
1-20-110   Private or public retirement funds or accounts.
9-3-426   Public employees.
9-3-620   Highway officers, criminal investigators, and game and fish wardens.
15-5-209   Payments being received by police officers and firefighters.

PUBLIC BENEFITS
1-40-113   Crime victims' compensation.
27-3-319   Unemployment compensation.
27-14-702   Workers' compensation.
42-2-113   AFDC; general assistance.

TOOLS OF TRADE
1-20-106   Motor vehicle, tools, implements, team and stock in trade to $2,000; library and implements of a professional up to $2,000.

INSURANCE
26-15-129   Life insurance proceeds if insured is not the beneficiary.
26-15-130   Disability benefits if policy prohibits use to pay creditors.
26-15-131   Group life or disability policy or proceeds.
26-15-132   Annuity contract proceeds up to $350 per month.
26-15-133   Life insurance proceeds if policy prohibits use to pay creditors.
26-29-116   Fraternal benefit society benefits.

MISCELLANEOUS
12-4-604   Liquor licenses and malt beverage permits.
17-13-502   Business partnership property.

The following publications and individuals can supply further information and services in asset protection. References for specific issues, such as forming a foundation or moving abroad are listed in the chapters discussing those subjects. The books can all be ordered through Sphinx Publishing's book store. The attorneys are those who have informed the author that are ready and able to provide asset protection services.

Newsletter:

The Jacobs' Report on Asset Protection Strategies
A monthly newsletter containing ongoing information and news on asset protection published by Vern Jacobs, C.P.A. $145 per year.
4500 W. 72nd Terrace
Prairie Village, KS 66208

Seminars for attorneys:

Asset Protection Planning
Professional Educational Systems, Inc.
P. O. Box 1208
Eau Claire, WI 54702

Books:

Asset Protection: Legal Planning and Strategies
Peter Spero
Warren Gorham & Lamont
950 pages, $115

Asset Protection Strategies: Tax and Legal Aspects
Lewis D. Solomon and Lewis J. Saret
John Wiley & Sons, Inc.
439 pages, $125

Freedom, Asset Protection and You
William Comer
Research Press, Inc.
4500 W. 72nd Terr., Box 8137
Prairie Village, KS 66208
$70 includes book, cassette tape and shipping

The SuperTrust
Henry Reardon
Nicholas Direct, Inc.
P.O. Box 877
Indian Rocks Beach, FL 34635
Tel: (813) 596-4966
Fax: (813) 596-6900

U.S. Attorneys:

Offshore Trusts:
Engel & Rudman, P.C.
5445 DTC Parkway #1025
Englewood, CO 80111
Telephone: (303) 741-1111
Fax: (303) 694-4028

Limited Partnerships & Valuations:
Larry W. Gibbs, Esq.
Croman Gibbs Schwartzman
5717 Northwest Parkway
San Antonio, TX 78249
Tel: (210) 690-8858
Fax: (210) 690-0024

U. S. Tax consultant:

Vern Jacobs, C.P.A.
4500 W. 72nd Terrace
Prairie Village, KS 66208
Tel: (913) 362-9667
Fax: (913) 362-4922

Bahamian attorneys:

Emanuel M. Alexiou, Esq.
Alexiou, Knowles & Co.
P. O. Box N 4805
Nassau, Bahamas
Tel: (809) 323-5600
Fax: (809)328-8395

Samuel E. Campbell, Esq.
Samuel Campbell & Co.
P. O. Box N 1649
Nassau, Bahamas
Tel: (809) 322-7511
Fax: (809) 325-0724

Theresa Haven-Edwards, Esq.
Graham, Thompson & Co.
P. O. Box N 272
Nassau, Bahamas
Tel: (809) 322-4130
Fax: (809)323-7276

Lynn P. Holowesko, Esq.
Higgs & Kelly
P. O. Box N 1113
Nassau, Bahamas
Tel: (809) 322-7511
Fax: (809) 325-0724

Mike A. Klonaris, Esq.
Callenders & Co.
P. O. Box N7117
Nassau, Bahamas
Tel: (809) 322-2511
Fax: (809) 326-7666

Peter D. Maynard, Esq.
Peter D. Maynard & Company
P. O. Box N 1000
Nassau, Bahamas
Tel: (809) 325-5335
Fax: (809)325-5411

Lennox M. Paton, Esq.
P. O. Box N 4875
Nassau, Bahamas
Tel: (809) 328-0563
Fax: (809)328-0566

L. Marvin B. Pinder, Esq.
P. O. Box N 345
Nassau, Bahamas
Tel: (809) 326-2730
Fax: (809) 328-4707

Harry B. Sands, Esq.
Harry B. Sands & Company
P. O. Box N 624
Nassau, Bahamas
Tel: (809) 326-5300
Fax: (809) 322-5554

Alfred M. Sears, Esq.
Sears & Co.
P. O. Box N 3645
Nassau, Bahamas
Tel: (809) 326-3481
Fax: (809)326-3483

E. P. Tooth, Esq.
E. P. Tooth & Associates
P. O. Box AB 20088
Abaco, Bahamas
Tel: (809) 367-3368
Fax: (809) 367-3923

Cayman Islands attorney:
W. S. Walker, Esq.
W. S. Walker & Company
P. O. Box 265
George Town, Grand Cayman
Cayman Islands
Tel: (809) 949-0100
Fax: (809) 949-7886

Gibraltar attorney:
Peter C. Montegriffo, Esq.
J. A. Hassan & Partners
P. O. Box 199
Gibraltar
Tel: 79000
Fax: 71966

Banks and Trust Companies:

Bahamas International Trust Co., Ltd.
P. O. Box N 7768
Nassau, Bahamas
Tel: (809) 322-1161
Fax: (809) 326-5020

Leu Trust and Banking
Contact: Lester M. Turnquest
P. O. Box N 3926
Nassau, Bahamas
Tel: (809)326-5054
Fax: (809) 323-8828

Standard Chartered Bank (Isle of Man) Ltd.
64 Athol Street
Douglas, Isle of Man
Tel: 0624 623916
Fax: 0624 623970

Uebersee Bank AG
Limmatquai 2
CH-8024 Zürich Switzerland
Tel: 01 267 55 55
Fax: 01 252 20 02

Appendix 5
Forms

As explained in this manual, there are several simple things you can do to protect yourself from lawsuits. Some of these require using certain legal language or forms in your affairs.

This appendix contains some of the most useful forms you can use in protecting yourself from claims. The forms and their uses are as follows:

Form 1: Addendum to Contract Attach this addendum to every contract you sign. It says that any dispute between the parties will be handled through arbitration, rather than in court. It will save you much time and a fortune in legal fees, unless, of course your spouse or child is a lawyer. In such a case you would probably rather go to court.

Form 2: Employment Contract 1 Use this agreement whenever you or a company you own hires an employee. It is meant to protect you from charges of discrimination sexual harassment, labor violations and other such charges.

Form 3: Employment Contract 2 This is a similar employment agreement but leaves out the trade secret and noncompete clauses. Employment contract 1 is better, and you should use it whenever possible, but if you do not want to be as harsh but still want to have some protections, use this contract.

Form 4: IRS Form SS-8 This form is used to determine if a person you treat as an independent contractor actually qualifies as such.

Forms 5 & 6: Tenancy by the Entireties Assignments 1 and 2 In states where tenancy by the entireties property is exempt from creditors, these forms will make property you own jointly with your spouse safe from claims by creditors against one of you. Use Part 1 to convey property owned by spouses separately and together to a third person such as an adult child or parent. Immediately thereafter have that person use Part 2 to convey it back to the spouses in an estate by the entireties.

Form 7: State Exemptions Worksheet Use this form to analyze your state's exemptions and whether what you own is exempt.

Form 8: IRS Form 720 This form is used when purchasing a Swiss annuity. The tax is 1% of the amount invested and is reported on line 30.

NOTE: *These forms are ready to photocopy and use. However, for a extra level of protection (except on IRS forms) you can retype them on your computer or typewriter. If they were created by you they look less like a fraud on creditors than if they came from an asset protection book!*

Addendum to Contract

This Addendum is made to that contract dated _____, be-
tween_____
and _____ as
follows:

ARBITRATION. In the event a dispute of any nature arises between the
parties to the contract, the parties hereto agree to submit the dispute to
binding arbitration under the rules of the American Arbitration Association.

An award rendered by the arbitrator(s) shall be final and binding
upon the parties and judgment on such award may be entered by either party
in the highest court having jurisdiction.

Each party hereto specifically waives his or her right to bring the
dispute before a court of law and stipulates that this agreement shall be
a complete defense to any action instituted in any local, state or federal
court or before any administrative tribunal.

_____   _____

_____   _____

_____   _____

Employment Contract

Employer, _____ agrees to employ _____ as employee and employee agrees to work for employer under the following terms and conditions:

Term. Either party is free to terminate this relationship at any time. Employee may resign at any time and for any reason and employer may terminate employee at any time and for any reason.

Duties. Employee is employed in the position of _____ to serve and perform such duties at such times and places and in such manner as employer may from time to time direct. Employee agrees to perform such duties to the best of his or her ability, to devote his or her ability, to devote full and undivided time during working hours to the employer's business, to remit promptly to employer all money or property belonging to employer, and to not engage in any activity in competition with employer's business.

Compensation. Employee shall initially be paid the sum of _____ per _____ as full payment for services performed for employer. This sum may be raised or lowered by agreement of the parties based upon the performance of the employee.

Probation. It is understood between the parties that the first _____ days of employment shall be probationary only and that if employee's services are not satisfactory to employer employment shall be terminated at the end of this probationary period.

Law. It is employer's intention to comply with all federal, state and local laws which apply to the business, including labor, equal opportunity, privacy and sexual harassment. Employee shall promptly report any violations encountered in the business. Employee shall at all times comply with any and all federal, state and local laws.

Trade Secrets. Employee understands that as part of the employment he or she will have access to confidential information of the employer and may participate in developing such information as part of the employment duties. Employee acknowledges that such information contains the valuable trade secrets of the employer. Employee agrees to at no time disclose them to anyone other than authorized employees, and to not remove from the premises any equipment or information without the consent of employer. Trade secrets of employer include but are not limited to customer lists, terms of payment, suppliers, methods, processes, or marketing plans.

Contracts. Employee shall not have the power to make any contracts or commitments on behalf of employer without express written consent of employer.

Noncompete. Employee agrees not to compete with employer's business for a term of _____ years in a radius of _____ miles from employer's business.

Waiver. In the event one party fails to insist upon performance of a part this agreement, such failure shall not be construed as waiving those terms and this entire agreement shall remain in full force

Arbitration. In the event a dispute of any nature arises between the parties to the contract, the parties hereto agree to submit the dispute to binding arbitration under the rules of the American Arbitration Association. An award rendered by the arbitrator(s) shall be final and binding upon the parties and judgment on such award may be entered by either party in the highest court having jurisdiction. Each party hereto specifically waives his or her right to bring the dispute before a court of law and stipulates that this agreement shall be a complete defense to any action instituted in any local, state or federal court or before any administrative tribunal.

Entire agreement. The parties agree that this document embodies the entire agreement between the parties and that no other oral or written representations or warranties have been made.

Reasonableness. Employee has read this contract and agrees that all clauses herein are reasonable to protect employer's business.

Severability. In the event any part of this agreement is found to be illegal, unenforceable, or against public policy, the parties agree that such part shall be modified or deleted so as to make this agreement enforceable.

In witness whereof, the parties have executed this agreement this _____ day of _____.

Employer: Employee:

By:_____   _____

201

Employment Contract

Employer, _____, agrees to employ _____ as employee, and employee agrees to work for employer under the following terms and conditions:

Term. Either party is free to terminate this relationship at any time. Employee may resign at any time and for any reason and employer may terminate employee at any time and for any reason.

Duties. Employee is employed in the position of _____ to serve and perform such duties at such times and places and in such manner as employer may from time to time direct. Employee agrees to perform such duties to the best of his or her ability, to devote his or her ability, to devote full and undivided time during working hours to the employer's business, to remit promptly to employer all money or property belonging to employer, and to not engage in any activity in competition with employer's business.

Compensation. Employee shall initially be paid the sum of _____ per _____ as full payment for services performed for employer. This sum may be raised or lowered by agreement of the parties based upon the performance of the employee.

Probation. It is understood between the parties that the first _____ days of employment shall be probationary only and that if employee's services are not satisfactory to employer employment shall be terminated at the end of this probationary period.

Law. It is employer's intention to comply with all federal, state and local laws which apply to the business, including labor, equal opportunity, privacy and sexual harassment. Employee shall promptly report any violations encountered in the business. Employee shall at all times comply with any and all federal, state and local laws.

Waiver. In the event one party fails to insist upon performance of a part this agreement, such failure shall not be construed as waiving those terms and this entire agreement shall remain in full force

Arbitration. In the event a dispute of any nature arises between the parties to the contract, the parties hereto agree to submit the dispute to binding arbitration under the rules of the American Arbitration Association. An award rendered by the arbitrator(s) shall be final and binding upon the parties and judgment on such award may be entered by either party in the highest court having jurisdiction. Each party hereto specifically waives his or her right to bring the dispute before a court of law and stipulates that this agreement shall be a complete defense to any action instituted in any local, state or federal court or before any administrative tribunal.

Entire agreement. The parties agree that this document embodies the entire agreement between the parties and that no other oral or written representations or warranties have been made.

Severability. In the event any part of this agreement is found to be illegal, unenforceable, or against public policy, the parties agree that such part shall be modified or deleted so as to make this agreement enforceable.

In witness whereof, the parties have executed this agreement this _____ day of _____.

Employer: Employee:

By:_____   _____

Form SS-8

(Rev. July 1993)

Department of the Treasury
Internal Revenue Service

Determination of Employee Work Status
for Purposes of Federal Employment Taxes
and Income Tax Withholding

OMB No. 1545-0004
Expires 7-31-96

Paperwork Reduction Act Notice

We ask for the information on this form to carry out the Internal Revenue laws of the United States. You are required to give us this information. We need it to ensure that you are complying with these laws and to allow us to figure and collect the right amount of tax.

The time needed to complete and file this form will vary depending on individual circumstances. The estimated average time is: **recordkeeping, 34 hr., 55 min., learning about the law or the form, 6 min.** and **preparing and sending the form to IRS, 40 min.** If you have comments concerning the accuracy of these time estimates or suggestions for making this form more simple, we would be happy to hear from you. You can write to both the **Internal Revenue Service,** Attention: Reports Clearance Officer, T:FP, Washington, DC 20224; and the **Office of Management and Budget,** Paperwork Reduction Project (1545-0004), Washington, DC 20503. **DO NOT** send the tax form to either of these offices. Instead, see **General Information** for where to file.

Purpose

Employers and workers file Form SS-8 to get a determination as to whether a worker is an employee for purposes of Federal employment taxes and income tax withholding.

General Information

This form should be completed carefully. If the firm is completing the form, it should be completed for **ONE** individual who is representative of the class of workers whose status is in question. If a written determination is desired for more than one class of workers, a separate Form SS-8 should be completed for one worker from each class whose status is typical of that class. A written determination for any worker will apply to other workers of the same class if the facts are not materially different from those of the worker whose status was ruled upon.

Please return Form SS-8 to the Internal Revenue Service office that provided the form. If the Internal Revenue Service did not ask you to complete this form but you wish a determination on whether a worker is an employee, file Form SS-8 with your District Director.

Caution: Form SS-8 is not a claim for refund of social security and Medicare taxes or Federal income tax withholding. Also, a determination that an individual is an employee does not necessarily reduce any current or prior tax liability. A worker must file his or her income tax return even if a determination has not been made by the due date of the return.

Name of firm (or person) for whom the worker performed services	Name of worker
Address of firm (include street address, apt. or suite no., city, state, and ZIP code)	Address of worker (include street address, apt. or suite no., city, state, and ZIP code)

Trade name	Telephone number (include area code) ( )	Worker's social security number — —

Telephone number (include area code) ( )	Firm's taxpayer identification number —	

Check type of firm for which the work relationship is in question:

☐ Individual ☐ Partnership ☐ Corporation ☐ Other (specify) ▶

Important Information Needed to Process Your Request

This form is being completed by: ☐ Firm ☐ Worker

If this form is being completed by the worker, the IRS **must** have your permission to disclose your name to the firm.

Do you object to disclosing your name and the information on this form to the firm? . . . . ☐ Yes ☐ No

If you answer "Yes," the IRS cannot act on your request. **DO NOT complete the rest of this form unless the IRS asks for it.**

Under section 6110 of the Internal Revenue Code, the information on this form and related file documents will be open to the public if any ruling or determination is made. However, names, addresses, and taxpayer identification numbers must be removed before the information can be made public.

Is there any other information you want removed? . . . . ☐ Yes ☐ No

If you check "Yes," we cannot process your request unless you submit a copy of this form and copies of all supporting documents showing, in brackets, the information you want removed. Attach a separate statement telling which specific exemption of section 6110(c) applies to each bracketed part.

This form is designed to cover many work activities, so some of the questions may not apply to you. You must answer ALL items or mark them "Unknown" or "Does not apply." If you need more space, attach another sheet.

Total number of workers in this class. (Attach names and addresses. If more than 10 workers, attach only 10.) ▶ _____

This information is about services performed by the worker from _____ to _____
(month, day, year)   (month, day, year)

Is the worker still performing services for the firm? . . . . ☐ Yes ☐ No

If "No," what was the date of termination? ▶ _____
(month, day, year)

1a Describe the firm's business ....

b Describe the work done by the worker ....

....

2a If the work is done under a written agreement between the firm and the worker, attach a copy.

b If the agreement is not in writing, describe the terms and conditions of the work arrangement ....

....

....

c If the actual working arrangement differs in any way from the agreement, explain the differences and why they occur ....

....

....

3a Is the worker given training by the firm? . . . . ☐ Yes ☐ No

If "Yes": What kind? ....

How often? ....

b Is the worker given instructions in the way the work is to be done (exclusive of actual training in 3a)? . ☐ Yes ☐ No

If "Yes," give specific examples. ....

c Attach samples of any written instructions or procedures.

d Does the firm have the right to change the methods used by the worker or direct that person on how to

do the work? . . . . ☐ Yes ☐ No

Explain your answer ....

....

e Does the operation of the firm's business require that the worker be supervised or controlled in the

performance of the service? . . . . ☐ Yes ☐ No

Explain your answer ....

....

4a The firm engages the worker:

☐ To perform and complete a particular job only

☐ To work at a job for an indefinite period of time

☐ Other (explain) ....

b Is the worker required to follow a routine or a schedule established by the firm? . . . . ☐ Yes ☐ No

If "Yes," what is the routine or schedule? ....

....

....

c Does the worker report to the firm or its representative?. . . . . ☐ Yes ☐ No

If "Yes": How often? ....

For what purpose? ....

In what manner (in person, in writing, by telephone, etc.)? ....

Attach copies of report forms used in reporting to the firm.

d Does the worker furnish a time record to the firm? . . . . ☐ Yes ☐ No

If "Yes," attach copies of time records.

5a State the kind and value of tools, equipment, supplies, and materials furnished by:

The firm ....

....

The worker ....

....

b What expenses are incurred by the worker in the performance of services for the firm? ....

....

c Does the firm reimburse the worker for any expenses? . . . . ☐ Yes ☐ No

If "Yes," specify the reimbursed expenses ....

....

6a Will the worker perform the services personally? . . . . ☐ Yes ☐ No

b Does the worker have helpers? . . . . ☐ Yes ☐ No

If "Yes": Who hires the helpers?   ☐ Firm ☐ Worker

If hired by the worker, is the firm's approval necessary? . . . . ☐ Yes ☐ No

Who pays the helpers?   ☐ Firm ☐ Worker

Are social security and Medicare taxes and Federal income tax withheld from the helpers' wages? . . ☐ Yes ☐ No

If "Yes": Who reports and pays these taxes? ☐ Firm ☐ Worker

Who reports the helpers' incomes to the Internal Revenue Service? ☐ Firm ☐ Worker

If the worker pays the helpers, does the firm repay the worker? . . . . ☐ Yes ☐ No

What services do the helpers perform?

7 At what location are the services performed? ☐ Firm's ☐ Worker's ☐ Other (specify) ....

8a Type of pay worker receives:

    ☐ Salary ☐ Commission ☐ Hourly wage ☐ Piecework ☐ Lump sum ☐ Other (specify) ....

  b Does the firm guarantee a minimum amount of pay to the worker? . . . . ☐ **Yes** ☐ **No**

  c Does the firm allow the worker a drawing account or advances against pay? . . . . ☐ **Yes** ☐ **No**

    If "Yes": Is the worker paid such advances on a regular basis? . . . . ☐ **Yes** ☐ **No**

  d How does the worker repay such advances? ....

9a Is the worker eligible for a pension, bonus, paid vacations, sick pay, etc.? . . . . ☐ **Yes** ☐ **No**

    If "Yes," specify ....

  b Does the firm carry workmen's compensation insurance on the worker? . . . . ☐ **Yes** ☐ **No**

  c Does the firm deduct social security and Medicare taxes from amounts paid the worker? . . . . . ☐ **Yes** ☐ **No**

  d Does the firm deduct Federal income taxes from amounts paid the worker? . . . . ☐ **Yes** ☐ **No**

  e How does the firm report the worker's income to the Internal Revenue Service?

    ☐ Form W-2 ☐ Form 1099-MISC ☐ Does not report ☐ Other (specify) ....

    Attach a copy.

  f Does the firm bond the worker? . . . . ☐ **Yes** ☐ **No**

10a Approximately how many hours a day does the worker perform services for the firm? ....

    Does the firm set hours of work for the worker? . . . . ☐ **Yes** ☐ **No**

    If "Yes," what are the worker's set hours? _____ am/pm to _____ am/pm (Circle whether am or pm)

  b Does the worker perform similar services for others? . . . . ☐ **Yes** ☐ **No** ☐ **Unknown**

    If "Yes": Are these services performed on a daily basis for other firms? . . . . . . ☐ **Yes** ☐ **No** ☐ **Unknown**

    Percentage of time spent in performing these services for:

    This firm .... % Other firms .... % ☐ **Unknown**

    Does the firm have priority on the worker's time? . . . . ☐ **Yes** ☐ **No**

    If "No," explain ....

  c Is the worker prohibited from competing with the firm either while performing services or during any later

    period? . . . . ☐ **Yes** ☐ **No**

11a Can the firm discharge the worker at any time without incurring a liability? . . . . ☐ **Yes** ☐ **No**

    If "No," explain ....

  b Can the worker terminate the services at any time without incurring a liability? . . . . ☐ **Yes** ☐ **No**

    If "No," explain ....

12a Does the worker perform services for the firm under:

    ☐ The firm's business name ☐ The worker's own business name ☐ Other (specify) ....

  b Does the worker advertise or maintain a business listing in the telephone directory, a trade

    journal, etc.? . . . . ☐ **Yes** ☐ **No** ☐ **Unknown**

    If "Yes," specify ....

  c Does the worker represent himself or herself to the public as being in business to perform

    the same or similar services? . . . . ☐ **Yes** ☐ **No** ☐ **Unknown**

    If "Yes," how? ....

  d Does the worker have his or her own shop or office? . . . . ☐ **Yes** ☐ **No** ☐ **Unknown**

    If "Yes," where? ....

  e Does the firm represent the worker as an employee of the firm to its customers? . . . . ☐ **Yes** ☐ **No**

    If "No," how is the worker represented? ....

  f How did the firm learn of the worker's services? ....

13 Is a license necessary for the work? . . . . ☐ **Yes** ☐ **No** ☐ **Unknown**

    If "Yes," what kind of license is required? ....

    By whom is it issued? ....

    By whom is the license fee paid? ....

14 Does the worker have a financial investment in a business related to the services performed? ☐ **Yes** ☐ **No** ☐ **Unknown**

    If "Yes," specify and give amounts of the investment ....

15 Can the worker incur a loss in the performance of the service for the firm? . . . . ☐ **Yes** ☐ **No**

    If "Yes," how? ....

16a Has any other government agency ruled on the status of the firm's workers? . . . . ☐ **Yes** ☐ **No**

    If "Yes," attach a copy of the ruling.

  b Is the same issue being considered by any IRS office in connection with the audit of the worker's tax

    return or the firm's tax return, or has it recently been considered? . . . . ☐ **Yes** ☐ **No**

    If "Yes," for which year(s)?

17 Does the worker assemble or process a product at home or away from the firm's place of business?   . ☐ Yes   ☐ No
If "Yes":

   Who furnishes materials or goods used by the worker? ☐ Firm   ☐ Worker
   Is the worker furnished a pattern or given instructions to follow in making the product? . . . . . ☐ Yes   ☐ No
   Is the worker required to return the finished product to the firm or to someone designated by the firm? . ☐ Yes   ☐ No

---

Answer items 18a through n only if the worker is a salesperson or provides a service directly to customers.

18a Are leads to prospective customers furnished by the firm? . . . . ☐ Yes   ☐ No   ☐ Does not apply
   b Is the worker required to pursue or report on leads? . . . . ☐ Yes   ☐ No   ☐ Does not apply
   c Is the worker required to adhere to prices, terms, and conditions of sale established by the firm? . . ☐ Yes   ☐ No
   d Are orders submitted to and subject to approval by the firm? . . . . ☐ Yes   ☐ No
   e Is the worker expected to attend sales meetings? . . . . ☐ Yes   ☐ No
   If "Yes": Is the worker subject to any kind of penalty for failing to attend? . . . . ☐ Yes   ☐ No
   f Does the firm assign a specific territory to the worker? . . . . ☐ Yes   ☐ No   ☐ Does not apply
   g Who does the customer pay? ☐ Firm   ☐ Worker
   If worker, does the worker remit the total amount to the firm? . . . . ☐ Yes   ☐ No
   h Does the worker sell a consumer product in a home or establishment other than a permanent retail
   establishment? . . . . ☐ Yes   ☐ No
   i List the products and/or services distributed by the worker, such as meat, vegetables, fruit, bakery products, beverages (other than milk), or laundry or dry cleaning services. If more than one type of product and/or service is distributed, specify the principal one. ....
   j Did the firm or another person assign the route or territory and a list of customers to the worker? . . ☐ Yes   ☐ No
   If "Yes," enter the name and job title of the person who made the assignment. ....

   ....
   k Did the worker pay the firm or person for the privilege of serving customers on the route or in the territory? ☐ Yes   ☐ No
   If "Yes," how much did the worker pay (not including any amount paid for a truck or racks, etc.)? $ ....
   What factors were considered in determining the value of the route or territory? ....
   l How are new customers obtained by the worker? Explain fully, showing whether the new customers called the firm for service, were solicited by the worker, or both. ....
   m Does the worker sell life insurance? . . . . ☐ Yes   ☐ No
   If "Yes":
   Is the selling of life insurance or annuity contracts for the firm the worker's entire business activity? . . ☐ Yes   ☐ No
   If "No," list the other business activities and the amount of time spent on them ....
   Does the worker sell other types of insurance for the firm? . . . . ☐ Yes   ☐ No
   If "Yes," state the percentage of the worker's total working time spent in selling other types of insurance .... %
   At the time the contract was entered into between the firm and the worker, was it their intention that the worker sell life insurance for the firm: ☐ on a full-time basis ☐ on a part-time basis
   State the manner in which the intention was expressed. ....
   n Is the worker a traveling or city salesperson? . . . . ☐ Yes   ☐ No
   If "Yes": From whom does worker principally solicit orders for the firm? ....

   If the worker solicits orders from wholesalers, retailers, contractors, or operators of hotels, restaurants, or other similar establishments, specify the percentage of the worker's time spent in this solicitation. .... %
   Is the merchandise purchased by the customers for resale or for use in their business operations? If used by the customers in their business operations, describe the merchandise and state whether it is equipment installed on their premises or a consumable supply. ....

   ....
19 Attach a detailed explanation of any other reason why you believe the worker is an independent contractor or is an employee of the firm.

Under penalties of perjury, I declare that I have examined this request, including accompanying documents, and to the best of my knowledge and belief, the facts presented are true, correct, and complete.

Signature ▶   Title ▶   Date ▶

If this form is used by the firm in requesting a written determination, the form must be signed by an officer or member of the firm.
If this form is used by the worker in requesting a written determination, the form must be signed by the worker. If the worker wants a written determination about services performed for two or more firms, a separate form must be completed and signed for each firm.
Additional copies of this form may be obtained from any Internal Revenue Service office or by calling 1-800-TAX-FORM (1-800-829-3676).

*U.S. Government Printing Office: 1993 — 343-034/80171

206

Assignment

Date:_____

    The undersigned, _____ and _____ in consideration of the sum of one dollar, receipt of which is acknowledged, and other good and valuable consideration, hereby assign, transfer and deliver to _____ the following goods:

Assignors: Assignee:

_____   _____

_____

Assignment
Tenancy by the Entireties

Date:_____

    The undersigned, _____ in consideration of the sum of one dollar, receipt of which is acknowledged, and other good and valuable consideration, hereby assigns, transfers and delivers to _____ and _____, husband and wife, in an estate by the entireties, the following goods:

Assignor: Assignees:

_____   _____

                                             _____

State Exemptions Worksheet

Homestead: $_____
Requirements & Limitations: _____
_____
_____

Tenancy by the entireties? _____
Applies to personal property? _____

Pensions: $ _____
Restrictions: _____
_____

Annuities: $ _____
Restrictions: _____
_____

Insurance: $ _____
Restrictions: _____
_____

Wages: $ _____
Restrictions: _____
_____

Tools of Trade: $ _____
Restrictions: _____
_____

Other: $ _____
Restrictions: _____
_____
_____
_____
_____

Form **720**	**Quarterly Federal Excise Tax Return**	Form 8 - IRS Form 720
(Rev. July 1994)	Use To Report Excise Taxes for 1994.	OMB No. 1545-0023
Department of the Treasury Internal Revenue Service	▶ For Paperwork Reduction Act Notice, see the separate instructions.	

If you are not using a preprinted label, enter your name, address, employer identification number, and calendar quarter of return. See the separate instructions. ▶

Name

Quarter ending

Number, street, and room or suite no. (If you have a P.O. Box, see page 2.)

Employer identification number

City, state, and ZIP code (If you have a foreign address, see page 2.)

FOR IRS USE ONLY

T	
FF	
FD	
FP	
I	
T	

Final Return: If this is a final return or a one-time filing, check this box ▶ ☐

Part I

IRS No.	Environmental Taxes (Attach Form 6627 for all environmental taxes.)			Tax	IRS No.
53	Domestic petroleum superfund tax and oil spill tax				53
16	Imported petroleum products superfund tax and oil spill tax				16
54	Chemicals				54
17	Imported chemical substances				17
98	Ozone-depleting chemicals (ODCs)				98
19	Imported products containing ODCs				19
IRS No.	**Communications and Air Transportation Taxes**			**Tax**	**IRS No.**
22	Toll telephone service, teletypewriter exchange service, and local telephone service				22
26	Transportation of persons by air				26
28	Transportation of property by air				28
27	Use of international air travel facilities				27
IRS No.	**Fuel Taxes**	Number of gallons	Rate	Tax	IRS No.
60	(a) Diesel fuel, tax on removal at terminal rack		.244		60
	(b) Diesel fuel, tax on taxable events other than removal at terminal rack, including tax on liquids blended with previously taxed diesel fuel		.244		
71	Dyed diesel fuel used in trains		.069		71
78	Dyed diesel fuel used in certain intercity buses		.074		78
61	Special motor fuels		.184/.183		61
79	Other alcohol fuels		(See instructions.)		79
62	(a) Gasoline, tax on removal at terminal rack		.184		62
	(b) Gasoline, tax on taxable events other than removal at terminal rack		.184		
	(c) Gasoline, tax on failure to blend or later separation		(See instructions.)		
58	Gasoline sold for gasohol production containing at least 10% alcohol		.1444		58
73	Gasoline sold for gasohol production containing at least 7.7% alcohol but less than 10% alcohol		.1542		73
74	Gasoline sold for gasohol production containing at least 5.7% alcohol but less than 7.7% alcohol		.1624		74
59	Gasohol containing at least 10% alcohol		.13		59
75	Gasohol containing at least 7.7% alcohol but less than 10% alcohol		.1424		75
76	Gasohol containing at least 5.7% alcohol but less than 7.7% alcohol		.1532		76
69	Aviation fuel (other than gasoline)		.219		69
14	Gasoline for use in noncommercial aviation		.01		14
77	LUST tax on aviation fuel (other than gasoline)		.001		77
101	Compressed natural gas (taxed at $.4854 per thousand cubic feet)				101

Cat. No. 10175Y

Form **720** (Rev. 7-94)

IRS No.	Retail Tax (Attach Form 8807.)				Tax	IRS No.
33	Truck, trailer, and semitrailer chassis and bodies, and tractors					33
IRS No.	**Ship Passenger Tax**	Number of persons		Rate	Tax	**IRS No.**
29	Transportation by water			$3 per person		29
IRS No.	**Other Excise Tax**	Amount of obligations		Rate	Tax	**IRS No.**
31	Obligations not in registered form			$ .01		31
IRS No.	**Luxury Tax (Attach Form 8807.)**				Tax	**IRS No.**
92	Passenger vehicles					92
IRS No.	**Manufacturers Taxes**	Number of tons	Sales price	Rate	Tax	**IRS No.**
36	Coal—Underground mined			$1.10 per ton		36
37				4.4% of sales price		37
38	Coal—Surface mined			$ .55 per ton		38
39				4.4% of sales price		39
66	Highway-type tires (See instructions.)					66
40	Gas guzzler tax (**Attach Form 6197.**)					40
IRS No.	**Vaccine Taxes**	Number of doses		Rate	Tax	**IRS No.**
81	DPT vaccine			$4.56		81
82	DT vaccine			.06		82
83	MMR vaccine			4.44		83
84	Polio vaccine			.29		84
IRS No.	**Foreign Insurance Taxes**	Premiums paid		Rate	Tax	**IRS No.**
	Policies issued by foreign insurers (See instructions.) Casualty insurance and indemnity bonds			$ .04		
30	Life insurance, sickness and accident policies, and annuity contracts			.01		30
	Reinsurance			.01		
1	**Total. Add all amounts in Part I. Attach Schedule A unless one-time filing** ▶				$	

Part II

IRS No.				Tax	IRS No.
41	Sport fishing equipment (**Attach Form 8807.**)				41
42	Electric outboard motors and sonar devices (**Attach Form 8807.**)				42
44	Bows and arrows (**Attach Form 8807.**)				44
IRS No.		Number of gallons	Rate	Tax	**IRS No.**
64	Inland waterways fuel use tax		$ .234		64
51	Alcohol sold as but not used as fuel (See instructions.)		.54/.40		51
IRS No.	**Floor Stocks Taxes**	Number of gallons	Rate	Tax	**IRS No.**
88	Diesel fuel, based on Jan. 1, 1994, inventory		$ .244		88
20	Ozone-depleting chemicals (floor stocks) (**Attach Form 6627.**)				20
2	**Total. Add all amounts in Part II** ▶			$	

Part III

3	Total tax. Add line 1, Part I and line 2, Part II.	3	
4	Adjustments and claims (See instructions. **Attach Schedule C.**)	4	
5	Tax as adjusted. (If no entry on line 4, enter amount from line 3.)	5	
6	Deposits you made for the quarter . . . . ▶	6	
7	Overpayment from previous quarter . . . . ▶	7	
8	Total deposits (add lines 6 and 7). . . . . ▶	8	
9	BALANCE DUE. If line 5 is greater than line 8, enter the difference. This amount must be paid with the return. Attach check or money order for full amount payable to "Internal Revenue Service." Write your EIN, Form 720, and the quarter on it . . . . ▶	9	
10	OVERPAYMENT. If line 8 is greater than line 5, enter the difference and check if you want it: ☐ **Applied to your next return, or** ☐ **Refunded to you.**	10	

Sign Here

Under penalties of perjury, I declare that I have examined this return, including accompanying schedules and statements, and to the best of my knowledge and belief, it is true, correct, and complete.

▶ _____ | _____ ▶ _____
Signature   Date   Title

(Please type or print name below signature.)   Telephone number (   )

211

Schedule A   Excise Tax Liability

Note: *You must file Schedule A if you have a liability for any tax in Part I of Form 720. Do not use Schedule A for taxes on bows and arrows, electric outboard motors and sonar devices, sport fishing equipment, alcohol sold as but not used as fuel, or inland waterways fuel use; for any floor stocks taxes; or for one-time filings.*

1 9-day-rule taxes (See instructions.)

(a) Record of Net Tax Liability	Period			
	1st–15th day		16th–last day	
First month	A		B	
Second month	C		D	
Third month	E		F	

(b) Net liability for 9-day-rule taxes. (Add the amounts for each semimonthly period.)

2 30-day-rule taxes (IRS Nos. 19 and 98)

(a) Record of Net Tax Liability	Period			
	1st–15th day		16th–last day	
First month	G		H	
Second month	I		J	
Third month	K		L	

(b) Net liability for 30-day-rule taxes. (Add the amounts for each semimonthly period.)

3 Collected taxes based on billings or tickets sold (IRS Nos. 22, 26, 27, and 28) (See instructions.)

(a) Record of Taxes Considered as Collected	Period			
	1st–15th day		16th–last day	
First month	M		N	
Second month	O		P	
Third month	Q		R	

(b) Collected taxes based on billings or tickets sold. (Add the amounts for each semimonthly period.)

4 14-day-rule gasoline and diesel fuel taxes (IRS Nos. 60, 62, 58, 73, 74, 59, 75, and 76) (See instructions.)

(a) Record of Net Tax Liability	Period			
	1st–15th day		16th–last day	
First month	S		T	
Second month	U		V	
Third month	W		X	

(b) Net liability for 14-day-rule gasoline and diesel fuel taxes. (Add the amounts for each semimonthly period.)

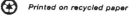

Printed on recycled paper   *U.S. Government Printing Office: 1994 — 301-628/00209

212

Appendix 6
Risk/Protection Chart

Common risks and possible protections

Risk	Protections (Dot indicates it could protect you):							
	Don't sign a guaranty	Corporation	Insurance	Contracts	Exempt property	Limited partnership	Offshore trusts	Gifts
Bills (Medical, legal, business, etc.)	●	●		●	●	●	●	●
Loans	●	●		●	●	●	●	●
Child support							●	●
Malpractice			●	●	●	●	●	●
Accidents		●	●		●	●	●	●
Acts of others		●	●	●	●	●	●	●
Torts (battery, slander)					●	●	●	●
Labor/ civil rights violations		●		●	●	●	●	●
Alimony				●	●	●	●	●
Environmental violations							●	●
Taxes				●			●	●

Note: This is an extremely simplified summary of the general rules of protection. In most cases you must follow strict procedures to be sure these devices will work for you. Not all of them are available in all states.

Index

Sphinx Publishing Presents
Self-Help Law Books
Laymen's Guides to the Law

Victims' Rights
The Complete Guide to Crime Victim Compensation
- Who qualifies
- How to qualify
- How to apply
- How much is available
- Rights of relatives
- Who to contact

William L Ginsburg
Attorney at Law

SELF-HELP LAW KIT
How to File Your Own Bankruptcy (or How to Avoid It)
With Forms
Includes
Chapter 7 (Discharge of Debts)
Chapter 13 (Payment Plan)
Edward A. Haman
Attorney at Law
SPHINX PUBLISHING

USA IMMIGRATION GUIDE
By Immigration Attorney RAMÓN CARRION

SELF-HELP LAW KIT
How to Register Your Own Trademark
With Forms
Includes
Choosing Your Mark
Searching Your Mark
State & Federal Registration
Protecting Your Mark
Mark Warda
Attorney at Law
SPHINX PUBLISHING

Every state has funds available to compensate victims of violent crime, but few are aware of this fact. Find out all about who qualifies, how much can be paid, and where and how to apply. Summary of laws for all states. 163 pages; $12.95.

Everything needed to file for bankruptcy in any state without a lawyer. Includes all of the forms and instructions for either Chapter 7 or Chapter 13 personal bankruptcies; with state-by-state exemptions. 138 pages; $19.95.

With forms and instructions, this books tells how the immigration system works, the types of visas, how to "buy" a visa by investing in a U.S. business or opening a U.S. office, and much more! 144 pages; $19.95. (Spanish edition avail.)

This complete guide to protecting a trademark explains state and federal registration, and protection available without registration. Includes all forms for filing your own federal registration. 140 pages; $19.95

What our customers say about our books:

"It couldn't be more clear for the lay person."   -R.D.

"I want you to know I really appreciate your book. It has saved me a lot of time and money." -L.T.

"Your real estate contracts book has saved me nearly $12,000.00 in closing costs over the past year." -A.B.

"...many of the legal questions that I have had over the years were answered clearly and concisely through your plain English interpretation of the law." -C.E.H.

"If there weren't people out there like you I'd be lost. You have the best books of this type out there." -S.B.

"...your forms and directions are easy to follow..." -C.V.M.

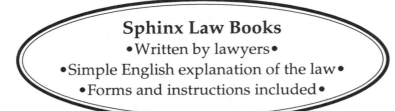

Sphinx Law Books
- •Written by lawyers•
- •Simple English explanation of the law•
- •Forms and instructions included•

Sphinx books are available directly from the publisher, or from your local bookstores.

Questions? Call us at 1-800-226-5291 or write P.O. Box 25, Clearwater, FL 34617

Our National Titles Are Valid In All 50 States

Living Trusts & Simple Ways to Avoid Probate $19.95
Simple Ways to **Protect Yourself From Lawsuits** $24.95
Help Your Lawyer **Win Your Case** $12.95
The Most Valuable **Business Forms** You'll Ever Need ...$19.95
Grandparents' Rights $19.95
Victims' Rights $12.95
Lawsuits of the Rich & Famous $10.95
Legal Research Made Easy $14.95
How to File Your Own **Divorce**, 2nd Ed. $19.95
Divorces From Hell $10.95
How to Write Your Own **Premarital Agreement** $19.95
U.S.A. Immigration Guide, 2nd Ed. $19.95

Guia de **Inmigración a Estados Unidos** $19.95
How to Form Your Own **Corporation** $19.95
The Most Valuable **Corporate Forms** You'll Ever Need $24.95
How to Negotiate **Real Estate Contracts** $14.95
How to Negotiate **Real Estate Leases** $14.95
Neighbor vs. Neighbor..$12.95
The **Power of Attorney** Handbook $19.95
Debtors' Rights, A Self-Help Guide, 2nd Ed. $12.95
How to Register Your Own **Copyright** $19.95
How to Register Your Own **Trademark** $19.95
Successful **Real Estate Brokerage Management** $19.95

Florida Legal Guides •With Florida Supreme Court-approved forms, where available•

Landlords' Rights and Duties in Florida, 5th Ed. ...$19.95
How to Win in **Small Claims** Court in Florida, 5th Ed. ..$14.95
Winning in Florida **Traffic Court** $14.95
How to **Start a Business** in Florida, 4th Ed. $16.95
How to Form a Simple **Corporation** in Florida, 3rd Ed. ..$19.95
How to Form a **Nonprofit Corporation** in Florida, 3rd Ed. $19.95
How to File a Florida **Contruction Lien**, 2nd Ed. $19.95
Land Trusts in Florida, 4th Ed. $19.95

How to File for **Divorce** in Florida, 3rd Ed. $19.95
How to **Modify Your** Florida **Divorce Judgment**, 2nd Ed. $19.95
Women's Legal Rights in Florida $19.95
Florida **Power of Attorney** Handbook ....$ 9.95
How to Make a Florida **Will**, 4th Ed. ....$ 9.95
How to **Probate** an Estate in Florida, 2nd Ed. $24.95
How to File a **Guardianship** in Florida $19.95
How to File an **Adoption** in Florida $19.95
How to **Change Your Name** in Florida, 3rd Ed. $14.95

Regional Books

✪ Southeastern Editions ✪

SELF-HELP LAW KIT

How to Register Your Own Trademark

With Forms

Southeastern Edition
- Alabama
- Florida
- Georgia
- Louisiana
- Mississippi
- North Carolina
- South Carolina
- Texas

Mark Warda
Attorney at Law

SPHINX PUBLISHING

$21.95

With detailed information for:

- Alabama
- Florida
- Georgia
- Louisiana
- Mississippi
- North Carolina
- South Carolina
- Texas

SELF-HELP LAW KIT

How to Form Your Own Partnership

With Forms

Southeastern Edition
- Alabama
- Florida
- Georgia
- Louisiana
- Mississippi
- North Carolina
- South Carolina
- Texas

Edward A. Haman
Attorney at Law

SPHINX PUBLISHING

$19.95

Texas

How to File for Divorce in Texas
$19.95

How to Make a Texas Will
$9.95

How to Start a Business in Texas
$16.95

Landlords' Rights & Duties in Texas
$19.95

How to Probate an Estate in Texas
$19.95

How to Form a Simple Corporation in Texas
$19.95

How to Win in Small Claims Court in Texas
$14.95

SELF-HELP LAW KIT

How to File for Divorce in Texas

With Forms

*Includes
Child Support
Child Custody & Visitation
Alimony & Property Division*

Karen Ann Rolcik
Edward A. Haman
Attorneys at Law

SPHINX PUBLISHING

North Carolina

How to File for Divorce in North Carolina
$19.95

How to Make a North Carolina Will
$9.95

How to Start a Business in North Carolina
$16.95

SELF-HELP LAW KIT

How to Start a Business in North Carolina

*Includes
Start-up Procedures
Laws and Regulations
Licensing and Taxes*

Wanda Naylor
and Mark Warda
Attorneys at Law

SPHINX PUBLISHING

Michigan

How to File for Divorce in Michigan
$19.95

How to Make a Michigan Will
$9.95

How to Start a Business in Michigan
$16.95

SELF-HELP LAW KIT

How to Make a Michigan Will

With Forms

*Includes
Last Will and Testament
Amendment (Codicil)
Designation of Patient Advocate*

Edward A. Haman
Mark Warda
Attorneys at Law

SPHINX PUBLISHING

Georgia

How to File for Divorce in Georgia
$19.95

How to Make a Georgia Will
$9.95

How to Start and Run a Georgia Business
$16.95

TAKE THE LAW INTO YOUR OWN HANDS

How to File for Divorce in Georgia

With Forms

Charles T. Robertson, II
and Edward A. Haman
Attorneys at Law

Sphinx Publishing
Self-Help Legal Guides Since 1983

Alabama

How to File for Divorce in Alabama
$19.95

How to Make an Alabama Will
$9.95

How to Start a Business in Alabama
$16.95

TAKE THE LAW INTO YOUR OWN HANDS

How to Start a Business in Alabama

With Forms

Gary G. Stanko
and Mark Warda
Attorneys at Law

Sphinx Publishing
Self-Help Legal Guides Since 1983

South Carolina

How to File for Divorce in South Carolina
$19.95

How to Make a South Carolina Will
$9.95

How to Start a Business in South Carolina
$16.95

TAKE THE LAW INTO YOUR OWN HANDS

How to Make a South Carolina Will

With Forms

Thomas P. Cullen
and Mark Warda
Attorneys at Law

Sphinx Publishing
Self-Help Legal Guides Since 1983

Books from other publishers

Represent Yourself in Court A step-by-step guide to preparing and trying a civil lawsuit. $29.95

Patent It Yourself, 3rd Ed. Explains every step of the patent process; a complete legal guide for inventors. $39.95

The Inventor's Notebook How to develop, document, protect, finance, and market your invention. $19.95

Plan Your Estate, 3rd Ed. For estates under $600,000, with specific instructions for preparing a living trust. $24.95

Make Your Own Living Trust For estates between $600,000 and $1,200,000. $19.95

How to Win Your Personal Injury Claim How to settle an injury claim on your own. $24.95

Beat the Nursing Home Trap: A Consumer's Guide to Choosing and Financing Long-Term Care $18.95
Explains how to choose and pay for long-term care, while protecting and conserving assets.

Social Security, Medicare & Pensions: The Sourcebook for Older Americans $18.95

The Living Together Kit, 7th Ed. Includes estate planning, living together agreements, buying real estate, etc. $24.95

Simple Contracts for Personal Use, 2nd Ed. Clearly written legal form contracts for all ocassions. $16.95

Stand Up to the IRS Know your rights when dealing with IRS: deductions, penalties, liens, and much more. $21.95

The Independent Paralegal's Handbook, 3rd Ed. $29.95
How to go into business helping consumers prepare their own paperwork in routine legal matters.

How to Write a Business Plan, 4th Ed. Finance your business and make it work. $19.95

A Legal Guide for Lesbian and Gay Couples, 8th Ed. $24.95

A practical guide covering living together, children, medical emergencies, estate planning, and more.

Your Rights in the Workplace: A Complete Guide for Employees, 2nd Ed. $15.95

Hiring, firing, wages, hours, family & medical leave, benefits, health & safety, discrimination, and more.

Sexual Harassment on the Job Explains the rights of employees who are sexually harassed. $14.95

Order Form

To order these publications, please fill in the information requested and send check or money order to Sphinx Publishing, PO Box 25, Clearwater, FL 34617 or call 800-226-5291.

☐ Check Enclosed   ☐ Money Order

We accept Visa, MasterCard, American Express and Discover cards.

Card number:

☐☐☐☐ ☐☐☐☐ ☐☐☐☐ ☐☐☐☐

Expiration date:

☐☐☐☐

☐ American Express   ☐ Visa
☐ MasterCard   ☐ Discover

Ship to:

Name_____

Address _____

City_____State_____

Zip_____ Phone_____

To order by credit card call:

1-800-226-5291

Or fax this form to (813) 586-5088

Quantity	Title		Price	Total Price

*Shipping: **In Florida:** UPS: (1-3 books) $3.25, each add'l .50¢
4th class mail: (1 book) $1.50 , each add'l. 50¢
[NOTE: Books from other publishers are only sent UPS]
Other States: UPS: (1-3 books) $3.75, each add'l .50¢

Subtotal: $_____
Sales Tax (FL residents) $_____
*Shipping: $_____
Total: $_____

Prices subject to change

_____
Signature